Live & Work

IN IRELAND

Live & Work
IN IRELAND

Dan Boothby

Distributed in the USA by
The Globe Pequot Press, Guilford, Connecticut

Published by Vacation Work, 9 Park End Street, Oxford
www.vacationwork.co.uk

LIVE & WORK IN IRELAND
by Dan Boothby

First edition 2004

Copyright © Vacation Work 2004

ISBN 1-85458-309-3

No part of this publication may be stored, reproduced or transmitted
in any form or by any means without the prior
written permission of the publisher

Cover design by mccdesign ltd

Typeset by Brendan Cole

Publicity: Charles Cutting

Printed and bound in Italy by Legoprint SpA, Trento

CONTENTS

SECTION I
LIVING IN IRELAND

GENERAL INTRODUCTION
    CHAPTER SUMMARY...17
    DESTINATION IRELAND – *Pros & Cons of Moving to Ireland*..18
    POLITICAL & ECONOMIC STRUCTURE – *Government – The European Parliament – Economy*...................20
    GEOGRAPHICAL INFORMATION – *Area – Population – Regional Divisions – Climate* 24
    INFORMATION FACILITIES...29
    GETTING THERE – *By Air – By Ferry*......................................31

RESIDENCE AND ENTRY REGULATIONS
    CHAPTER SUMMARY...35
    THE CURRENT POSITION 35
    IRELAND IMMIGRATION RULES – Entry for EEA Nationals – Entry for US & Canadian Nationals – Permission to Remain on Entry to Ireland – Work Authorisation Scheme – Work Visas – Application Process – Renewing Work Visas – Registration & Permission to Remain in Ireland – Working Holiday Permit – Irish Citizenship 36
    USEFUL ADDRESSES AND WEBSITES..................................44
    CUSTOMS REGULATIONS..46

SETTING UP HOME
    CHAPTER SUMMARY...49
    THE IRISH WAY OF LIFE..50
    RENT OR BUY? 51
    FINANCE – *Mortgages – Fixed or Variable Rate Mortgages – Commercial & Buy-to-Let Mortgages – Redemption Charges –*

Mortgage Interest Relief at Source – Non-Mortgageable Properties – Buying Land 52
FINDING A HOME – *Finding a Property – Estate Agents – The Internet – Old Property – New Property – Self-Build – Other Sources of Property* 57
PURCHASING & CONVEYANCING PROCEDURES – *Solicitors – The Costs of Buying Property* 64
RENTING PROPERTY – *Letting Agents – Tenancy Agreements – Rental Costs – Deposits* 68
UTILITIES – *Electricity – Gas – Oil & Solid Fuel – Water & Sewerage – Refuse Collection* 72
REMOVALS – *Storage Depots – Customs Regulations* 75
IMPORTING YOUR CAR 78
IMPORTING PETS – *Quarantine – Approved Quarantine Premises – Pet Travel Scheme* 79

DAILY LIFE
CHAPTER SUMMARY 83
LANGUAGE – *Gaelic* 84
SCHOOLS & EDUCATION – *Pre-school & Nursery Education – Primary Education – Secondary Education – Special Education – Home Education – Examinations – International Schools – School Transport & Meals – Further Education* 84
HIGHER EDUCATION – *Universities – Colleges of Education – Independent Colleges – Technical Colleges – Admissions, Tuition Fees & Grants* 96
MEDIA – *Newspapers – Magazines – Television & Radio – Satellite & Cable Television* 99
COMMUNICATIONS – *Post – Telephones – The Internet* 103
CARS & MOTORING – *Roads & Signage – Driving Regulations – Driving Tests – Driving Licences – Endorsements & Disqualification – – Insurance – National Car Test – Motoring Organisations – Car Rental – Fuel* 110
PUBLIC TRANSPORT – *Rail – Bus & Coach Services – Taxis & Minicabs* 119
BANKS & FINANCE – *Choosing a Bank – Bank Accounts –*

Opening An Account – Plastic Money – Building Societies & the Post Office – Credit Unions – The Euro – Foreign Currency – Transferring Funds..121
TAXATION – *Income Tax – Double Taxation Agreements – National Insurance (PRSI) – PPS Numbers – Income Tax Rates – Value Added Tax – Other Taxes – Further Information*...128
HEALTH – *The Irish Health Service – Medical Cards – Health Boards – Private Health Care – General Practitioners – Drugs & Medicines – Dentists – Disability Benefit* 134
LOCAL GOVERNMENT – *The Vote & Elections* 141
CRIME & THE POLICE – *The Police (Guardaí) – The Prison Service – Emergency Services* 143
ENTERTAINMENT & CULTURE – *Food & Drink – Arts & Culture – Music & Dancing – Museums, Galleries & Historical Monuments – Sport*..146
RELIGION 149
SHOPS & SHOPPING – *Opening Times* 150
PUBLIC HOLIDAYS – *Local Fairs and Festivals* 151
TIME..153
METRICATION..153

RETIREMENT

CHAPTER SUMMARY..155
BACKGROUND INFORMATION 157
PENSIONS – *State Pensions – Contributory Pension – Old Age Non-Contributory Pension – Widow's and Widower's Pension* 157
TAXATION – *Double Taxation Agreements – Capital Acquisitions Tax*...161
LEAVING ONE'S FAMILY 162
HEALTH CONSIDERATIONS & SOCIAL SERVICES 163
BUYING A RETIREMENT HOME – *Sheltered Housing, Residential & Nursing Homes*..164
DAILY LIFE, HOBBIES & INTERESTS 165
WILLS & LEGAL CONSIDERATIONS..............................167
DEATH 169

SECTION II
WORKING IN IRELAND

EMPLOYMENT
- CHAPTER SUMMARY 175
- THE EMPLOYMENT SCENE 176
- RESIDENCE & WORK REGULATIONS – P*ermit-Free Employment – Working Holidaymakers – Au Pairs – Work Permits – Work Authorisation Scheme/Fast Track Visa Programme* 178
- SKILLS & QUALIFICATIONS – EU/EEA *Nationals – Nationals of Other Countries* 183
- TRADE & PROFESSIONAL BODIES IN IRELAND 185
- SOURCES OF JOBS – *The Employment Service – EURES – Newspapers – Professional & Trade Publications – The Internet – Employment Agencies – Company Transfers* 188
- APPLYING FOR A JOB – *Application Forms & Letters – The Curriculum Vitae – References – Interview Procedure – Useful Books & Websites* 199
- ASPECTS OF EMPLOYMENT – *Benefits & Perks – Sample Salaries – Working Hours, Overtime & Holidays – Employment Contracts – Termination of Employment – Redundancy – Rights of Part-time, Temporary & Seasonal Workers* 205
- TELEWORKING & E-WORKING 211
- TRADE UNIONS & PROFESSIONAL ASSOCIATIONS .. 212
- INCOME TAX & PAY RELATED SOCIAL INSURANCE (PRSI) – *Social Security and Unemployment Benefits* 213
- WOMEN IN WORK – *Maternity Leave – Maternity Benefit – Parental Leave – Childcare – Useful Addresses & Websites* 214
- COMPANY PENSION SCHEMES 217
- **Permanent Work** – *Professional & Executive – Civil Service – Financial & Business Services – Administrative – Medical – Teaching – Computers & IT – Police – Tourism – Agriculture & Fishing – Construction – The Environment* 219
- **Temporary & Seasonal Work** – *Tourism – Working as an Au Pair – Agriculture & Fishing – Secretarial & Clerical* 233

TRAINING, WORK EXPERIENCE & EXCHANGE
SCHEMES – *Sources of Advice* 236
Business & Industry Report 238
Regional Employment Guide – *Connaught –
Munster – Leinster – Ulster – Regional Authorities – City
Councils – Regional Assemblies* 240
Directory of Major Employers – *Communications – Computers
– It & Electronics – Construction – Finance & Banking – Food &
Drink – Fuel & Energy – Hotel, Bar & Restaurant Chains – Media
– Public Transport – Research & Technology – Retail – The Best 50
Companies in Ireland 2004 – Useful Websites* 261

STARTING A BUSINESS

CHAPTER SUMMARY 275
RESIDENCE REGULATIONS 276
CREATING A NEW BUSINESS – *Planning Permission* 276
BUYING AN EXISTING BUSINESS – *Finding Premises or
an Existing Business for Sale* 279
PROCEDURES INVOLVED IN STARTING A
BUSINESS – *Business Structures* 280
SOURCES OF FINANCE – *City & County Enterprise
Boards – Loan Finance – Equity Capital* 283
WRITING A BUSINESS PLAN 288
IDEAS FOR NEW BUSINESSES – *Tourism – Retail –
Garages – Franchises – Computer Services – Trades – Working as
a Freelance* 290
E-COMMERCE 295
RUNNING A BUSINESS – *Taxation – Employing Staff –
Business Insurance – Data Protection – Intellectual
Property – Accountancy & Legal Advice* 297
SOURCES OF ADVICE & ASSISTANCE 303

PERSONAL CASE HISTORIES 309

MAPS
MAJOR TOWNS AND CITIES OF IRELAND 19
PROVINCES AND COUNTIES OF IRELAND 25
REGIONAL AUTHORITY AREA BOUNDARIES 259

ACKNOWLEDGEMENTS

A number of people have assisted me during the researching and writing of this book. In particular, I should like to thank Gary Hetzler, James Pengelly, Freya Forrest, E. Wood and Daphne Ballantine for sharing their experiences of living and working in Ireland. I would also like to thank Peter Ingram and Sylvia Scarlett; and the Mitchell family and Mike Kreciela for hospitality. Thanks also to S. O'Neill and G. Davies for providing me with a splendid place in which to live and work.

NOTE: the author and publishers of this book have every reason to believe in the accuracy of the information given in this book and the authenticity and correct practices of all organisations, companies, agencies, etc. mentioned; however situations may change and telephone numbers etc. can alter, and readers are strongly advised to check facts and credentials for themselves. Readers are invited to write to Vacation Work, 9 Park End Street, Oxford OX1 1HJ or e-mail with any comments or corrections.

PREFACE

Do not underestimate the people of Ireland for it was they who built the foundations on which present-day Australia stands and they were integral to the building of modern-day America.

The myth of Ireland is one of a country and a people living far away from the stresses of urban life, on an unpolluted, rural and remote island in the Atlantic Ocean, where the views are fine and life is simpler, friendlier, less class conscious than 'back home', and where everyone has time for everyone else. A place where, historically, though the population was a poor one and life was hard, a shared faith and a common bond won through. And Ireland does, still, in places, bear some resemblance to this myth, but do not be fooled; Ireland has reinvented herself and over the last 20 years has become one of the most highly regarded economic success stories in the world. Emigrants are returning to the island and immigrants are tapping at the visa providers' doors to be let in and today the country has the fastest growing (and youngest) population in the European Union.

To be sure, the Irish are a friendly, polite and inquisitive people, with a unique humour and logic about them, and you should find a welcome, or a hundred thousand welcomes (*'céad mile fáilte'*) throughout the land. You'll find the *Mulligan's Drinking Establishment*s and the *seisiúns*, the horse fairs and the blarney; but you will also find a country that is fast changing. The unspoilt romantic Ireland of the tourist brochures and recent memory is fast disappearing, yet for those looking to take part in the most recent economic success story in the world, Ireland offers golden opportunities. Freedom of movement within the EU means that it has never been easier for European nationals to relocate to Ireland, though regulations make immigration from other parts of the world more problematic unless you have specific skills to offer. For those who wish to study or gain work experience in Ireland, opportunities are greater now than they have been in the past. In Ireland, the grass really is greener.

Dan Boothby
Valentia Island, Co. Kerry
April 2004

TELEPHONE NUMBERS

Please note that the telephone numbers in this book are written as needed to call that number from inside the same country. To call these numbers from outside the country you will need to know the relevant international access code; these are currently 00 from the UK and Ireland and 011 from the USA

To call Ireland: dial the international access code +353 and the number given in this book minus the first 0.

To call the UK: international access code +44 then the number given in this book *minus the first 0.*

To call the USA: international access code +1 then the complete number as given in this book.

THE EURO

Since January 1st 2002 the Euro has been the legal currency of Ireland, replacing the Irish punt. The value of the Euro against the UK £ and the US $ varies from day to day: at the time of going to press one Euro is worth UK £0.67 or US $1.21

Section I

LIVING IN IRELAND

GENERAL INTRODUCTION

RESIDENCE AND ENTRY REGULATIONS

SETTING UP HOME

DAILY LIFE

RETIREMENT

GENERAL INTRODUCTION

CHAPTER SUMMARY

- Ireland is equivalent in size to the state of Maine in the USA, or to Austria.
- Winters in Ireland are mild and the summers are cool.
- Airfares to and from Ireland are at their highest during the summer tourist season and at weekends.
- Dublin is the nation's capital and home to 40% of the total population of Ireland.
- **Politics**. Ireland's political system is based on the British system.
  - The two-chamber parliament consists of a House of Representatives and a Senate in addition to the Office of the President.
  - There is one TD (Member of Parliament) for every 21,000 people in Ireland.
- **Economy**. Ireland's unemployment rate of 3.6% is one of the lowest in Europe.
  - Half the country's labour force is under 25 years of age.
  - Ireland is the second most expensive country in the 12-nation eurozone.

DESTINATION IRELAND

Pros and Cons of Moving to Ireland

Emigration from Britain to the Republic of Ireland is high. According to the Irish Central Statistics Office, of the 44,000 people who moved to Ireland in 1998, 21,000 were from Britain. This figure has continued to grow with the continued prosperity of Ireland pulling in those who wish to work and live in the vibrant, new Ireland. People are drawn to live and work in Ireland for a number of reasons: some immigrants are second-generation Irish who have decided to return to their roots; others are drawn by employment prospects, or a relationship, or the promise of a new way of life. Some, desperate to escape the rat run of a life spent working in a large town or city, decide that they prefer the working environment, and work ethic, of the more rural parts of Ireland to that back home.

In both the cities and rural areas of Ireland – and especially in Dublin – job prospects with international companies continue to be good. Microsoft, Dell, Hewlett Packard, Intel and Gateway Computing have all set up offices in the capital and a number of Northern Irish companies with markets in the Republic have relocated south the border to take advantage of operating in the eurozone. Many multinationals have also located plants and European headquarters in many parts of Ireland.

The 'Celtic Tiger' economy, together with the assistance of European grants, has transformed both the land and the economy of Ireland in the last decade. Long-term unemployment is low – the figures for January 2004 show an unemployment rate of 3.6%, one of the lowest in Europe, and the economy is expected to grow by 5% over the next couple of years. Many companies are struggling to fill vacancies. On the downside, the knock-on effect of the Tiger's rampage has been a massive increase in traffic congestion and house prices, especially in Dublin. Ireland has become far more cosmopolitan that it was a decade ago, with even the more remote regions developing a savvy and 'Modern' attitude that was scarce before.

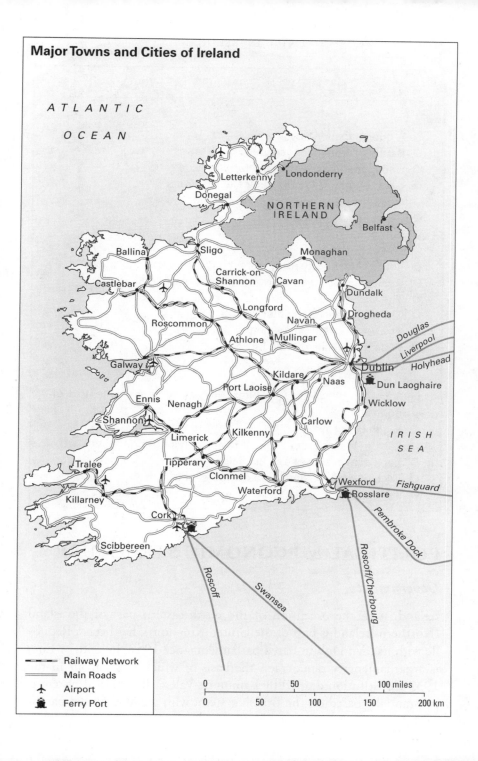

THE PROS & CONS OF IRELAND

Pros
- A booming economy
- Beautiful, varied landscape
- Cheap and easy flights and ferry services
- Good and reliable communication systems
- Good business and employment opportunities
- Good education system
- Low crime rate
- Low pollution
- Low traffic density away from the larger towns and cities
- Residence and work permit procedures straightforward
- The *Craic*
- The Irish people and their culture
- The youth of the population
- Wide availability of outdoor sports

Cons
- A certain sense of isolation if living away from the centres of population
- High cost of living
- Lack of a support network of family and long-term friends
- Lack of available cheap housing
- Lack of work in some areas of the country
- The changeable weather

POLITICAL & ECONOMIC STRUCTURE

Government

Ireland, with the exception of the north-eastern part of the island (Northern Ireland is part of the United Kingdom), has been a Republic with its own Dublin-based parliament since 1949. Ireland, or Eire, is a parliamentary democracy, the basis of which was set out in the 1937 Constitution drafted by Éamon de Valera. Its political system is substantially based on the British system, with a two-chamber parliament consisting of a House of Representatives and a Senate, in addition to the Office of the President.

The House of Representatives (*Dáil Éireann*) is made up of 166 members elected by the people of Ireland through a system of proportional representation. Members of the Dáil Éireann are called *Teachtaí Dála*, or TDs, and serve five-year terms of office. The 26 counties of Ireland are divided into 41 Dáil constituencies, which each elect between three and five TDs to the House of Representatives. At present there is one TD for every 21,000 people in Ireland.

The Senate (*Seanad Éireann*) has a total of 60 members – 49 elected by Trinity College and the National University of Ireland, and existing senators, TDs and councillors who sit on five vocational panels representing various sectors of Ireland's economy. A further 11 senators are nominated by the Prime Minister. Members of the senate serve a five-year term in office. The Seanad is more a forum for political debate than a legislative office and the main political power rests with the Dáil.

The President (*an Uachtarán*) of Ireland is the supreme commander of the defence forces, appoints the Prime Minister and cabinet on the advice of Parliament, is the guardian of the Constitution and carries out largely ceremonial duties (meeting visiting dignitaries and so forth). The Office of the President is a post held for a period of seven years, though a President may be elected for a second term. The President of Ireland is Mary McAleese, who succeeded the first woman President of Ireland to the post, Mary Robinson, in 1997.

The President is elected by popular vote and all Irish citizens over the age of 18 on the day the Electoral Register comes into force (15 February) may vote in both Presidential elections and European Parliament elections. Fundamental changes of national importance to the laws of the country, such as that on the loosening of legalisation relating to abortion, are put to the country as a whole through a referendum.

The six main parties in Irish politics are *Fianna Fail, Fine Gael*, the Labour Party, the Progressive Democrats, the Green Party, and *Sinn Fein*. The current Prime Minister (*an Taoiseach*) is Bertie Ahern whose party, Fianna Fail, has been in a coalition government with the Progressive Democrats since 1997. Bertie Ahern was re-elected in the general election of May 2002, when the coalition became the first government to win re-election in Ireland in over three decades.

The European Parliament

The European Parliament promotes the interests and defends the rights of the 375 million citizens of the EU. It has substantial legislative, budgetary and supervisory powers and under the legislative procedure of 'co-decision' no law can be enacted without the agreement of the European Parliament and the Council of Ministers (the primary legislative and budgetary body of the EU) acting jointly and equally as co-legislators. The European Parliament shares responsibility with the Council of Ministers for establishing and shaping the annual EU budget.

The European Parliament approves the appointment of the President of the European Commission, and supervises the Commission as it spends the budget and implements EU policies. Members of the European Parliament (MEPs) can put written and oral questions to the European Commission and to the Council of Ministers. The European Parliament can also establish temporary committees of inquiry and hold public hearings on matters of concern to the general public.

Members of the European Parliament elected in EU member states serve a five-year term. Fifteen of these MEPs are elected from Ireland. For the purposes of the European Parliament, Ireland is divided into the four constituencies of Dublin, Leinster, Munster, and Connacht-Ulster in Northern Ireland. Dublin, Leinster and Munster each have four MEPs while Connacht-Ulster (counted as part of the UK representation) returns three MEPs.

The first direct elections to the European Parliament were held in 1979 and continue to be held every five years. They take place over a four-day period all over the EU, with the next elections taking place in June 2004. The responsibility for conducting the election in each of the four Irish constituencies rests with a returning officer appointed by the Minister for the Environment who must also be a County Registrar or a City or County Sheriff. There are, in addition, local returning officers who are responsible for the many polling stations in each county and city.

MEPs travel weekly from their constituencies to Brussels or Strasbourg. They spend two weeks every month on committee work in Brussels while an additional week is set aside for meetings of the political groups. A further week is spent each month at the plenary sessions in Strasbourg. Parliament also holds additional plenary sittings in Brussels.

The European Parliament has offices in the capital of each EU member state to inform the public about the European Parliament and to facilitate media coverage of Parliament's debates and activities. The European Parliament office in Dublin liaises with the Dáil and Seanad, Government departments and other public bodies, and provides public access to the records of Parliamentary proceedings (minutes, debates, votes, resolutions, declarations, etc.,) as well as to Ireland's MEPs. The European Parliament Office in Ireland is located at 43 Molesworth Street, Dublin 2 (☎ 01-605 7900; fax 01-605 7999; www.europarl.ie) and is open 9am-1pm and again from 2pm-5pm, Monday-Friday.

Economy

The Irish economy continues to grow at a rate unparalleled in the rest of Europe. Fourteen years ago Ireland was, per capita, one of the world's great debtor nations with International Monetary Fund (IMF) inspectors poised to take over its management. However, with cuts in business and personal taxes, massive investment from overseas companies and the commitment to enter the eurozone, Ireland's economic boom is of a size unsurpassed since Germany rebuilt its economy after the Second World War. There is a large software industry, many entrepreneurs, and it is estimated that three new millionaires are created in Ireland every week.

Ireland has been a member of the European Community since 1973. The country is rich in natural resources and is justifiably famous for the beauty of its countryside and the hospitality of its people. It has a young, well-educated and highly skilled labour force and offers tariff-free access to the vast European Union market of over 320 million people. Half the labour force is under 25 years of age; and half of all third-level students are studying business, technological or computing skills. The present Irish government has created a favourable operating environment for business and industry and Ireland's success in attracting international investment is due in large part to the financial and tax incentives offered.

For those looking to move to Ireland, the downside of all this investment and economic strength is that the price of property, especially in Dublin, has been affected by the boom. There are now literally thousands of houses in the capital valued at more than £1million – something unheard of less than five years ago. Additionally, according to a study by *Forfás*, the Irish Government's enterprise policy advisory board, Ireland is the second most expensive country in the 12-nation eurozone – only marginally less expensive than Finland – with prices 12% above average.

GEOGRAPHICAL INFORMATION

Area

The Republic of Ireland lies in the North Atlantic Ocean, separated from Great Britain to the east by the Irish Sea, and nothing but 3,200 km of ocean dividing it from the USA to the west. At just 304 km (189 miles) at its widest point and 485 km (302 miles) at its longest, (by comparison the distance between Land's End and John O'Groats in Britain is 874 miles (1,406 km) as the crow flies) Ireland is a relatively small country covering a total area of 27,133 sq. miles (70,273 sq. km) – equivalent in size to the state of Maine in the USA, or Austria.

The interior of the country is made up of a central low-lying limestone plain surrounded by a rim of mountains and hills with numerous expanses of moorland, lakes (*loughs*), bogs and river systems. Quiet sandy beaches, sea cliffs, and bays warmed by the Gulf Stream make up the 5631 km (3,500 miles) of coastline. Ireland's highest mountain, Carrauntoohil, near Killarney in County Kerry in the southwest of the country, measures 1,041 metres (3,414 feet) above sea level. The River Shannon drains almost a fifth of the country on its 336 km journey from source to sea. Off the west coast there are a number of rocky islands. Granite is the predominant rock in the northwest

counties of Connemara, Mayo and Donegal and in the eastern county of Wicklow. The country's natural resources are zinc, lead, natural gas, barite, copper, gypsum, limestone, dolomite, peat and silver, while about 20% of the island is given over to arable land. Its main exports are machinery and equipment, foodstuffs and chemicals. Ireland has a strategic location in the world as it is on the major air and sea routes between North America and northern Europe.

Population

Between the 1840s – the years of the Great Famine – and the middle of the twentieth century, the population of Ireland fell from eight million to four million and reached its zenith of 2.8 million in 1961. Today, Ireland's population stands at just under four million (approximately 3,880,000 were recorded by the 2003 census). It has a population density of 55.2 per sq. km, which makes it one of the most thinly populated countries in Europe. Over 40% of the total population resides within 100 km (60 miles) of Dublin, the Republic's capital. According to the latest figures published by the United Nations the life expectancy for males in Ireland is around 74 years; 80 years for females. Approximately 42% of the population are under 25 years of age and Ireland has the fastest growing population in the EU.

Regional Divisions (Provinces & Counties)

Ireland is divided into the three southern provinces of Connacht (Connaught), Leinster and Munster, and the northern province of Ulster (most of which has remained part of the United Kingdom since the founding of the Irish Free State in 1921). These ancient provinces of Ireland are, in turn, subdivided into 32 counties, 26 of which make up the Republic. The other six counties make up the UK province of Northern Ireland (which since 1973 have been replaced by the 26 districts). Today, for most administrative purposes the Republic is divided into regional districts (Eastern, North-Eastern, Midland, etc.), though the traditional provinces are often referred to and are still of importance when discussing Ireland, both in a cultural and social context.

The province of Connacht, situated in the northwest of the Republic, consists of five counties.
- County Galway
- County Leitrim
- County Mayo
- County Roscommon
- County Sligo

The province of Leinster is situated on the east coast and consists of twelve counties. There are several ferry ports along its coastline and the province includes the capital of the Republic, Dublin.
- County Carlow
- County Dublin
- County Kildare
- County Kilkenny
- County Laois
- County Longford
- County Louth
- County Meath
- County Offaly
- County Westmeath
- County Wexford
- County Wicklow

The province of Munster in the southwest of Ireland consists of six counties and is the largest of the four provinces. The province has some of the most beautiful scenery of the island with ranges of hills, a fantastic coastline and lakeland.
- County Clare
- County Cork
- County Kerry
- County Limerick
- County Tipperary
- County Waterford

Of the nine counties that make up the province of Ulster, only three (Co. Cavan, Co. Donegal and Co. Monaghan) form part of the Republic.
- County Antrim

- County Armagh
- County Cavan
- County Derry
- County Donegal
- County Down
- County Fermanagh
- County Monaghan
- County Tyrone

The Pale. The Pale was a term that defined the territory under English control from the time of the Anglo-Norman settlement until the early 17th century. The boundaries fluctuated, but at its height the Pale's reach stretched from Dundalk in County Louth in the north to Waterford city in the south. Those within the Pale upheld the English values, customs and interests. In Elizabethan times, Gaelic chieftains 'beyond the Pale' were allowed to keep their lands if they agreed to raise their heirs within the Pale.

Climate

A country such as Ireland, with its lush green landscape, lakes and surfeit of places to sit beneath a roof drinking and talking, doesn't get called the 'the Emerald Isle' for nothing. The truth is that Ireland is one of the wettest countries in Europe, with the west coast especially receiving bucket loads of the stuff annually – straight off the Atlantic Ocean. The weather isn't always great in this land where one can expect it to be humid and overcast for about 50% the time. Away from the mountain areas, the annual rainfall of the west averages around 1,000-1,300mm; around 800mm of rainfall is recorded annually in the east. Up in the mountains, much higher averages are recorded – with annual rainfall figures in regions such as the Wicklow Mountains and around Kerry rising as high as 3,000mm per annum. The area around Dublin has the least rainfall; with annual figures often showing less than 750mm.

April is the driest month (generally) in Ireland and although rain is a fairly constant factor on the island the climate is a constantly changing one, with a downpour often followed by bright spells and rainbows. Winters are mild and the summers cool, due in part to the prevailing south-westerly winds that buffet the island. The country has a temperate climate as all areas are also relatively close to the seas, which are warmed by the Gulf Stream. Winter water temperatures range from 10°C off the southwest coast to less than 7°C off County Wexford in the southeast corner of the country. During the summer these temperatures rise to around 15°C and 13°C respectively.

January and February see the coldest weather in Ireland, with temperatures ranging between 4°C in the northeast and 7°C in the southwest. Snow rarely lies for long upon the ground except up on the high mountains. During the warmest months – July and August – temperatures rise to around 14-16°C, though it's a fairly rare occurrence for the mercury to show a reading of over 25°C. Northern Ireland gets the least sunshine; the southeast gets the most. The sunniest months in Ireland are May and June, when you can expect between five and seven hours of sunshine a day. Unlike in say, England, the state of the weather is a much less often-expressed topic of conversation in Ireland where, if in doubt, expect a light shower of rain.

INFORMATION FACILITIES

Practically every town in Ireland has a tourist office whose offerings will range from large buildings full of free brochures, maps, area guides, local transport information and an accommodation booking service, to small kiosks with limited information facilities. Globally, the Irish Tourist Board (*Bord Failté*) has offices in many countries worldwide and a presence on the Internet at www.ireland.ie. Its main office in Dublin is located at Baggot Street Bridge, Dublin 2 (☎01-602 4000; fax 01-602 4100; for postal enquiries write c/o PO Box 273, Dublin 8). The Irish Tourist Board also has a list of over 8,000 recommended places to stay, with their website providing a searchable database of options from the basic to the all-inclusive.

Bord Failté Addresses

United Kingdom

Nations House, 103 Wigmore Street, London W1U 1QS; ☎0800-397000/0207-518 0800; fax 0207-493 9065; www.tourismireland.com.

All Ireland Desk, British Visitor Centre, 1 Regent Street, London SW1Y 4NS (walk-in office only, no telephone enquiries).

James Millar House, 7th Floor, 98 West George Street, Glasgow G2 1PJ; ☎0800-0397 000; fax 0141-572 4033; www.tourismireland.com.

53 Castle Street, Belfast BT1 1GH; ☎01232-327 888; fax 01232-240 201; www.tourismireland.com.

8 Bishop Street, Derry BT48 6PW; ☎01504-369 501; fax 01504-369 501; www.tourismireland.com.

United States of America

Ireland House, 17th Floor, 345 Park Street, New York, NY 10154; ☎800-223 6470; fax 212-371 9052; www.tourismireland.com.

Canada

2 Bloor Street, West, Suite 1501, Toronto M4W 3E2; ☎800-223 6470; fax 416-925 6033; www.tourismireland.com.

Australia

5th Level, 36 Carrington Street, Sydney NSW 2000, Australia; ☎02-9299 6177; fax 02-2996 323; www.tourismireland.com.au.

New Zealand

Level 6, 18 Shortland Street, Private Bag 92136, Auckland 1; ☎09977 2255; fax 09977 2256; www.tourismireland.com.

South Africa

c/o Development Promotions, Everite House, 7th Floor, 20 De Korte Street, Braamfontein 2001, Gauteng; ☎011 3394865; fax 011 3392474; www.tourismireland.com.

GETTING THERE

There are various options open to those wishing to travel to Ireland – from a cheap, no frills flight with an airline company such as Ryanair or easyJet, to travelling by car, coach or train to Wales, Liverpool or Scotland and taking a ferry across the Irish Sea. The cheapest way for North Americans or Antipodeans to reach Ireland is to travel to London and then get a connecting flight or ferry over to Ireland.

By Air

Ireland has four main international airports: Cork, Dublin, Shannon and Belfast, and a number of regional airports – Donegal, Galway, Kerry, Knock, Sligo, Waterford, City of Derry and Belfast City. Dublin is by far the busiest of the airports, with around five million passengers passing through its doors annually. More than 30 airlines serving over 70 destinations fly in and out of Ireland. There are frequent flights from a number of UK airports to both the international and regional airports in Ireland and a number of connecting flights leave from Dublin and Shannon to many European and transatlantic destinations. A flight from New York to Dublin takes around six hours. You can reach Dublin by air from most of the UK airports in about an hour. The Aran Islands, out on the northwest coast of Ireland, are served by a daily flight operated by *Aer Arann* from Galway.

Airfares to and from Ireland are at their highest during the summer tourist season (early June-late August) and over bank holidays and weekends. Cheaper fares can be found by travelling midweek and at unsociable hours of the day or night, though in most cases you will need to book well in advance to take advantage of such discounted fares. Advance booking is also often essential during peak commuter times. Additional taxes on return flights from the UK to Ireland add an extra surcharge onto the price of a ticket. Flight-only websites and directories are a very good place to look for cheap flights to Ireland, with companies such as www.deckchair.com, www.travelocity.co.uk, and www.expedia.com able to searching out a range of airlines and fares dependent on the date, time and type of flight required.

There is a regular bus service from Dublin Airport to the central bus station in Dublin City, and the majority of airports also have bus and taxi services linking them to the nearest city. Airports have car rental offices. The Republic's national airline is *Aer Lingus*, which flies both international and domestic services.

AIRLINES SERVING IRELAND

Aer Arann, ☎ 0800-587 2324; www.aerarann.com.
Aer Lingus, ☎ 0845-084 4444; www.aerlingus.com.
Air Wales, ☎ 0870-777 3131; www.airwales.co.uk.
bmi british midland, ☎ 0870-6070 555; www.flybmi.com.
bmibaby, ☎ 0870-264 2229; www.bmibaby.com.
British Airways, ☎ 0870-850 9850; www.ba.com.
Eastern Airways, 01652-680 600; www.easternairways.com.
easyJet, ☎ 0870-600 0000; www.easyjet.com.
Euromanx, ☎ 01624-822 123; www.euromanx.com.
Flybe, ☎ 08705-676 676; www.flybe.com.
Luxair, ☎ 01293-596 633; www.luxair.lu.
MyTravelLite, ☎ 08701-564 564; www.mytravellite.com.
Ryanair, ☎ 0871-246 0000; www.ryanair.com.

By Ferry

A somewhat slower but often more economical way of travelling to and from Ireland – and necessary if you want to take your car over the Irish Sea – is by ferry. Ireland has six main ferryports – Dublin Port, Dun Laoghaire, Belfast, Larne, Cork and Rosslare – with a number of different companies operating the ferries and SeaCats that traverse the Irish Sea. There are also ferries travelling between Cherbourg, Le Havre & Roscoff in France and Rosslare & Cork in Ireland. In addition, there are summer only sailings between Cherbourg and Cork, and St Malo and Cork.

Fares vary considerably depending upon the time, date and type of craft on which you wish to travel. As with flights, cheaper fares can be had by travelling outside the holiday season, or midweek or at unsociable times of the day or night. Some of the ferry operators offer discounted rates to seniors and families; and some offer youth/student fares. Single tickets for adult foot passengers range from €28-€55. (approx. £18.65-£36.65/US $33-$65) Note that ferry passengers from the Republic are taxed an additional €6.50 when travelling home from Britain.

FERRY COMPANIES SERVING IRELAND

Irish Ferries, ☎0870-517 1717; www.irishferries.com.
Isle of Man Steam Packet Co., ☎0870-5523 523; www.steam-packet.com.
Norse Merchant Ferries, ☎0870-600 4321; www.norsemerchant.com.
P&O Irish Sea, ☎0870-242 4777; www.poirishsea.com.
Sea Cat, ☎0870-552 3523; www.seacat.co.uk.
Stena Line, ☎0870-400 6798; www.stenaline.com.
Swansea Cork Ferries, ☎01792-456 116; www.swansea-cork.ie.

RESIDENCE & ENTRY REGULATIONS

CHAPTER SUMMARY

- Residence permits can be obtained from police stations.
- A work authorisation scheme has been introduced in order to facilitate the recruitment of suitably qualified people from non-EEA countries for sectors of the economy where skill shortages are particularly acute.
- A work visa or work authorisation is usually valid for multiple re-entries for a period of two years.
- Citizens of Australia and New Zealand aged 18-30 may enter Ireland on a Working Holiday Visa.
- US and Canadian passport holders do not need a visa to enter Ireland but will need a permit in order to take up employment.

THE CURRENT POSITION

The Employment Permits Act, which came into force in April 2003, provides for the freedom of movement of nationals of the 10 EU Accession States (Malta, Slovenia, Hungary, Lithuania, Slovakia, Poland, Czech Republic, Estonia, Latvia and Cyprus) after Accession, for purposes of work. This means that with effect from the date of EU enlargement (1st May 2004) employers will no longer require work permits to employ nationals of these States. In addition, The EU Accession Treaty contains a provision that requires EU Member States, when considering applications for work permits, to give preference to applications in respect of Accession State nationals. With the expansion of the European Union and the accession of more countries into the Union immigration rules will continue to be subject to change and expansion and readers – especially those from non-EU member states – are advised to check immigration regulations with their nearest Irish embassy or consulate for the most up-to-date rulings.

IRELAND IMMIGRATION RULES

Entry for EEA Nationals

If you are a national of the European Union or European Economic Area (the EEA includes Iceland, Liechtenstein and Norway in addition to the EU member States) you have the right to stay in Ireland and, regardless of your economic circumstances, you have the right to an Irish residence permit. If you plan to stay in Ireland for three months or less you do not need to apply for any special visa, but if you plan to stay in Ireland for a period of between three months and one year, or for a longer period, you should apply for a residence permit. However, note that you may be refused a residence permit if you act in such a way as to be a danger to public order or security, or on public health grounds. Having a criminal record is not, in itself, grounds to be refused a residence permit.

Residence permits can be obtained from police stations. You will need to show a valid passport or identity card and any other documents that relate to your specific circumstances. When applying for a residence permit you will be asked to produce various documents to support your application, and those asked for will depend on your circumstances. If you are employed in Ireland you will be asked for a signed statement from your employer or proof of your self-employed status. If you are studying, you will be asked for evidence of registration on an approved course, in addition to proof of a health insurance policy and proof that you possess sufficient funds to provide for yourself and any family dependants who are with you while you are resident in Ireland. If you are retired or unemployed, you will be asked for evidence of health insurance and sufficient funds to support yourself and any dependents while you remain in Ireland.

Applying for a residence permit can take time as the authorities may decide to check your application, in which case a decision on whether you will be granted a permit will be deferred. In such cases, by law you are entitled to receive a decision on your application within six months of application.

Your family (defined as a spouse, children under 21 if they are dependent on you, and your parents and your spouse's parents if they are also dependent on you), whatever their nationality, also have the right to live with you in Ireland. If your family members are not EU nationals, however, then they may require an entry visa, which should be provided free of charge.

Entry for US & Canadian Nationals

US and Canadian passport holders do not need a visa to enter Ireland but will need to be in possession of a valid passport, have a round trip ticket and must be able to show evidence of sufficient funds to support themselves for the duration of their stay. Those US and Canadian citizens entering Ireland in order to attend a course of study must be able to present a letter of registration from the relevant education institution in Ireland verifying the duration and the nature of the course of study, and evidence that the requisite fees have been paid. Prospective students must also present evidence that they are covered by medical insurance for the period of their proposed stay in Ireland.

US or Canadian citizens entering Ireland for the purposes of employment must present to the immigration authorities at the port of arrival a copy of a valid work permit or a copy of confirmation from the Irish Department of Enterprise, Trade and Employment that a work permit will be issued. Those US or Canadian citizens entering Ireland to establish a business or to work on a self employed basis must be able to present a valid Business Permission from the Irish Department of Justice authorising them to operate a business in Ireland.

Permission to Remain on Entry to Ireland

Permission to enter Ireland is given by an Immigration Officer at the port of entry. When entering Ireland you will receive a stamp in your passport permitting you to remain in the country for a particular purpose for a period of up to 90 days. Those intending to stay in Ireland for more than 90 days (for study, employment or to operate a business, etc.) need to seek permission to do so within 90 days of their entry into the country from the Aliens Registration Office, *An Garda Síochána* (Police Office), Harcourt Street, Dublin 2, Ireland or if staying outside the Dublin area, from the local Police Superintendent's Office. You will need to provide a completed Aliens Registration Form (available from local police offices), a valid passport, four passport photographs and evidence of sufficient funds of support for the duration of the stay (e.g. a statement of earnings, bank statements, credit cards, ATM cards, travellers' cheques, etc.). Unauthorised overstays of the 90-day period could result in prosecution, imprisonment and a fine. Students and those intending to take up employment in Ireland will need to provide additional documentation (see below). Further information on residency permits is obtainable from the Immigration Section of the Department of Justice, Equality and Law Reform (72-76 St. Stephen's Green, Dublin 2, Ireland; ☎602 8202).

Holders of passports of the following non-EEA countries do not require a visa to travel to Ireland

Andorra	Argentina	Australia	Bahamas
Barbados	Botswana	Brazil	Brunei
Canada	Chile	Costa Rica	Croatia
El Salvador	Grenada	Guatemala	Holy See
Hong Kong SAR	Israel	Jamaica	Japan
Republic of Korea	Lesotho	Malawi	Malaysia
Mexico	Monaco	Nauru	New Zealand
Nicaragua	Panama	Paraguay	San Marino
Singapore	South Africa	Swaziland	Switzerland
Tonga	Trinidad & Tobago	USA	Uruguay
Venezuela	Western Samoa	Zimbabwe	

Work Authorisation Scheme

A work visa and work authorisation scheme has been introduced in order to facilitate the recruitment of suitably qualified people from non-EEA countries for designated sectors of the employment market in Ireland where skill shortages are particularly acute. The scheme makes it possible for prospective employees with job offers from employers in Ireland to obtain immigration and employment clearance in advance of their arrival in Ireland from Irish embassies and consulates in their home country. The scheme is a much faster alternative to the work permit procedure, although the latter is still available to employers in Ireland. Businesses in Ireland that wish to employ people from non-EEA countries will need to obtain work permits from the Department of Enterprise, Trade and Employment (Davitt House, 65a Adelaide Road, Dublin 2; ☎01-631 3079; fax 01-631 3268).

Work Visas

The rapid growth of the Irish economy in recent years has resulted in shortages of skilled personnel in some sectors of the economy, such as the information and technology industry, construction and nursing. Websites such as that of *FÁS*, the State Training and Employment Authority (www.fasjobs-ireland.com) and *Forfás* (www.askireland.com), the State body promoting industrial and technological development, have information on skill shortages and job vacancies in Ireland. In addition, some of the Irish daily newspapers and their sister websites, such as the *Irish Examiner* (www.examiner.ie), the *Irish Independent* (www.loadza.com), the *Irish Times* (www.ireland.com), the *Sunday Business Post* (www.sbpost.ie) and the *Sunday Tribune* (www.tribune.ie) have information on job vacancies.

A citizen of a country requiring a visa to enter Ireland and who has an offer of employment in one of the designated sectors (i.e. information and computing technologies, architecture, construction, surveying, town planning, nursing) from an employer in Ireland may be given a work visa by an Irish embassy or consulate.

A work visa or work authorisation is usually valid for multiple re-entries and for two years (three months in the case of a temporarily registered nurse). Authorisation to continue to work and reside in Ireland for a further two years may be granted to a holder of a work permit at the end of the first period of its validity. Holders of work visas and of work authorisations are allowed to change employers after arrival in Ireland for as long as they continue to have authorisation to work and reside in the country.

Application Process

Anyone applying for a work visa or work authorisation should present to Department of Enterprise, Trade and Employment the following:

- A completed application form
- A job offer from an employer in Ireland, corresponding to the designated skills category in which the applicant is qualified, which states the starting date and salary to be earned
- A passport valid at least until the expiry date of the relevant working visa or work authorisation
- A photograph
- The work visa or work authorisation application fee

An applicant who is a nurse must also present a certificate of temporary or full registration issued by the Nursing Board (*An Bord Altranais*). Applicants with job offers in the information and computing technologies sector must possess third-level (university or equivalent) qualifications.

Renewing Work Visas

Except in the case of temporarily registered nurses, at the end of the initial two-year period in Ireland, holders of work visas wishing to renew their work visa must apply to the Visa Office of the Department of Foreign Affairs at Hainault House, 69-71 St. Stephen's Green, Dublin 2 (☎01-4082 143; fax 01-4751 201). Those resident outside Dublin wishing to renew work authorisations will need to apply to a Superintendent of the *Garda Síochána* at their nearest police station.

Temporarily Registered Nurses. Nurses with qualifications from countries other than Australia, Canada, New Zealand and the United States must undertake a period of supervised clinical practice in an Irish hospital before they will be eligible for full registration in Ireland. The Nursing Board (An Bord Altranais) issues certificates of temporary registration allowing nurses to apply for work visas or work authorisations valid for three months. Temporarily registered nurses who do not qualify for full registration within three months will not be allowed to remain in Ireland.

Subject to their having satisfactorily completed periods of supervised clinical practice and obtaining full registration with An Bord Altranais, nurses can obtain new work visas for multiple re-entries valid for a further 21 months after which further work visas will be valid for two years at a time. These visas are obtainable from the Immigration Registration Office, Harcourt Square, Dublin 2 (☎ 01-475 5555; fax 01-478 5509) or at any office of a Superintendent of the *Garda Síochána*.

Registration and Permission to Remain in Ireland

Nationals of non-EEA countries must register with the *Garda Síochána* in the areas in which they intend to reside within three months of arriving in Ireland. In the Dublin area, registration is done at the Immigration Registration Office, Harcourt Square, Dublin 2 (☎ 01-475 5555; fax 01-478 5509). Those living outside the Dublin area should register at the Garda Superintendent's Office in the relevant Garda district.

Dependants. In general, the holder of a work authorisation may be joined by a spouse and any minor dependant children once the holder is in employment and has resided in Ireland for three months. The holder of the work authorisation must be in a position to be able to support the family members in question without the need for them to take up paid employment.

Working Holiday Permit

The Working Holiday Permit covers work of a casual or temporary nature only and is valid for an overall period of one year. The holder of a Working Holiday Permit must not engage in work with any one employer for a period in excess of three months. Applicants must be Australian or New Zealand citizens aged between 18-30 years old (a permit expires on the holder reaching 30) and single or married without children. Applicants will need to have sufficient funds to support themselves for at least the initial part of the holiday and immigration officials may request evidence of sufficient funds at the point of entry to Ireland. Taking out private medical insurance to cover hospitalisation costs in the event of an accident or illness while in Ireland is recommended, though not obligatory.

The majority of those who travel to Ireland on a Working Holiday Permit are aged between 24 and 30. The Irish Embassy in Canberra is authorised to process, on behalf of the Department of Enterprise, Trade and Employment, applications for Working Holiday Permits from Australian citizens and applications should normally be made in Canberra so that permits can be issued prior to departure for Ireland. For Australian applicants who fail to apply for a permit before departure from Australia, the Department of Foreign Affairs in Dublin (Visa Section, Hainault House, 69-71 St. Stephen's Green, Dublin 2) offers a courtesy 'postbox' service and will, on request issue application forms and explanatory leaflets, accept completed application forms and supporting documents, check passports, forward applications to Canberra for a decision and convey that decision and/or permit to an applicant in due course. Applicants will need to allow at least six weeks for an application to be processed.

In Australia any queries in relation to an application should be addressed to the Embassy of Ireland (20 Arkana Street, Yarralumla, Canberra ACT 2600; ☎ +612 6273 3022; fax +612 6273 3741).

Irish Citizenship

The Irish Nationality and Citizenship Act of 2001 created significant changes in the law affecting those wishing to obtain Irish citizenship through marriage to an Irish citizen or through naturalisation. Irish law has no objections to a person holding dual or multiple citizenship with Ireland and another State; however, other countries have citizenship laws that do not permit the holding of another citizenship alongside their own. In general a person is eligible to acquire Irish citizenship through:

- *Birth* – due to birth in the island, the islands and seas, of Ireland. This includes anyone born in Northern Ireland or born in an Irish registered aeroplane or ship, regardless of location;
- *Descent* – if one of his or her parents was an Irish citizen at the time of the person's birth, irrespective of the place of birth, or he or she was born outside Ireland to an Irish citizen who was also born outside Ireland, but who had a grandparent born in Ireland.
- *Marriage* – a non-national who was married to an Irish citizen prior to 30 November 2002 may be entitled to make a declaration of post-nuptial citizenship after three years of marriage. A non-national who has married an Irish citizen on or after 30 November 2002 can only apply for citizenship through the naturalisation process

Full details of the citizenship process are set out in information leaflets available from the Citizenship Section of the Department of Justice, Equality and Law Reform (13/14 Burgh Quay, Dublin 2, Ireland; ☎01-616 7700; fax 01-616 7701; email info@justice.ie). A helpline is available from 10am-12.30pm, Tuesdays and Thursdays only.

Naturalisation. A person who fulfils certain conditions, including residing in the State of Ireland for at least five of the preceding nine years (the last year of which must have been one of continuous residence), is 18 years of age or older, and who is of good character, may apply to the Minister for Justice, Equality and Law Reform for a certificate of naturalisation. Persons studying in Ireland may not make an application for naturalisation, though time spent studying in Ireland may be counted towards the five-year naturalisation criterion if the applicant subsequently finds employment and settles in the State.

Irish Passports. The Department of Foreign Affairs processes all applications for passports, either through the Passport Office at Molesworth Street in Dublin if the applicant is resident in Ireland, or from the nearest Irish embassy or consular office if the applicant is resident abroad. Passport applications need to be supported by documentation showing that the applicant is, or is entitled to be, an Irish citizen. Further information about obtaining a passport is available from the Department of Foreign Affairs' website at www.irlgov.ie/iveagh.

USEFUL ADDRESSES AND WEBSITES

Ireland has 43 embassies in 107 countries. Below are a list of Irish embassies and consulates in some of the English-speaking countries. A full list can be obtained from the Department of Foreign Affairs (80 St. Stephen's Green, Dublin 2; ☎01-478 0822) and at www.irlgov.ie/iveagh/embassies/abroad.asp.

Irish Embassies and Consulates Abroad

United Kingdom
Irish Embassy, 17 Grosvenor Place, London SW1X 7HR; ☎020-7235 2171; fax 020-7235 2851.
Irish Consulate, 16 Randolph Crescent, Edinburgh EH3 7TT; ☎0131-226 7711; fax 0131-226 7704.
Irish Consulate General, Brunel House, 2 Fitzalan Road, Cardiff CF24 0EB; ☎0207-225 7700; fax 0207-225 7778.

United States of America
Irish Embassy, 2234 Massachusetts Avenue NW, Washington, DC 20008-2849; ☎+1-202-462-3939; fax +1-202-232-5993.
Irish Consulate General, Ireland House, 345 Park Avenue, 17th Floor, New York, NY 10154-0037; ☎+1-212 319-2555; fax +1-202-980-9475.
Irish Consulate General, Chase Building, 535 Boylston Street, Boston, MA 02116; ☎+1-617-267-9330; fax +1-617-267-6375.
Irish Consulate General, 400 North Michigan Avenue, Chicago, IL 60611; ☎+1-312-337-1868; fax +1-312-337-1954.

RESIDENCE AND ENTRY REGULATIONS

Irish Consulate General, 100 Pine Street, 33rd Floor, San Francisco, CA 94111; ☎+1-415 392-4214; fax +1-415-392-0885.
Honorary Consul, 920 Schelbourne Street, Reno, NV 89511; ☎+1-775-853-4497; fax +1-775-853-4497.
Honorary Consul, 222 Central Central Avenue, St Louis, MO 63105; ☎+1-314-727-1000; fax +1-314-727-2960.
Honorary Consul, 2711 Weslayan, Houston, TX 77027; ☎+1-713-961-5263; fax +1-970-925-7900.
Honorary Consul, 751 Seadrift Drive, Huntington Beach, Los Angeles, CA 92648-4163; ☎+1-714-658-9832; fax +1-714-374-8972.

Canada

Irish Embassy, Suite1105, 130 Albert Street, Ottawa, K1P 5G4, Ontario; ☎+1-613-233-6281; fax +1-613-233-5835.
Irish Consulate General, 3803-8A Street SW, Calgary AB, T2T 3B6; ☎+1-403-243-2970; fax +1-403-287-1023.
Honorary Consul, 401-1385 West 8th Avenue, Vancouver, British Colombia V6H 3V9; ☎+16-04-6839233; fax +16-04-6838402.
Honorary Consul, Canadian Helicopters, Hangar No. 1, Torbay Air Base, St. John's, Newfoundland A1C 5V5; ☎+17-09-570-0511; fax +17-09-570-0506.
Honorary Consul General, Suite 1210, 20 Toronto Street, Toronto, Ontario M5C 2B8; ☎+1-416-366-9300; fax +1-416-947-0584.
Consulate General, 13 Glenmeadow Crescent, St Albert AB, T8N 3AT; ☎+1-780-458-0810; +1-780-458-6483.

Australia

Irish Embassy, 20 Arkana Street, Yarralumla, ACT 2600, Canberra; ☎+612-6273-3022; fax +612-6273-3741.
Honorary Consul General, P.O. Box 250, Floreat, Forum, WA 6014; ☎+618-9385-8247; fax +618-9385-8247.
Consulate General, Level 30, 400 George Street, Sydney 2000; ☎+612-9231-6999; fax +612-9231-6254.

New Zealand

Honorary Consul General, 6th Floor, 18 Shortland Street, Auckland 1001; ☎+64-9-977-2252; fax +64-9-977-2256; www.ireland.co.nz.

All diplomatic representation for New Zealand is handled by the Irish Embassy in Australia.

South Africa
Irish Embassy, First Floor, Sothern Life Plaza, 1059 Schoeman Street (Corner Festival Street), Arcadia 0083, Pretoria (Postal Address: PO Box 4174, Pretoria 0001); ☎+27-12-342-5062; fax +27-12-342-4752.

Embassies and Consulates in the Republic of Ireland

United Kingdom, 29 Merrion Road, Dublin 4; ☎01-205 3700; fax 01-205 3885.
United States of America, 42 Elgin Road, Ballsbridge, Dublin 4; ☎01-668 8777; fax 01-668 9946.
Canada, 4th Floor, 65/68 St. Stephen's Green, Dublin 2; ☎01-478 1988; fax 01-478 1285.
Australia, 2th Floor, Fitzwilton House, Wilton Terrace, Dublin 2; ☎01-676 1517; fax 01-668 5266.
South Africa, Chargé d'Affaires, 2nd Floor, Alexandra House, Earlsfort Centre, Earlsfort Terrace, Dublin 2; ☎01-661 5553; fax 01-661 5590.

CUSTOMS REGULATIONS

Customs officers in Ireland are allowed to carry out selective checks on all travellers at all points of entry to Ireland (air and sea) to ensure that prohibited or restricted goods are not being carried and to combat smuggling.

Since June 1999, the sale of duty-free goods to those travelling within the European Union has been abolished, although such goods are still available to those travelling to destinations outside the EU. What this means is that any goods bought within the EU (with the exception of food, drink and tobacco bought for on-board consumption) will now be subject to normal rates of excise duty and VAT. Travellers will not be charged any extra duty or VAT on purchases where the duty and VAT has been paid (e.g. on goods bought in shops, supermarkets, etc.)

in another EU country, provided the goods are for personal use only.

If a traveller's purchases are equivalent to or less than the quantities stated below, they would usually be regarded as being for personal use only. However, if these quantities are exceeded, Customs will need to be convinced that the goods are indeed only for personal use. Receipts should be kept as proof that duty and VAT has been paid. Those aged less than 17 years are not entitled to alcohol or tobacco allowances.

GOODS AND ALLOWANCES

Goods	Maximum quantity allowed
Cigarettes	800
Cigarillos	400
Cigars	200
Smoking tobacco	1 kg
Spirits (whisky, vodka, gin, etc.)	10 litres
Intermediate Products (e.g. sherry, port, etc., excluding sparkling wine)	20 litres
Wine (only 60 litres of sparkling wine allowed)	90 litres
Beer	110 litres

Those travelling to Ireland from countries outside the EU (including the Canary Islands, the Channel Islands and Gibraltar) are allowed to take in to Ireland the goods shown in the table below subject to maximum limits. The goods in question may have been bought either duty-free/tax-free or duty-paid/tax-paid outside the EU.

GOODS AND ALLOWANCES

Goods	Maximum quantity allowed
Cigarettes	200g
Cigarillos	100g
Cigars	50g
Tobacco	250g
Spirits (whisky, vodka, gin, etc.)	1 litre
Intermediate products (sherry, port, sparkling wine, etc.)	2 litres

Still wine	2 litres
Perfume	60 mls (50g)
Eau de toilette	250 mls (0.25 litre)
Other goods, including beer, gifts and souvenirs	€175 per adult and €90 per child under 15 years

Certain goods cannot be imported to Ireland, or can only be imported under licence. The main items that cannot be imported or must be imported under licence are:

- Firearms
- Ammunition
- Explosives
- Offensive weapons
- Indecent or obscene material (books, periodicals, prints and video recordings)
- Plants or bulbs
- Live animals or dead animals (including cats and dogs)
- Birds or poultry
- Endangered species
- Hay or straw (even if used as packing)

It is an offence to import or carry controlled substances (i.e. drugs including cannabis, cocaine, heroin and amphetamines) when travelling to or from Ireland. The Customs National Drugs Team has dog units located at airports and ferryports trained to sniff out drugs.

Useful Addresses

The Office of the Collector of Customs and Excise, Dublin Castle, Dublin 2; ☎01-647 5000; www.revenue.ie.

Customs and Excise Information Office, Irish Life Centre, Lower Abbey Street, Dublin 1; ☎01-817 1920; www.revenue.ie

SETTING UP HOME

CHAPTER SUMMARY

- **Housing.** About 80% of the population of Ireland own their own homes.
  - In the early 1990s Ireland had the smallest housing stock – relative to its population – in the EU.
- **Buying Property.** Property in Ireland is sold on the understanding of *Caveat Emptor* ('Let the Buyer Beware').
  - A cottage located in the Midlands will sell for far less than one in the same state of repair on the East Coast.
  - Many properties are sold at auction in Ireland.
- **Services.** Utility companies in Ireland generally bill for the provision of electricity, gas and the telephone every two months.
- **Importing a Car.** If you import a vehicle into Ireland you will need to register your vehicle at a Revenue Vehicle Registration Office and pay a Vehicle Registration Tax based on the resale value of the vehicle.
- **Quarantine.** Animals being imported into Ireland from the UK, the Channel Islands or the Isle of Man are not subject to quarantine requirements.

THE IRISH WAY OF LIFE

Some 80% of all homes in Ireland are owned by the residents, compared with 69% in England, 62% in Scotland, 72% in Wales and 68% in Northern Ireland. The average price paid for a house in Ireland in February 2004 was €237,179 (approx. £157,988.US $280,346). The average price paid for a house in Dublin was €309,347 (approx. £206,085/US $365,666); outside Dublin the price was €207,335. The year-on-year increase in national prices to the end of February 2004 was 13.3%. The rate of house price growth outside Dublin (at 1%) was more than twice that experienced within the Dublin area (0.4%). Houses in Ireland are most definitely not as cheap as they were and there is something of a housing shortage nationwide.

With the population of Ireland increasing through immigration and natural demographics, the number of young people reaching the age when they are thinking about buying their own home (with half the population of the country under 25) is pretty high. With increased social and economic independence, more young people than ever before want to move out of the family home and live in their own home yet many people in their 30s are still living with their parents because they cannot afford to buy. As has happened in the UK, house prices have gone beyond the reach of many of those who want to own their own home.

Over 30% of the Irish population live in homes built since 1990 and the spread of new housing throughout the country is evident for all to see. This building boom has been necessary, as there is still a shortfall of available housing, but the increasing demolition of old rural houses to make way for new bungalows and neo-Edwardian dwellings is a reflection of the Irish tendency to associate all things old with the poverty and discontent of a colonial past. An interesting footnote to this building boom and the Irish craving for all things new is that although Ireland has a larger number of historical place names than any other country in Europe, this hasn't deterred property developers and builders from pandering to the desire of some of the Irish to live in new housing schemes with upmarket sounding monikers such as Cambridge Close or Chelsea Terrace.

RENT OR BUY?

Whether you decide to rent or buy a property on arrival in Ireland will partly depend on financial factors: Do you have the capital available in order to buy? Have you obtained equity from a property that you have sold or will you need a mortgage in order to purchase? If so, can you satisfy the financial criteria demanded by a lender? There are also practical considerations to take into account: Are you committed to moving to Ireland by a certain date – to take up employment, for example? Are you in the process of selling your property in your home country? Will it sell before you leave and if not, can you afford to buy a place in Ireland before it does?

When relocating to another country it seems sensible to move into a long-let property in the area of your choice to begin with, and then scout around for a suitable property to buy (assuming you have the capital) once you have got to know the area, and prices. If you own a property in your home country then rent it out to begin with, as you may decide that life in Ireland isn't what you expected/hoped for and you want to return home. Burning bridges is always a risky idea. If you are moving to Ireland to take up a job then the employer may be able to provide you with accommodation as part of a relocation package, and will at least be able to help you locate rental agencies.

It can be harder to find rented accommodation in the remoter regions of Ireland, although in the more touristy areas it is often possible to negotiate a long winter let in one of the cottages let during the summer for holiday accommodation. Most rented accommodation is let furnished.

Obviously, once you are settled in an area and decide to stay, it makes sense to buy a property. With a mortgage, your monthly outgoings are likely to be fairly similar whether you rent or buy, and buying property is one of the best, relatively risk-free investments you can make. About 80% of the population of Ireland own their own homes (around 40% own their homes outright – with no mortgage repayments outstanding), and with a young population looking to get its feet on the property ladder, houses prices in Ireland are higher than they have ever been. Prices for both new and second-hand homes are expected to increase by 3%-6% in 2004.

FINANCE

Mortgages

Mortgages in Ireland are available from building societies and banks but be aware that practices vary between different mortgage lenders so it is important to shop around.

There are several types of mortgage available in Ireland. As a general guideline, the maximum amount that a bank or a building society will consider lending is 90%-92% of a property's value or 2.5-3 times the primary annual gross salary and 1 times the secondary annual gross salary where there are two partners working, or 3.25 times the annual gross salary of a single buyer. However, as house prices have increased lenders have increased the amounts they are prepared to lend. The minimum cash deposit needed will usually be at least 8% of the value of the property, and in addition the costs of conveyancing (stamp duty, legal fees, etc.) will need to be found. The larger the deposit, the smaller the loan, and therefore the least interest accrued. The maximum mortgage term that most lenders will consider is 35 years; and they will require a mortgage to be paid off by the time the borrower has reached the age of 65.

Only a third of Irish residential mortgages are bought through independent mortgage brokers (compared to two-thirds in the UK), but going through a broker can save you time and money, as a broker will be able to survey a number of mortgage companies and then offer you the best option available. However, find out if your broker deals with all the mortgage lenders, or only some of them. Some people are denied mortgages because of bad credit ratings or uncertain incomes – the self-employed in particular may have problems finding a mortgage, especially if going through a bank or building society, and will at the very least need to produce three years' accounts so that the lender can determine the risk they may pose. For people in such circumstances it may be easier to use the services of a mortgage broker, who will know those lenders that can assist those who do not conform to the standard picture of a model house buyer. Irish Mortgage Corporation (118 Lower Baggot Street, Dublin 2; ☎ 01-676 3654; fax 01-661 9102) is an independent brokerage company with a website at www.irishmortgage.ie that has a search facility allowing you to you to rank the top lenders in the mortgage lending category of most interest to you.

If you are unable to get a loan from a building society or bank, and you are resident in Ireland, you may be eligible for an annuity mortgage from your local authority. These loans can be up to 95% of the price of a house, capped at €126,974 (approx. £84,587/US $150,086, and subject to repayments of not more than 35% of the household net income (after tax and PRSI deductions). To be eligible for a local authority mortgage you will need to meet certain criteria concerning your income and housing status.

At the beginning of 2004 the rate of variable rate mortgages offered by the lending companies ranged from 3.30% from Allied Irish Banks to 3.55% from Permanent TSB. Fixed mortgage rates ranged from 2.59% for a one-year fixed mortgage from the Bank of Ireland to a 4.19% three-year fixed rate from Irish Nationwide.

Repayment Mortgages. The repayment, or annuity, mortgage is the most common type of mortgage. The loan is gradually repaid over the length of the period of the mortgage, with the borrower repaying on a monthly basis both the interest on the loan and a portion of the outstanding loan amount. As the outstanding loan reduces, the element of interest to be paid also reduces and the balance changes to a down payment of the loan as the period progresses until the loan is fully paid at the end of the mortgage term. Annuity mortgages are by far the most popular way of buying property in Ireland, especially as they attract tax relief on the interest charges.

Endowment Mortgages. The loan amount remains the same throughout the mortgage term and interest is paid on the total amount of the loan for the whole of the mortgage period. The amount of interest will fluctuate with changes in interest rates. Alongside the mortgage, a life assurance policy is taken out and the borrower's monthly premiums, less charges, are paid to an insurance company, which then invests them in shares, bonds and other assets. Premiums are set at a level that should ensure that the accumulated investment funds pay off the loan in full at the end of the mortgage period. However, there is no guarantee that this will be the case and you may end up with a shortfall. If the insurance company is doing its job properly it should monitor the progress of investments and, if necessary, increase the monthly premiums payable and of course it is also possible that you may end up with a surplus, which will be payable to you as a tax-free lump sum at the end of the mortgage period. In the event of the death of the borrower, the mortgage is paid off in full. Where there is more than one party to the mortgage, i.e. if a married couple take out a joint mortgage, the mortgage may be paid off in the event of the death of either party and the surviving borrower will own the property outright even if the mortgage still has a period to run.

It is strongly advised that you get good advice from a mortgage broker before deciding on an endowment mortgage. There has been concern in recent years that endowment mortgages may not be performing well enough to pay off the full amount of the mortgage. Due to adverse publicity regarding the whole concept of this type of mortgage, financial institutions have ceased selling them, and others are introducing lower charge endowment plans.

Pension Mortgage. Pension mortgages are similar to endowment interest-only mortgages but are only available to the self-employed or those in non-pensionable employment. A pension plan rather than an endowment policy supports the mortgage in this case, with the lump-sum portion of a pension plan used to repay the mortgage in full at the end of the mortgage term. A borrower has the advantage of gaining tax relief at the highest tax rate on the pension premiums.

Low-Start Mortgage. This type of mortgage postpones the repayment of some of the interest that is normally paid at the beginning of the loan by adding it to the amount of the loan, so that the loan increases over time after a fixed period. First-time buyers on a low income may be drawn to this kind of mortgage, but it is important to be sure that you will be able to afford the increased repayments. And if interest rates rise, an outstanding loan may end up being worth more than the value of the house.

Foreign Currency Mortgage. It is possible to obtain a mortgage in a foreign currency such as Swiss francs, US dollars or Japanese yen. The way such mortgages work is that instead of lending the borrower the money to buy a house in Ireland in Euros, a bank will lend Swiss francs, for example. The borrower then sells the Swiss francs for Euros in order to buy the house. The debt will still be in Swiss francs and the borrower will pay Swiss franc interest rates, not Euro interest rates. When the borrower receives the interest charge in Swiss francs he or she simply sells some Euros and buys some Swiss francs to repay the interest on the loan. There will be a commission to pay each time the borrower converts Euros to the foreign currency in which the loan is held.

With historically low interest rates, this type of mortgage has provided large savings for borrowers in the past. The downside is that interest rate gains can be lost due to currency swings, although shifting the mortgage between a variety of currencies should minimise losses. Such loans are usually only available to very high earners and for a maximum of 60% of a property's value. Consult a financial advisor before deciding whether to apply for this kind of mortgage.

Fixed & Variable Rate Mortgages

Whether you decide on an endowment or repayment mortgage, you can also choose between a fixed rate and a variable rate loan. Interest on fixed rate loans is fixed for a specified period of years (generally between one and ten years), whereby payments remain constant. Interest on variable rate loans can rise or fall depending on changes decided by the mortgage company and rate changes determined by base interest rates set by the European Central Bank. Some mortgage companies can offer a combination of fixed and variable rate repayment options.

Commercial & Buy-to-Let Mortgages

If you are looking to find a mortgage to buy commercial premises for business purposes then you will need to approach mortgage lenders with copies of your business' accounts or, if the business is a start-up, then a business plan and information about finances and expected turnover, etc. Rates on commercial loans are not as favourable as those on home loans.

Some lenders have special mortgage schemes for those who wish to invest in a residential property for letting purposes without paying commercial rates. Such mortgages work out more expensive than those for buying your own home, however, they have the advantage that when deciding how much you can borrow, they take into account a percentage of the expected rental income on the property.

Redemption Charges

Although it may be desirable, as your circumstances change, to pay off a mortgage before the mortgage term is to end, or to switch to a more competitive mortgage, in many cases a redemption fee will be charged by the lender to offset their loss in interest payments over the remaining period of the loan. This charge may be as much as five or six percent of the loan, or 12 months' interest. The charges are higher the earlier you repay the loan. High redemption charges are particularly likely with mortgages offering low fixed-interest rates for the first few years, or those with discounts of standard variable rates.

Mortgage Interest Relief at Source

Since January 2002 the mortgage lender, rather than the Revenue, gives you tax relief on mortgage interest paid, which means that any mortgage repayments will be reduced by the amount of tax relief. The mortgage lender then reclaims the tax relief from the Revenue Commissioners. Tax relief on a mortgage is available for a period of seven years and is subject to upper limits, which depend on personal circumstances and whether or not you are a first-time buyer. Borrowers who take out new mortgages must complete Form TRS1, avaiable from the Tax Relief Section, Collector-Generals, Sarsfield House, Francis Street, Limerick (☎ 1890-463 626; www.revenue.ie). It is not necessary to claim mortgage interest relief in an annual tax return. The maximum amounts of interest relief allowable at the time of going to print for first-time mortgage holders was €4,000 for a single holder and €8,000 for a widowed or married holder; for non first-time buyers the rates were €2,540, and €5,080 respectively.

Non-Mortgageable Properties

Before a mortgage company will lend you money to buy a property it will want to be satisfied that the property is worth the money you intend to pay for it. The mortgage company will have a survey carried out – at a cost to you – to determine the value of the property. Any amount that a mortgage company agrees to lend you will take this evaluation into account. In some cases lenders may refuse a mortgage on a property, particularly if you wish to buy a run-down or semi-derelict property requiring a great deal of renovation, or a property that is not of approved construction. If this is the case then shop around as you may find another mortgage company prepared to lend the money.

Buying Land

If you satisfy requirements regarding income and so forth, there should be no difficulty getting a mortgage if you wish to buy a plot of land and build a house on it immediately (assuming of course that there is planning permission to do so). The amount of the mortgage would be based on the combined value of the land and the house you build, together with the cost of running services such as mains water and electricity to the site. However, if you wish just to buy a building site, with the intention of building on it at some later date, you would not be granted a mortgage on the land alone. In this case you would have to find the cash or look for some other form of loan to purchase the land, probably at a higher rate of interest.

FINDING A HOME

There is something at once both joyful, but also bleak about searching for a property to buy. The experience is the same wherever the location, and looking for property in Ireland is no exception. In the early 1990s Ireland had the smallest housing stock – relative to its population – in the EU, together with the highest average household size. A housing shortage ensued. To make up for this there was a massive building boom (between 1992 and 2002 around 420,000 houses were built – a third of the housing stock currently available today) but despite this accommodation is still in short supply in Ireland. This historic lack of dwellings, as well as increased immigration from returning expats and others, is at the root of the cause of shortages of housing and the rising house prices experienced today.

Finding a Property

The obvious way to find a suitable property is to contact all the auctioneers and estate agents who are selling properties in your chosen area, tell them what you want in terms of location, size and price and ask them to inform you of any suitable properties that they have on their books, and to keep you in mind when new properties come on to the market. Some estate agents maintain mailing lists while others do not, so often it will be up to you to keep proactive and visit agents' offices regularly in addition to keeping an eye on the property pages of local newspapers. It is also a good idea to take a regular look around your target area to keep a lookout for properties that you may have missed while visiting estate agents. Perhaps an agent unknown to you has a property for sale, or an owner is selling a property privately without using an agent, or you may find a vacant property, which might be for sale if you find the owner to ask.

Most properties in Ireland are sold through estate agents, or 'auctioneers' as they are generally known, while a small percentage are sold at public auction. Properties that come up for sale at auction will have a reserve price set, which must be met or exceeded by the bidders. This reserve is often not disclosed by the auction house and need not necessarily be anywhere near the actual price accepted for a property on the day of the auction. If you find and covet a property coming up for auction you will need to get a solicitor to check the contracts of the property, which will be held by the vendor's own solicitor. Auctions are advertised in advance in the local press, which give potential buyers time to arrange a surveyor's report of the property and to discover any legal, financial or practical reasons why the property may be a bad investment.

Because properties can often sell for far more than their true market value at auction (people get carried away) it is important to honestly evaluate all costs associated with the purchase of a property before deciding to engage the services of estate agents, surveyors, solicitors, etc. Once a property has gone to the highest bidder he or she will have to pay on the day the required 10% deposit. The balance is paid after the legal formalities have been completed on the purchase, which can take between 6 and 12 weeks. Note that vendors are entitled to withdraw their property from an auction at any time.

Estate Agents

The majority of estate agents in Ireland belong to a professional body such as IPAV (the Irish Professional Auctioneers and Valuers, 129 Lower Baggot Street, Dublin 2; ☎01-678 5685; fax 01-676 2890; www.ipav.ie) or IAVI (the Irish Auctioneers and Valuers Institute, 38 Merrion Square, Dublin 2; ☎01-661 1794; fax 01-661 1797; www.iavi). IPAV is the representative body for qualified, licensed auctioneers, valuers and estate agents throughout Ireland and is affiliated with the Confederation of European Estate Agents (CEI), which represents 25,000 estate agents throughout Europe. IAVI represents over 1,550 real estate agents and auctioneers in Ireland. A listing of all IAVI members across Ireland is available from the Institute.

Property in Ireland is sold on the understanding of *Caveat Emptor* ('Let the Buyer Beware'). An estate agent's job is to get the best price possible for a property so that his client will receive a good price for the property and his firm can take a good commission, which means that an estate agent who voluntarily discloses information about his client's property that would prove detrimental to the sale would be in breach of his contract of agency. However, although an agent cannot volunteer negative facts about a property under sale, a prospective buyer may *elicit* information by asking an agent the right questions.

Estate agents charge the vendor a certain percentage of the final sale price of a property (usually between 2% and 3.5%, but negotiable) for their services, so as a buyer you will not be charged directly for using an estate agent's services (though indirectly you will, as the fee will be passed on to you by the vendor through the purchase price!). The estate agent will arrange accompanied viewings of properties you wish to see.

www.property.ie

Ireland's Premier property website

Advertising properties sold through estate agents and properties being sold privately throughout Ireland

Email: info@property.ie
Tel: +353 90 6482818
Fax: +353 90 6482819

The Internet

There are a large number of websites advertising property for sale in Ireland, either privately or through estate agents' sites. One important website is www.property.ie, which advertises properties throughout Ireland; it covers all types of residential property, holiday homes, commercial property and plots for development.

Other sites include www.niceone.com – Ireland's Internet directory, which holds a listing of numerous estate agents throughout the country, and www.irishpropertywebsites.com. There are many similar sites on the Internet, with new ones coming online all the time. A search for 'Irish Property' using any of the search engines such as google.com or yahoo.com will lead you to more.

Old Property

If it's character in a property you're after, then you will be looking to buy an old property. As with all property there are pros and cons to this sort of purchase and you will at the very least need to get a structural survey of such a property done before proceeding to purchase. Structural soundness can never be guaranteed on an old property. A lot of the time the price of a property will depend very much on location and the state of repair. A picture postcard stone cottage on the western seaboard with stunning views is not going to sell for a song, however pokey the actual living accommodation. Such properties will attract both romantics from abroad looking to 'live the life' as well as the well-heeled Irish looking for a holiday home. However, a cottage in the same condition but located in the unfashionable Midlands will sell for far less. Anything within commutable distance of the main cities of Dublin, Limerick, Cork, Waterford and Galway will come at a premium. Since the seventies West Cork has been a particular favourite haunt of those looking to buy old properties in need of repair. Such places may have needed extensive renovation work but they were cheap to buy and were often located in suitably dramatic and beautiful scenery. These days even a shell of an old property in such a location could set you back about €70,000.

A renovation project can be an exceedingly fulfilling occupation for those with the knowledge and know-how, and can also prove quite profitable. Older, traditional properties may need repairs undertaken costing both time and money, and unless fitted with central heating they are usually more expensive to heat; fixtures and fittings may also have to be replaced. There is a stamp duty payable on second-hand properties (see *Conveyancing* below).

New Property

There are certain advantages in buying a new house: they tend to be built to higher standards than older houses and come with thermal insulation, double glazing, modern central heating and adequate ventilation, which may not always be the case with an older property. They are often sold complete with luxury fitted kitchens, bathrooms and bedrooms, together with the full range of kitchen appliances such as fridges, freezers, dishwashers and so forth. Many property developers tend to build small 'estates' or 'developments' of around a dozen or more similar houses, which may be a disadvantage if you prefer to keep some distance between you and the neighbours. Newly built bungalows have spread all over Ireland like a rash in recent years.

The process of buying a new house is exactly the same as buying any other property but it has the advantage that you will not find yourself caught in a chain of buyers – i.e. where the house you want to buy will not be available until its current occupants can take occupation of the house they are buying, which may not become available until the owners of that house can move into the house that they are negotiating to buy, etc, etc. In such cases you can find yourself in a chain of several different parties, all waiting on the party at the top of the chain to reach the stage of vacating their property. If any one of the links in such a chain pulls out, this can result in all the other sales falling through.

The is no stamp duty to be paid by owner occupiers on most new homes and in addition new homes are covered by a 'Home Bond' or 'Premier Guarantee', which covers the property for structural soundness for a period of ten years. The downside of buying a new property, apart from a lack of character, is that the houses and the accommodation tend to be smaller than second-hand homes and gardens are also often rather small.

Self-Build

The term 'self-build' does not mean that you have to physically design and construct a house yourself – although those who have the skills may do all or part of the building or fitting-out work themselves. You may hire a building contractor to undertake all the work, or you may wish to employ a number of different tradesmen and craftsmen to work on various parts of the project. What it does mean is that you will have overall control of the build from start to finish and you can work with an architect or builder to produce a building to suit your individual requirements.

So, what if you come across a plot of land for sale that has a perfect view and you say to yourself, 'What a perfect place to build a house.' Well, you'll first of all need to investigate whether the plot has planning permission, or whether it will be possible to obtain planning permission from the local authorities; otherwise all your dreams will come to nothing. And plots of land that already have planning permission will cost a lot more than land without. Planning permission must be applied for from the Chief Officer of the Planning Department of the local authority.

A self-build project is not something to be entered into lightly, and you will need to make sure that you have the budget available to complete the build. In addition to the costs of the building work there are the costs of buying the land and of installing services such as electricity, water and sewerage on site. There are also likely to be other unforeseen costs that arise due to the topography of the land and to changing planning regulations. You will need to be able to crack the whip with tradesmen, should they decide to let standards and punctuality slip, and will have to find somewhere to live while the project is underway. For reasons such as these, together with the vagaries of the Irish climate, delays to the completion of the project are likely and costs can creep up, and up. If you decide to build your own home, remember there are only two things of which you can be certain: the project will take longer than you initially expected, and it will cost more. However, you should also end up with a unique house, tailored to your specific needs and, especially if you can do part of the work yourself, you may end up with a property costing less than a similar one bought from an estate agent.

A fact sheet, *'Making a Planning Application'* can be obtain from local authorities and from the the Department of the Environment and Local Government (Custom House, Dublin 1; ☎ 01-888 2000; www.environ.ie).

Other Sources of Property

Property for sale and to rent can also be found advertised by estate agents and auctioneers in local and national newspapers. If money is no object, very expensive and exclusive properties and large country estates are advertised for sale in glossy magazines such as *The Field*, *Country Life*; Ireland's quarterly *Irish Countrysports and Country Life* magazine (www.countrysportsandcountrylife.com), and in the national daily or Sunday broadsheet newspapers such as *The Telegraph*, *The Observer*, *Irish Independent*, *Irish Examiner*, etc. Electronic online versions of some of these newspapers have their own property for sale sections, e.g. www.telegraph.co.uk, www.unison.com. Dedicated Irish property portals such as www.propertyfile.net, www.myhome.ie and www.irishpropertynews.com are also a good starting point when researching the market, as are the monthly property magazines such as *Irish Property Buyer* and *Irish Property Monthly* (www.irishpropertymonthly.com).

It can be very difficult to find a property to buy in a rural area from a distance and some vendors look to sell their property without advertising it beyond the local area. Some houses for sale are only advertised in local newspapers, which have a small circulation so it is useful to have a contact 'on the ground' who can sniff out these properties for you.

PURCHASING & CONVEYANCING PROCEDURES

Before you make an offer on a house (especially a second-hand house) you will want to carry out a structural survey to make sure it meets the required standards and that you are not buying a white elephant. A surveyor will evaluate the accessible and visible parts of the property, including the roof space, to ensure that it is structurally sound and then complete a standard valuation report for the mortgage lender, if you have one. If you are looking to buy a second-hand property the surveyor will look for serious structural problems of the property such as subsidence, dry rot or collapsed drains. If the property is new, the surveyor will compile a 'snag list' indicating what needs to be done before the property is suitable for occupation. The fees a surveyor will charge will depend on the age and size of the house. Once a survey has been carried out and you are happy to go through with the purchase, you can make an offer. There may then follow a period of haggling over price. Once your offer has been accepted by the vendor, a Contract of Sale will be prepared which binds both parties to the completion of the sale, a deposit (typically of 10% of the purchase price) will be paid and a date set for the payment of the balance and the handing over of the keys.

Solicitors

Since there is no fixed rate of charges for legal fees in Ireland solicitors can offer competitive rates for conveyancing work and quotes will vary from law firm to law firm. Shop around and ask friends in Ireland for recommendations. Solicitors may charge a flat fee or a percentage of the purchase price and so you will need to be clear by which method you are to be charged. Note that there may be other costs associated with the legal process involved in the conveyancing process, such as land registry fees and search fees to determine a property's history and that VAT (at 21%) is also payable on legal fees.

Make sure that the solicitor you hire is not also representing the vendor of the property, as a clash of interests could ensue. Names and addresses of solicitors can be found in the Golden Pages directory and through the Law Society of Ireland. A solicitor's duty over the conveyancing procedure is to:

- Check if there are legal issues attached to the property, i.e. Boundary disputes, planning regulation restrictions, flouting of the law in respect to building standards, etc.
- Check the title of the property to ensure that the vendor is the legal owner and entitled to sell the property.
- Ensure that all fixtures and fittings included in the negotiated price are also included in the legal documents.
- Ensure there is no outstanding mortgage on the property, and that all utility bills have been paid up in full and that any debts against the property have been cleared.
- Ensure that there is no compulsory purchase order on the property.
- Ensure that the client fully understands all documents before signing them.
- Ensure that stamp duty is paid.
- Oversee the exchange of contracts.

Once your solicitor has received satisfactory replies to the checks carried out (the 'Requisitions on Title') a Deed of Conveyance will be drawn up, and, if involved, the mortgage company will be contacted by your solicitor to issue the approved loan. Once the remaining balance of the purchase has been received by the vendor's solicitor, the title deeds and keys to the premises will be handed over to your solicitor.

Once the sale is completed, the deeds of the property, showing the new ownership details, and mortgage details if relevant, are presented to the Revenue Commissioners, who determine how much stamp duty is due. Once this amount has been paid to the Revenue

Commissioners, the deeds are stamped and must then be registered with either the Registry of Deeds or the Land Registry. The timescale of the conveyance procedure will depend on individual circumstances but is usually between 8-12 weeks, though sometimes it can be less.

The Costs of Buying Property

Solicitors. The standard conveyancing fee has always been around 1% of the purchase price of a property but as the nature of the business is competitive solicitors these days are more willing to negotiate a fixed fee.

Survey Fees. If you are hoping to buy a second-hand house then a survey of the property is a must. Costs vary, and range from around €135 to €400 depending on the amount of work to be undertaken by the surveyor. Shop around.

Estate Agents. The buyer should not have to pay anything to the estate agent who is selling the property. Estate agents charge fees only to the vendor, and these will vary from company to company but generally fall within the range of 2%-3.5% of the selling price, but are negotiable. The fees are used towards producing a brochure with a photograph and details of the property, advertising the property in the agent's offices and in newspapers, placing an advertising board outside the property, showing prospective purchasers round the property and acting as the intermediary between buyer and seller when an offer is made.

Stamp Duty. Stamp duty is a tax payable based on the value of the property and the status of the buyer (first-time buyer, investor, etc). The duty is due when deeds are presented to the Revenue Commissioners after the closing of a sale. The solicitor calculates the amount of stamp duty to be paid on the property and requests this from the purchaser prior to the closing of the sale. Stamp duty is calculated as a percentage of the purchase price and ranges between 3% and 9%, depending on the value of the property. There is also a stamp duty of €1 for every €1,000 borrowed, to be paid on any mortgage worth more than €254,000.

Lending Agency Fees. These may include an application fee (typically of 0.5%); the cost of a survey of the property and a valuation report; any searches required on the property; mortgage loan costs and an indemnity bond (to ensure that if the lender has to repossess the property it won't make a loss).

Land Registry Fees. These are due once a property has changed hands. The details of the new owner are registered to prove ownership of the property.

LAND REGISTRY FEES	
House Price	**Land Registry Fee**
€1-€13,000	€125
€13,001-€26,000	€190
€26,001-€51,000	€250
€51,001-€225,000	€375
€255,001-€385,000	€500
€385,001+	€625
Land Registry fee on Mortgage	€125
Land Registry fee to open new folio	€50

Buildings Insurance. A property and its contents should be adequately insured against fire and general household risks and in any case it is a condition of any mortgage that a property is fully insured against structural and other damage for the full term of the loan. It is also advisable to obtain Insurance Protection so that, in the case of unexpected death, any mortgage repayments outstanding will be cleared by the insurance company. There are a number of companies offering these Household Policies. Premiums payable vary depending on individual circumstances, the area in which you live, the size and type of the property and the insurance company.

When insuring commercial properties it is advisable to not only consider the usual risks of fires, malicious damage, etc. but to also take out an adequate level of cover in respect of Public Liability and Employer Liability.

RENTING PROPERTY

It is always a good idea to initially rent a property in a place where you are intending to settle, rather than rushing headlong into buying a place. The reasons for this are twofold; first of all, renting a property will allow you to get a feel for the area and people around the locale where you are thinking of buying. If you find that you're not too happy with the pace of life, cost of property, services or climate in one area you can always move to another and check out the situation there. Additionally, buying a property is a major financial commitment and therefore not something to be entered into lightly by most of us mortals.

Looking for a flat or house to rent in Ireland is a far less complicated procedure than looking for a place to buy and will be challenging or easy depending on location and personal tastes. The range of property available for rent will depend on the locality – larger cities and towns will have more to offer than smaller towns and villages in both type of property available, and rental price. In general, rental prices outside the larger urban areas are lower. Not all rental properties will be available fully – or even part – furnished

The property sections of local newspapers is a good place to look for rental accommodation but you should buy these newspapers on the day that they are published as the best deals are often snapped up very quickly. You may also find 'accommodation for rent' notices displayed in shop windows or on notice boards in supermarkets. Depending on what you are looking for, colleges often have notice boards offering accommodation in shared houses. The cost of renting a room in a student house can be very cheap though it will depend on your age and stamina whether you can live with the mess and noise that students tend to generate.

In more rural areas of Ireland it is worth talking to locals in pubs, shops and post offices to see if they know of anywhere locally. Even if they don't, they may know of someone who may be able to help you in this respect.

Once you have found a property that you consider suitable contact the landlord and arrange a time and date for you to view the property. When considering whether to take a property or not you should consider the following:

- Are there any signs of dampness?
- Do the windows open?
- What security is available (i.e., window locks, burglar alarm)?
- Is a smoke detector provided and is it functioning?
- Are bills (heating, lighting, water and telephone) inclusive in the rental cost?
- Is there adequate hot water, heating provision?
- Who is responsible for repairs to fixtures and fittings should they need replacing?
- If there are repairs needed, will the landlord carry them out before your tenancy begins?
- Are the cooker and fridge clean and in working order?
- Is there adequate storage space?
- Parking amenities for a car, bicycles, pram?
- How far is the property from a bus route or public transport point?
- Are shops and facilities nearby?

Landlords will usually ask for a deposit, which typically will be a month's rent. Make sure that you get a receipt for any deposit or rent that you pay in advance and find out how and when the landlord would like rent to be paid. A deposit may be kept by a landlord if you leave a property without giving the proper notice period, if you leave before the end of a fixed term lease (usually of six or twelve months), if you cause damage to the accommodation beyond that considered to be normal wear and tear (this latter will very much depend on the landlord), or if you leave the property at the end of the agreed rental period with bills or rent left unpaid.

Before agreeing to rent a property make sure you can afford the rent being asked and find out what rights you are entitled to as well as what your obligations are in respect to renting the property. These should be set out in the rental contract but if you are unsure or unclear about anything contained in the contract ask before signing. Contracts tend to contain a great deal of almost indecipherable legalese jargon, but don't skim over anything that may end up committing you to more than you are happy with.

If the landlord wants you to sign a fixed term lease of six months or a year, don't agree to this unless you are sure that you want to stay that long, as you may lose your deposit if you decide to leave before the end of a fixed term lease. At the same time you should agree with the landlord a list of fixtures and fittings, furnishings and appliances that have been provided with the property. Having a written and signed itemised inventory will help to prevent future possible disagreements or disputes with a landlord. If the property shows any signs of damage caused by previous tenants make sure that this is noted too.

Note that if you will be claiming help with paying the rent from local authorities make sure that you know the local maximum rent level allowed by the Health Board and let the landlord know that you will be claiming it, since not all landlords will take tenants on rent supplement.

Free, confidential advice on housing rights in Ireland can be obtained from Threshold (21 Stoneybatter, Dublin 7; ☎ 01-6786 096; fax 01-677 2407; www.threshold.ie), a charitable organisation with offices in Dublin, Galway and Cork, and from Citizens Information Centres throughout Ireland.

Letting Agents

A more direct route to finding rental accommodation, and one that could save you a lot of legwork, is to go through an accommodation or letting agency. Agencies act as intermediaries between the landlord and the tenant and generally charge a fee (often a week's rent) for helping you find private rented accommodation. Agencies tend to offer accommodation that may be more expensive than that advertised privately in newspapers or on notice boards. Often an agency will have a regularly updated list of properties available for rent in the area.

Some properties are run by property management companies where the owners pass over responsibility for the day to day maintenance as well as the collection of rents. These are particularly often found in connection with buildings containing a number of flats owned by different people. The management company will charge service charges to both owners and tenants for maintenance and repairs to the building, in addition to administration charges for the collection and transferral of rents.

If you are asked to pay a fee before the agency has found you a property make sure that the agency is licensed and find out what services you will be offered and under what circumstances you be entitled to a refund. Ensure that you are given a receipt for any money you pay an agency.

Tenancy Agreements

When a property is rented, a tenancy agreement must be signed by both the landlord and the tenant. It is a legal contract, so both parties who sign it agree to abide by the conditions contained within it and if they fail to do so the other party can take legal action against them. For this reason it is essential to read the tenancy agreement closely, and to obtain the advice of a solicitor if there is anything you are unsure or unhappy about.

Rental Costs

The tenancy agreement will detail how often and in what form the rent is to be paid. This is normally payable in advance for one month at a time. The agreement will state the length of time the tenant agrees to take the property, and rent is payable for the whole of this period. If the tenant leaves early he or she will have to continue to pay the rent and outgoings for the property until a new tenant is found. The tenancy agreement may state a period after which your rent may be reviewed or increased.

The landlord should issue you with a rent book, in which all rental payments made are recorded. If you are not given a rent book, it is wise to pay only by cheque and insist on a receipt. This provides evidence if there is ever a dispute about rental payments.

Depending on the conditions of the agreement, in addition to the monthly rental payments, tenants are responsible for paying for other outgoings such as contents insurance, as well as for gas, electricity and telephone bills. Buildings' insurance will normally be paid by the landlord.

Deposits

A landlord will ask for a deposit of a week or a month's rent before handing over the keys to their property. Depending on how you look after the property this should be refunded to you in full when you give up the tenancy. If you are in receipt of a welfare payment from the Irish Government you may get help with paying the deposit from your community welfare officer, though you are likely to have to foot some of the bill yourself.

UTILITIES

The utility companies in Ireland generally bill for the provision of electricity, gas and the telephone every two months, but payments may be made by monthly direct debit payments through a bank account. Paying by direct debit allows for easier budgeting, as regular equal payments are made throughout the year, levelling out the fluctuations of large bills (especially for fuel) in the winter and smaller bills in the summer months. Utility providers all levy a standing charge for their services in addition to the payments for actual consumption.

When moving into a property, you will need to have the meters read and new accounts set up in order to ensure that you do not pay for electricity, gas or telephone calls used or made by the previous owner or tenant. You should give the company two weeks notice to arrange this. Where a property has been left empty for some time, services may have been disconnected and there may be a small reconnection charge. If you are moving into a new property, you will be liable for connection charges.

Electricity

The standard electricity voltage in Ireland is 230 Volts AC, 50Hz. If you are moving to Ireland from outside Europe you will need to check that any electrical appliances you wish to use in Ireland are compatible, or buy a transformer. Plugs are of the 3-pin (UK) variety.

At present, electricity services in Ireland are provided by the Electricity Supply Board (ESB, Lower Fitzwilliam Street, Dublin 2;

☎1850-372372; www.esb.ie) – a state, Governemnt-owned body. However, the electricity market was opened to competition in 2000 and will be fully open to competition from 2005, when tariffs should begin to drop. Electricity consumed is measured by a meter supplied and installed by the ESB. Readings are taken or estimated, and bills issued every two months. There are several tariffs available from the ESB based on the standing charge, the Public Service Obligation (a levy on the purchase by ESB of certain renewable, sustainable or alternative forms of energy) and the amount of units of electricity (measured in Kilowatt/hour or kWh) used by a consumer.

Gas

Mains gas in Ireland is supplied by Bord Gáis (PO Box 51, Gasworks Road, Cork; ☎021-453 4000; fax 021-453 4001; www.bordgais.ie). If there is an existing gas pipe and meter in the property, you will need to get in touch with Bord Gáis to register with them and make an appointment for them to turn on the meter. If the property has a gas pipe fitted but no meter you will need to get a meter installed. If there is no gas pipe in the property then Bord Gáis will be able to tell you how much it will cost to be connected to the mains gas service. Cost of connection will depend on the distance your property is from a main pipeline – a charge of €250 is made if the property is within 15 metres of a pipeline; €74 per metre if it is further away. Bills for domestic gas use are issued every two months and are calculated on a standing charge of €31 plus €2.5 per kWh unit of gas consumed.

If your property is not connected to the mains gas supply you can use bottled gas, which comes in bottles of various sizes and is available from supermarkets and other suppliers throughout the country. Alternatively you could have a tank installed on the premises.

Oil & Solid Fuel

In the remoter areas off the mains, many heating systems are oil-fired. Local suppliers will deliver oil, which must be stored in approved tanks outside the property. Coal, smokeless fuel and logs for open fires and solid-fuel cooking and heating appliances are available from local suppliers. Some people still dig and burn peat from their traditional peat cuttings, but its back-breaking work and not recommended for the weedy. Some local firms will supply ready bagged peat – worth trying at least once. Peat doesn't produce a great deal of heat on its own, so generally it is best augmented with coal. Suppliers can be found in the local area phone book or Golden Pages.

Water & Sewerage

Domestic water charges were abolished in Ireland in 1997 and for the majority of those living in domestic properties water from the public mains is now supplied free of charge. However, for those who use their property for business purposes, a commercial water charge is still levied by the local authority. Businesses pay a flat rate bi-annually, or have a metered account whereby the business is subject to a minimum annual charge in addition to the rental fee for the meter.

In rural areas where there is no access to the mains water system, group water schemes are established where the water is supplied from a souce such as a well or reservoir. Water charges are then levied by the local authoritiy in order to maintain and improve the water and wastewater systems. If you decide to sink your own well you may be entitled to a small grant from the local authority – who will need to come and test the water before you can consume it.

Refuse Collection

Refuse collection is supervised by local authorities who may provide the collection service themselves or outsource the collection to private firms. Household garbage is usually collected weekly and wheelie bins are provided. The vast majority of households with a refuse collection service are charged (rates vary depending on the authority; some authorities provide the service for free). You may claim tax relief on waste charges.

REMOVALS

It should take only a few days to have your belongings shipped from continental Europe, around four weeks from the east coast of the US, six weeks from the west coast. From Far Eastern countries it should take around six weeks; eight weeks or so from Australasia.

When choosing a removal company, it is wise to ensure that they are members of the International Federation of Furniture Removers (FIDI), the Overseas Moving Network International (OMNI), the National and Overseas Movers of Ireland (NAOMI) or of the British Association of Removers (BAR). You should then be covered by insurance and guarantees of safe delivery.

The British Association of Removers provides a free and useful leaflet *Now that you're ready to move...* which covers most of the issues you may face and ends with the advice, 'Relax...', which unfortunately no-one moving home will find easy to do. The British Association of Removers can also provide the names and telephone numbers of reputable removals companies throughout the country that are members of BAR and specialise in overseas operations. The cost of transporting a packing carton measuring 61x51x41cm from the UK to Ireland is approximately €135 with each additional carton costing a further €60, however, quotes for furniture removals can vary widely from company to company so it always pays to shop around. Don't agree to pay for removal insurance before you have checked your home contents policy as you may already be covered, but make sure that you are covered in the event of losses and damages to your belongings.

If your new home is situated down a narrow, single-track road you should inform the removal company of this fact as they may need to use a smaller van, or arrange to transfer your belongings to a smaller van at one of their depots. If you don't have a lot of possessions it will be a lot less hassle to rent a van and gather a couple of friends to help you move your life across the Irish Sea. The addresses and phone numbers of some Irish removals firms are given below.

CHECKLIST FOR MOVING HOUSE

- Confirm dates with removal company
- Sign and return contract together with payment
- Book insurance at declared value
- Arrange a contact number where you can be reached at all times
- Arrange transport for pets
- Dispose of anything you don't want to take with you
- Start running down freezer contents
- Contact carpet fitters if needed
- Book disconnection of mains service
- Cancel all rental agreements
- Notify dentist, doctor, optician, vet.
- Notify bank and savings/share accounts of change of address
- Inform telephone company
- Ask the post office to re-route mail
- Tell TV licence, car registration, passport offices of change of address
- Notify hire purchase and credit firms
- Make local map of new property for friends/removal company
- Clear the loft/basement
- Organise your own transport to new home
- Plan where things will go in new home
- Cancel the milk/newspapers
- Clean out the freezer/fridge
- Find and label keys
- Send address cards/e-mails to friends and relatives
- Separate trinkets, jewellery and small items
- Sort out linen and clothes
- Put garage/garden tools together
- Take down curtains/blinds
- Collect children's toys
- Put together basic catering for family at new house

Addresses of Removals Firms & Representative Bodies.
Allen Removals & Storage, Greenhills Road, Tallaght, Dublin 24; ☎01-451 3585; fax 01-459 9039; www.allenremovals.ie.
Oman Overseas Moving & Storage, 8 City Link Park Forge Hill, Kin-

sale Road, Cork, Co. Cork; ☎021-431 0088; fax 021-431 0084; www.oman.ie.

Emerald Movers International, Unit 21 Ashbourne Industrial Park, Ashbourne, Navan, Co. Meath; ☎01-835 3314; fax 01-835 3317.

Nat Ross Ltd, Monahan Road, Cork; ☎021-968 539; fax 021-312 418; www.natross.com.

Careline, Whitehall, Parteen, Limerick; ☎061-326 070; fax 061-326 030; www.careline.ie.

The British Association of Removers (BAR), 3 Churchill Court, 58 Station Road, North Harrow, London HA2 7SA; ☎020-8861 3331; www.bar.co.uk.

National and Overseas Movers of Ireland (NAOMI), Airton Road, Tallaght, Dublin 24; ☎02-889 656; fax 02-889 989; www.fedemac.com.

Overseas Moving Network International (OMNI), Priory House, 45-51 High Street, Reigate, Surrey RH2 9AE; ☎01737-222 022; fax 01737-241 767; www.omnimoving.com.

Fédération Internationale des Déménageurs Internationaux (FIDI), 69 Rue Picard B5, 1080 Brussels, Belgium; ☎+32 2 426 51 60; fax +32 2 426 55 23; www.fidi.com.

Storage Depots

If you are moving into rented accommodation temporarily while looking for a property to buy, you may need to arrange to have your belongings put into storage. If so, you must ensure your goods are properly insured. Storage is charged at a monthly rate depending on the size of the consignment. If you need to access any items during the storage period you will have to pay a fee to have the container opened, so it is as well to be sure you only put items you will not need for some time into storage. There are storage depots in most of the larger Irish cities. If possible try to ensure your belongings will be stored as near as possible to your abode for convenience; this will also cut down on the cost when you finally have your belongings delivered to your permanent address. The largest firm of removers in the UK is Allied Pickfords (Heritage House, 345 Southbury Road, Enfield EN1 1UP; ☎020-8219 8343; www.pickfords.co.uk), who deal in international removals and have storage depots throughout the UK.

Customs Regulations

If you are using a removals company, the company should advise you on the customs formalities and be able to deal with them at both the port of exit and the port of entry. If you are moving to Ireland from a country within the EU then you will not have to pay duty on the importation of any personal effects as duty will have already been paid on these in the country of origin.

If you are moving to Ireland from a country outside the EU, import charges will not be incurred on importing personal effects if you lived at your place of normal residence outside the EU for a continuous period of at least 12 months. The personal property to be imported must have been in your possession for a minimum period of six months prior to moving to Ireland. You will be free to continue to import effects without having to pay customs duty for a period of twelve months from the date of first moving to Ireland. Items less than six months old will be subject to duty and VAT. Note that any goods imported free of import charges cannot be disposed of (i.e. sold, hired out, etc.) for the twelve months following their importation into Ireland. Irish Customs and Excise can be contacted at the Customs and Excise Information Office, Irish Life Centre, Lower Abbey Street, Dublin 1 (☎ 01-878 8811; fax 01-874 7608; www.revenue.ie).

IMPORTING YOUR CAR

All new motor vehicles imported into Ireland (with the exception of those brought in temporarily) are subject to a Vehicle Registration Tax (VRT) and must be registered with the Revenue Commissioners. The VRT payable on a vehicle is calculated as a percentage of the expected retail price of the vehicle. If the vehicle is new there will also be VAT to pay.

Once in Ireland, you will need to register your vehicle at a Revenue Vehicle Registration Office and pay VRT by the end of the next working day following the vehicle's arrival in Ireland. Once the tax has been paid you will be issued with a Vehicle Registration Certificate so that you can obtain a new Irish number plate and road tax. You will then need to obtain and display the new Irish vehicle registration plates within three days. There are 32 Vehicle Registration Office around the country; all are open from 9am-12.45pm & from 2-4pm Monday to Friday. In Dublin contact the Vehicle Registration Office at St John's House, Tallaght, Dublin 24 (☎ 01-4149 777; fax 01-4147 720; www.revenue.ie).

IMPORTING PETS

Animals being imported into Ireland from the UK, the Channel Islands or the Isle of Man are not subject to quarantine requirements. However, if you want to import a dog or cat into Ireland from elsewhere you must have an import licence, which will necessitate your pet either being put into an approved quarantine in Ireland for at least six months or, if the animal has come from certain countries and meets certain requirements (i.e. has a current rabies vaccination certificate), put into an approved quarantine for a period of one month, followed by a further five months' quarantine at the residence of its owner, provided that there is a suitable facility that has been approved in advance by the Veterinary Inspectorate of the Department of Agriculture and Food. Note that all the costs of quarantine, veterinary fees, transport, etc. must be met by the animal's owner and that any arrangements for quarantine and transport must be in place before an import licence is granted.

An animal cannot travel without an import licence. Import laws change at intervals and you are advised to check with the Animal Health and Welfare Division of the Department of Agriculture and Food (Floor 6 East, Agriculture House, Kildare Street, Dublin 2; ☎ 01-607 2827; www.agriculture.gov.ie) nearer the time of your decision to move to Ireland.

Under the terms of the 1986 Control of Dogs Act, a dog licence is required for any dog over four months old. Dog licences cost €12.70, are valid for one year from the date of issue and can be bought at the post office. All dogs must wear a collar and bear the name and address of the owner.

Quarantine

The animal to be imported into Ireland under the quarantine scheme must be transported by air to Dublin. If it is transported to Cork or

Shannon airports it will need to be taken on by air to Dublin if necessary. Transportation from the airport to the Public Quarantine, and if necessary from the Public Quarantine to the Private Quarantine, can only be undertaken by the sole authorised carrying agent, Kelly Couriers (30 Selskar Avenue, Skerries, Co. Dublin; ☎01-849 0807).

Approved Quarantine Premises

Lissenhall Quarantine Kennels and Catteries is the only Government-approved Public Quarantine premises and details of costs and availability can be obtained from them at Lissenhall, Swords, Co. Dublin (☎01-840 1776; fax 01-840 9338). Quarantine costs will vary depending on the size of the animal but expect to pay around €1,400 for a cat or €1,700 for a small dog for six months' quarantine.

Pet Travel Scheme

Pets that have been through the UK Pet Travel Scheme are free to travel to and from Ireland without quarantine. Under the Pet Travel Scheme, which came into operation in 2000, quarantine arrangements have been dispensed with for dogs and cats entering or re-entering the UK from member states of the EU, the EEA, the USA, Canada and rabies-free islands. Pets from these countries are instead now subject to microchip identification, vaccination, blood testing, and health certification. Further information can be obtained from the Pet Travel Scheme Helpline, Department for Environment, Food and Rural Affairs, Area 201, 1a Page Street, London SW1P 4PQ (☎0870-241 1710; fax 020-7904 6206; www.defra.gov.uk/animalh/quarantine/pets).

If you decide to take your pet out of Ireland (for instance on an extended holiday abroad), in order to get your pet back into Ireland under the Pets Scheme you will need a PETS Certificate to show the transport company when checking your pet in at the point of departure. A PETS Certificate is valid six months after the date of the blood test up to the date the animal's booster rabies shot is due (a dog has to be at least three months old before it can be vaccinated). You should obtain the PETS Certificate from a government-authorised vet and you can obtain a list of these from DEFRA's website (www.defra.gov.uk/animalh/quarantine/pets/contacts.htm). Immediately (24-48 hours) prior to leaving Ireland the animal must be treated against ticks and tapeworm by a vet. This has to be done every time your pet enters the UK. The vet will issue an official certificate bearing the vet's stamp with the microchip number, date and time of treatment, and the product used.

If your pet originated from outside the UK, where different systems for identifying dogs and cats are in force, it will need a microchip insert for entry to the UK. Pets that have had other forms of registration (e.g. an ear tattoo) must be vaccinated; blood-tested and have a microchip insert. To enter the UK the animal must have the PETS Certificate showing that the vet has seen the registration document.

PET TRAVEL SCHEME

The procedures involved are

- Vet inserts a tiny microchip just under the animal's skin (cost £20-£30).
- Vet administers a rabies shot, or two, given two weeks apart. (£50 x 2; second shot possibly cheaper).
- Vet takes a blood sample from animal and sends it to a DEFRA-approved laboratory. (£70-£80 including vet's handling charge). Note: If the blood test is negative, your pet must be vaccinated and tested again.
- Vet issues a PETS 1 Certificate, which you have to show to the transport company (e.g. airline, ferry, channel tunnel, etc).
- When taking pets from Britain to Ireland you will need a PETS 5 certificate (this replaces a separate Export Health Certificate) which is issued at the same time as PETS 1 (see above).
- Total cost about £200.

Useful Addresses

Airpets Oceanic, Stanwell Moor, Staines, Middlesex TW19 6BW; ☎01753-685 571; fax 01735-681 655; www.airpets.com. Pet exports, pet travel schemes, boarding, air kennels, transportation by road/air to and from all UK destinations.

Animal Airlines, Mill lane Cottage, Mill Lane, Adlington, Cheshire SK10 4LF; ☎01625-827 414; fax 01625-827 237; info@animalairlines.co.uk.

Breeny Boarding & Quarantine Kennels, Belfast, Northern Ireland; ☎+44 (2890) 402 068; fax +44 (2890) 705 775; e-mail lisnabreenypets@aol.com.

Department of Agriculture and Food, Information Division, Agriculture House, Kildare Street, Dublin 2; ☎01-607 2000; www.agriculture.gov.ie.

Independent Pet and Animal Transport Association, Route 5, Box 747, Highway 2869, 2-364 Winding Trail, Holly Lake Ranch, Big Sandy, Texas 75755 USA; ☎903-769-2267; fax 903-769-2867; www.ipata.com. An international trade association of animal handlers, pet moving providers, kennel operators, veterinarians and others who are dedicated to the care and welfare of pets and small animals during transport locally, nationwide and worldwide. Citizens of the USA can contact this address for a list of agents dealing in the transport of pets from the USA to Ireland.

Irish Animals, www.irishanimals.ie. Independent online resource relating to animals in Ireland.

Jets4Pets, 99A High Street, Yeadon, Leeds, West Yorkshire LS19 7TA; ☎0113-250 1162; fax 0113-250 1192; www.jets4pets.com.

Par Air Services Livestock Ltd, Warren Lane, Stanway, Colchester, Essex C03 0LN; ☎01206-330 332; fax 01206-331 277; www.parair.co.uk. Handles international transportation and quarantine arrangements. Can arrange door-to-door delivery of pets by specially equipped vans.

Pet Travel Scheme, Department for the Environment, Food and Rural Affairs, Area 201, 1a Page Street, London SW1P 4PQ; ☎0870 241 1710; fax 020-7904 6834; www.defra.gov.uk.

DAILY LIFE

CHAPTER SUMMARY

- **Language.** Irish is a Celtic language related to Welsh, Scottish Gaelic and Breton.
- **Education.** Participation rates in Irish Education are very high. Around 90% of all children are enrolled in secondary education schooling. Approximately 55% of these will go on to third-level education.
  - Tuition fees for third-level educational courses were abolished in 1994.
- **Media.** Around 5 million national papers are sold in Ireland every week.
  - British radio and television programming can be picked up over much of the country and satellite and cable channels are widely available.
- **Tax.** Personal circumstances dictate the amount of tax credits (personal allowance, private health insurance premiums, mortgage interest, etc.) that you are be entitled to.
  - VAT is payable on most goods and services at a standard rate of 21%. The current rate of Capital Gains Tax is 20%.
- **Health Services.** Anyone from an EEA member state or who is deemed to be ordinarily resident in Ireland is entitled to free or subsidised public health services.
  - There are currently ten Health Boards responsible for the provision of health, community care and personal social services to the people in their area.
- **The Irish.** Traditional Irish sports such as Gaelic football, hurling and camogie attract huge crowds of supporters.
  - Religion is deeply embedded in the national psyche of Ireland.

LANGUAGE

Gaelic

Officially the Republic of Ireland is bilingual, with official documents and road signs presented in both English and Irish (*Erse*). Irish is a Celtic language related to Welsh, Scottish Gaelic and Breton (the language spoken in north-western France) and is now a compulsory curriculum subject in schools. Because the areas where Irish is spoken were some of the worst affected areas by the famine of the 1800s, many of the inhabitants of these areas left for the cities to find work and adopted English as their first language, thus bringing about a decline in the number of Gaelic speakers. Today much of the population of Ireland only speak English, although the inhabitants of a few areas of the country continue to have Irish as their first language.

The *Gaeltacht* are the regions where Irish is spoken as a first language, though all speakers (fewer than 100,000 in number) are now also fluent in English. This region is the responsibility of the Minister for the Gaeltacht and the inhabitants are given certain tax benefits. The Irish speaking population are located on some but not all of the islands off the west coast of the country, along the sparsely populated regions such as Donegal and Connemara along the western seaboard, and in a few communities of West Cork and County Waterford. Road signs in Gaeltacht regions are often in Irish only.

SCHOOLS & EDUCATION

Schooling in Ireland has traditionally been organised along denominational lines, with the Catholic Church being the leading provider of education to the country's children, followed by the Anglican Church. Participation rates in Irish Education are very high and around 90% of all children are enrolled in secondary education schooling. Approximately 55% of these will go on to third-level (university or equivalent) education. These days there are more co-educational and multi-denominational primary and secondary level schools than there were in the past, and State-funded education is available at all levels. There are also private (fee-paying) schools and colleges, and schools where children are taught in Irish (Gaelscoileanna). Tuition fees for third-level educational courses were abolished in 1994; however, there is no guarantee that tuition fees will not be reintroduced in the future.

There are around 58 fee-paying schools in Ireland – 21 of which are run by the Anglican Church. Listings of both private and state schools in Ireland can be obtained from the Department of Education and Science, Marlborough Street, Dublin 1 (☎ 01-8734 700; fax 01-8786 712; www.education.ie).

Pre-School & Nursery Education

Although children in Ireland under the age of six are not obliged to attend school, almost all children begin going to school in the September following their fourth birthday. Approximately 50% of four-year-olds, and almost all five-year-olds, are enrolled in the infant classes of primary schools and much of what is considered pre-school education in other countries is provided, free of charge, for all children in Ireland.

Public provision for early childhood education in Ireland is still limited, with the Department of Education and Science's involvement in this area focusing primarily on those children with special needs or from disadvantaged backgrounds (the traveller community is a good case in point). Nursery schools, crèches and playgroups are generally privately or community run affairs, financed by parents though in some cases with the help of public funding from health boards or FÁS.

All forms of childcare provision are subject to the requirements of the Child Care Act of 1991, which states that regional health boards are responsible for the welfare and development of children attending pre-school services such as playgroups, day nurseries, crèches, day care facilities or other similar services. By law, anyone providing a pre-school service to four or more children must notify the local health board and abide by regulations relating to minimum standards in space and staffing, record keeping, first aid and safety procedures, equipment and materials and insurance. Officials from health boards routinely carry out inspections to ensure compliance with these standards.

When looking to place your child with a childcare provider it is always best to look for the childcare facility nearest home. If you can't locate one nearby, get in touch with the IPPA (the Irish Pre-school Playgroups Association), which has been a pioneer in the provision of early childhood education and care in Ireland and has a membership of over 2,000 playgroups, parent and toddler groups, day care groups, after- and out of-school groups and individuals. The IPPA is a nationwide organisation and represents its members at local level through its branches nationwide. IPPA has its main offices at Unit 4, Broomhill Business Complex, Broomhill Road, Tallaght, Dublin 24; (☎ 01-463 0010; fax 01-463 0045; www.ippa.ie).

There are several things to look for when choosing a prospective childcare facility. In addition to the training, experience and continuity of staff, check out the size of the group, the ratio of children to staff, evidence of curriculum development, management practice, opportunities for family involvement and the physical surroundings of a centre. Interview those who will be responsible for looking after your child, check their references and talk to other parents who use the facility to get there views on the place. The National Children's Nurseries Association (Unit 12c, Bluebell Business Park, Old Naas Road, Bluebell, Dublin 12; ☎ 01-460 1138; www.ncna.net) can provide information about crèches and day nurseries in Ireland, while information about Irish-speaking pre-school playgroups can be obtained from *Naonrai An Comhchoiste Reamhscolaiochta Teo* (7 Cearnog Mhuirfean, Baile Atha Cliath 2; ☎ 01-6763 222; e-mail comhchoiste@eircom.net). The Irish Montessori Education Board (Togal House, 1-3 Callaghan's Lane, Dun Laoghaire, Co. Dublin; ☎ 01-280 5705; fax 01-280 5705; www.imebtrust.org) was formed in consultation with the Department of Education to provide an overall accreditation body for the Montessori schools and teachers in Ireland and acts as a regulatory body for Montessori schools in Ireland.

As yet there is no national curriculum for the whole early childhood period from birth to six years. Various service providers and umbrella organisations have devised curricula and work programmes for use within early years classes, and infant classes in the formal education system follow the Primary School Curriculum. In December 1999 a White Paper on Early Childhood Education, *Ready to Learn*, was published, which has provided a blueprint for developing and implementing a comprehensive early education policy. In 2001 the Minister for Education and Science established the Centre for Early Childhood Development and Education to develop a quality framework for early childhood education and for those children who are educationally disadvantaged or have special needs. The Centre for Early Childhood Development & Education can be contacted at Gate Lodge, St. Patrick's College, Drumcondra, Dublin 9 (☎ 01-8842110; fax 01-8842111; www.cecde.ie).

Primary Education

Up until 1975 the majority of national schools in Ireland were established under the patronage of the local Bishop and were usually run by a local clergyman. However, the introduction of Boards of Management and trustees granted opportunities for partnerships of parents, teachers, Patrons' representatives and community representatives to undertake the management of schools.

Currently, approximately 450,000 children in Ireland receive their primary education at the 3,200 national state-funded schools. Although children are not legally required to attend school until the age of six, nearly all schools have two years of infant classes and much of what is termed pre-school education in other countries is carried out by the primary education sector. Children attend primary school from the age of four or five until they are twelve or thirteen years of age. The Irish primary school year generally runs from 1 September to 30 June.

There are several different types of Irish primary schools: state-funded primary schools or national schools, special schools, and private schools. Included within the state-funded education sector are religious schools, non-denominational schools and, in recent years, multi-denominational schools. There are also a significant number of national schools in which pupils are taught the curriculum through the medium of Irish, both in the Gaeltacht but also in others where Gaelic speakers are rarer. These *Gaelscoileanna* are under the separate patronage of *Foras Pátrunachta na Scoileanna LánGhaeilge*.

Most of the primary schools are under the patronage of one religious denomination or another; the majority of schools are Roman Catholic. Schools of one denomination will accept children from different religious backgrounds and pupils do not have to attend religion classes. The general aims of primary education in Ireland as stated by the Department of Education and Science are:

- To enable a child to live a full life and realise his or her potential as a unique individual;
- To enable a child to develop as a social being through living and co-operating with others and so contribute to the good of society;
- To prepare a child for further education and lifelong learning.

The primary school curriculum in Ireland was revised in 1999, the first complete revision of the curriculum since 1971 and the present curriculum is designed to nurture the child in all dimensions of his or her life – spiritual, moral, cognitive, emotional, imaginative, aesthetic, social and physical, as well as reflecting the educational, cultural, social and economic aspirations and concerns of Irish society. The curriculum also takes into account the changing nature of society and aims to help children to adjust to these changes. The primary curriculum is divided into key areas of language; mathematics; social, environment and scientific education; arts education – including visual arts, music and drama; physical education; and social, personal and health education. The provision for the teaching of modern languages in primary schools (French, German, Spanish and Italian especially) has become more important in recent years.

You should, in theory, be able to send your child to the school of your choice in Ireland, however, the amount of choice you actually have in this respect will depend upon the area in which you live. All schools operate their own admissions policy and it is always a good idea to ask for this when looking to place your child with a particular school. Some secondary schools give priority to the students from certain primary schools, while state-funded primary schools tend to give priority to children living in the immediate area. Multi-denominational schools, non-denominational schools and Gaelscoileanna each decide their own admissions policy.

As the majority of primary schools are state-funded, children are educated gratis. However, many schools often need to raise extra funds for additional resources such as computers, sports equipment or improved facilities and parents may be asked to make a contribution or to take part in fund-raising activities. Some schools ask pupils' families to pay for books and extra-curricular activities. Private schools charge annual fees, which can vary considerably from school to school. Note that should you choose to do so, you have a constitutional right to educate your child at home.

Secondary Education

The Irish secondary school curriculum is generally five or six years long and consists of a three-year junior cycle followed by a two or three-year senior cycle. Children begin secondary school education around the age of 12 and leave around the age of 17 or 18. School attendance is compulsory up to the age of 16. Whilst attending secondary school pupils take two state exams. The Junior Certificate examination is taken on completion of the three-year Junior Certificate course, which aims to give pupils a balanced course of study in a wide variety of curricular areas and to prepare them for senior cycle education. Pupils then pass into the Senior Cycle, at the end of which they take the final Leaving Certificate exams. Most schools in Ireland now offer students the option of a Transition Year after they have completed the junior cycle, which allows pupils to explore other, non-academic interests of a social, creative or business nature.

Secondary-level educational institutions in Ireland, comprising secondary, vocational, community and comprehensive schools, are privately owned and managed. The trustees of the majority of these schools are from religious communities (mainly Roman Catholic, though teachers are generally lay staff) or are made up of Boards of Governors. Vocational schools are administered by Vocational Education Committees, while community and comprehensive schools are managed by Boards of Management. The majority of secondary schools are free, but there are also fee-paying schools for both day pupils and boarders. There are also a small number of private international schools in Ireland. A list of schools in Ireland is available from the Department of Education and Science (Marlborough Street,

Dublin 1; ☎ 01-889 6400; www.education.ie). In both private and state-funded second-level schools parents will be expected to pay for their child's schoolbooks, school uniforms and extra-curricular activities.

Vocational schools and community or comprehensive schools tend to provide both academic and technical education and often also additional further education opportunities for school-leavers and adults in the local community. The Irish secondary school year runs from the first week in September to the first week in June, unless a child is going into a Junior Certificate Class or a Leaving Certificate class – in which case he or she will not finish until the end of June, when the exams for these classes take place.

As with choosing a primary school, it is wise to gather as much information as possible about the schools in which you are interested and to enrol your child as far as possible in advance of the beginning of the school year. Check out the admissions policy of a school, as this can vary from school to school – different management styles, with differing degrees of emphasis placed on exams, sports, the arts, personal development, religion, social affairs, European languages and practical skills acquisition, etc. There may even be an entrance exam. Remember that some schools may have a waiting list or may favour children who have a relative attending the school. Some schools favour children from particular primary schools.

Special Education

As well as a number of classes in primary and post-primary schools for children with disabilities and special needs, there are also over 100 special needs schools in Ireland. Special needs teachers and assistants are available to classes and schools and there are also special transport arrangements for children with disabilities attending school. Pupil-teacher ratios in special schools and special classes are lower than in the mainstream schools and even lower for children with a severe or profound mental handicap. Remedial teachers are available to all primary schools (some are visiting teachers with responsibility for a number of schools in their area while others work in individual schools) to look after the needs of pupils with hearing and visual impairment.

Second-level students with dyslexia and other reading difficulties, and their teachers, receive help and advice. In addition, there are post-primary schools in Dublin (for both day pupils and boarders) serving the needs of the visually and hearing impaired. There are also a small number of schools for students with physical disabilities, and the emotionally disturbed. Students in these schools usually take the Junior Certificate and Leaving Certificate examinations though the schools also make provision for students whose level of disability would make it very difficult for them to benefit from these programmes.

Several universities have disability officers whose job it is to give support and advice to students with disabilities. The Association for Higher Education Access and Disability – AHEAD (Newman House, 86 St. Stephens Green, Dublin 2; ☎01-475 2386; fax 01-475 2387; e-mail ahead@iol.ie), a voluntary organisation promoting the participation of students with disabilities in third-level education, produces a handbook giving information for students at third-level with disabilities and learning difficulties. A complete listing of special schools in Ireland is available on the *Comhairle* website (www.comhairle.ie).

Home Education

If you decide to take your child out of school to educate him or her at home, you will need to write to inform the school of your actions within three days of the withdrawal of the child. Under the Education Act of 2000 you should receive a form from the Education Welfare Officer concerning registration with the National Educational Welfare Board. You will need to register with the Board within three months of beginning the education of your child at home, providing details of the educational provision for your child. Although as a home educator you do not need a formal teaching qualification curriculum, or to provide formal lessons or a designated schoolroom, registration with the National Educational Welfare Board is not an automatic process and it may be refused (though there is an appeal process). Under the Education Act of 2000 school attendance officers have become Education Welfare Officers and the Gardai no longer have jurisdiction concerning school attendance matters. For more information about educating children at home in Ireland contact the Home Education Network (92 Meadow Mount, Churchtown, Dublin 16; www.binf.org/hen/).

Examinations

Although there are no formal exams at the end of the primary level of education, pupils will be assessed by their teachers. Pupils in post-primary education take two sets of examinations during their time at school, the exam system having been altered in the last few years with the more flexible Junior Certificate exams replacing the Intermediate Certificate examination. Final year students can now choose from three different Leaving Certificate programmes: the traditional *Leaving Certificate*; the *Leaving Certificate Vocational Programme*; and the *Leaving Certificate Applied Programme*. Both of the latter exams focus on a student's more practical and technical abilities. Students normally sit for the Leaving Certificate examination at the age of 17 or 18 following the established Leaving Certificate programme of at least five subjects, including Irish. The Leaving Certificate Vocational Programme (LCVP) is a Leaving Certificate with a strong vocational element. Pupils take two Leaving Certificate subjects from one of the LCVP subject groupings, a Leaving Certificate Modern European Language or a Vocational Language Module, in addition to mandatory link modules. Pupils following this programme take at least five Leaving Certificate subjects, including Irish. The Leaving Certificate Applied is a distinct, self-contained two-year Leaving Certificate programme involving a cross-curricular, rather than a subject-based, approach. Although graduates of the Leaving Certificate Applied do not have direct access to Higher Education through the Central Applications Office (CAO – see below), those who progress to an approved further education award can become eligible for admission to some third-level courses in the institutes of technology, and to some of the degree courses offered by the institutes of technology and universities.

As in the UK, the Irish educational system is very exam-focused. Any child wishing to go on to study at a university or another third-level institution will need to score sufficient points in second-level exams to gain a place. Points needed for third-level courses depend on the subject to be studied. For example, competition for a place on courses to study veterinary medicine, dentistry and law is fierce, and most institutions ask for students who have scored in excess of 500 points in their exams (the highest possible number of points being 600).

There are support facilities in place for those with special needs when sitting their exams, for example arrangements can be made for a pupil to take an exam while in hospital, or using voice-activated computers, tape recorders or scribes, or an enlarged or Braille version of question papers. Those with hearing difficulties may be exempted from the aural part of certain examinations.

International Schools

There are a small number of private international schools in Ireland. These include *St Kilian's German School* (Roebuck Road, Clonskeagh, Dublin 14; ☎01-288 3323; fax 01-288 2138; www.kilians.com); a Japanese school – *Sundai Ireland International School* (Curragh Grange Green Road, Curragh, Co. Kildare; ☎045-441 888; fax 045-441 306), a French school (*Lycée Français D'Irlande*, Foxrock Avenue, Dublin 18; ☎01-289 4063; fax 01-289 8319; www.lfi.ie), an Islamic School (*The Muslim National School*, 19 Roebuck Road, Dublin 14; ☎01-296 1340), a Spanish School (*Elian's Spanish School*, Jubilee Hall, Ballyman Road, Bray, Co. Wicklow; ☎01-282 1230; fax 01-282 3910; www.elians.com) and a Jewish School (*Zion Parish School*, Bushy Park Road, Dublin 6; ☎01-491 0065).

There are two international colleges affiliated to the European Council of International Schools where pupils prepare for the Irish Leaving Certificate Higher Level or the International Baccalaureate Diploma exams. *St Andrew's College* (Booterstown Avenue, Blackrock, Co. Dublin; ☎01-288 2785; fax 01-283 1627; www.st-andrews.ie) is a co-educational, multi-denominational day school with approximately 1,200 pupils ranging in age from 4 to 18; fees are in the region of €3,650-€4,580 per annum. *Sutton Park School* (St Fintan's Road, Sutton, Dublin 13; ☎01-832 2940; fax 01-832 5929; www.suttonpark.ie) is a non-denominational, co-educational day and boarding school; fees for day pupils are in the region of €3,935-€4,940 per annum; for boarders around €11,000 per annum). Both colleges are experienced in handling admissions to American colleges and pupils can be prepared for SATs.

School Transport & Meals

The School Transport Scheme caters for over 130,000 pupils on some 5,600 routes nationwide and receives funding from the Department of Education and Science of around €82.2 million annually. In order to qualify for free school transport, a child must be living more than two miles/3.2km from the nearest suitable national school. If a child is attending a school that has more than one teacher and there is a one-teacher school nearer the home, that fact will not usually disqualify the child from using the school transport scheme. Special arrangements can be made to cater for children in remote areas and those who have religious reasons for attending a certain school. For a school transport service to be established there must be at least seven children wishing to use the service on a daily basis.

Bus Éireann runs school transport for post-primary students who are eligible for the school transport scheme. When a pupil enrols in a second-level school, the school principal makes arrangements to have the pupil placed on *Bus Éireann's* register. The parents will then receive an invoice for the term's fare from *Bus Éireann*, which must be paid before the start of term. The Department of Education and Science decides the fares for each school year, which for eligible students in 2002/2003 were around €33 per term for Junior Certificate pupils and €50 per term for Leaving Certificate students. Dublin Bus operates a special fare for post-primary students living in Dublin. Transport fees may be waived if the pupil's family has a Medical Card.

For pupil's living two miles or more from the nearest pick-up point for transport services, remote area grants are paid by the Department of Education and Science. Parents must arrange to take their child to the nearest pick-up point on a bus route and to collect them after school. To apply for the remote area grant parents must apply in writing to the School Transport Section of the Department of Education and Science (Portlaoise Road, Tullamore, Co. Offaly; ☎ 0506-21363; fax 0506-41052). There are also special transport arrangements in place to provide for students with disabilities.

In 2003, the School Meals Scheme, which provides free meals

to approximately 60,000 primary school children in 400 schools nationwide, was extended to include second-level schools.

Further Education

Further Education refers here to any education or training which occurs after second-level schooling other than third-level higher education, such as post Leaving Certificate courses, Vocational Training Opportunities Scheme for the unemployed, Youthreach for early school leavers, Senior Traveller Training Centre programmes for young and adult travellers who have left school early, adult literacy and community education and self-funded part-time adult programmes in second-level schools. Further education programmes are delivered locally by community organisations, Vocational Education Committees, second-level schools and a range of training agencies such as FÁS, CERT and TEAGASC. National certification is provided by the Further Education and Training Awards Council. Programmes, though not necessarily purely academic in content, can also be offered leading to Junior or Leaving Certificates. Under the Back to Education Initiative, introduced during the 2002/3 school-year, there has been an expansion of flexible and part-time options right across the further education sector aimed at adults with less than upper second-level education. In addition, the National Adult Learning Council was set up in 2002 to promote the development of adult learning and to ensure a co-ordinated strategy across the different sectors and agencies of education, training, employer, trade union, learner and community and voluntary interests.

The Irish Vocational Education Association (McCann House, 99 Marlborough Road, Donnybrook, Dublin 4; ☎01-496 6033; fax 01-496 6460; www.ivea.ie) has committees throughout the country and delivers education and training programmes. Learning Ireland (2nd Floor, 31-33 Ranelagh, Dublin 6; ☎01-496 2484; www.learningireland.ie) publishes the annual *National Guide to Nightcourses* every July. The guide covers courses in Arts & Crafts, Business Studies, Distance Learning, Health & Personal Development, IT Training, Languages, and Sports & Leisure, costs €4.99 and is available in six regional editions (Dublin, Cork, South-East, South-

West, West & North West, and 04 Area – the counties surrounding Dublin). The guide is available from bookstores, newsagents, filling stations, and other retail outlets, as well as direct from Learning Ireland.

HIGHER EDUCATION

The number of second level students enrolling in higher education courses in Ireland has increased dramatically in recent decades and today an estimated 55% go on to higher education – one of the highest participation rates in the world. Entry to third-level education is based upon performance in the final second-level examination, the Leaving Certificate. The third-level education system in Ireland is broad in scope and encompasses universities, technological colleges, education colleges and private independent colleges. The first three of these providers – which comprise 34 institutions – are autonomous and self-governing but substantially state funded.

HETAC – the Higher Education and Training Awards Council – awards qualifications and sets and monitors standards at all levels of higher education and training up to PhD level. The qualifications awarded by HETAC are internationally recognised by academic, professional, trade and craft bodies.

The third-level academic year in Ireland typically runs from September to June and is divided into two, and sometimes three, semesters with holidays in December (for Christmas) and April (for Easter).

Universities

There are seven universities in Ireland: Trinity College, Dublin; Dublin City University; the University of Limerick; the National University of Ireland (which has four constituent universities – University College Dublin, University College Cork, National University of Ireland, Galway, and National University of Ireland, Maynooth). Universities in Ireland offer the usual degrees at Bachelor, Master and Doctorate levels and undergraduate and postgraduate diplomas. Universities award their own degrees using external examiners to ensure consistency of standards. There is also a Higher Education Authority (HEA), which oversees the work of the universities on behalf of the Department of Education and Science.

Colleges of Education

There are several colleges of education offering the recognised qualification for primary school teachers in Ireland – a three-year full-time course leads to a Bachelors of Education degree. Proficiency in the Irish language is currently an entry requirement for courses in primary teacher education. Trainee second-level schoolteachers normally take a university degree followed by a one-year Higher Diploma in Education. Some colleges offer particular specialisations. A list of Colleges of Education can be obtained from the Department of Education and Science, Athlone, Co. Westmeath; ☎0902-74621; fax 0902-78024; www.education.ie.

Independent Colleges

There are a number of independent institutions in Ireland involved in the provision of business and professional educational training. Many of the programmes offered by these colleges are validated by the Higher Education and Training Awards Council (HETAC) and some have links with universities and/or professional associations through which the courses on offer are accredited.

Technological Colleges

There are 14 colleges of technology, in addition to the Tipperary Rural and Business Development Institute and the Tourism College in Killybegs. These institutions provide programmes of education and training from craft to professional level and courses, offered at degree, national diploma and national certificate levels, cover sectors such as business, science, information technology, engineering, linguistics and music. Most colleges also have courses leading directly to the examinations of professional institutes and many colleges also run postgraduate programmes. In addition, some institutes have developed special programmes in areas such as Humanities & Languages, Paramedical Studies and Healthcare, Art & Design, and Tourism. Programmes in all these institutions are validated by HETAC.

Admissions, Tuition Fees & Grants

Applications are processed centrally by the Central Applications Office (CAO – Tower House, Eglinton Street, Galway; ☎091-509 800; fax 091-562 344; www.cao.ie), which processes applications to the majority of higher education institutions providing undergraduate degree, diploma, and certificate courses. Applicants may choose up to ten courses from a degree list and an additional ten from the diploma/certificate list, in order of preference. The participating institutions retain the right to make the final decisions on all admissions. Entry requirements for students from abroad are determined individually by each institution and are generally based on national examination performance and English language aptitude.

Tuition fees are not payable by EU students pursuing a full-time approved undergraduate programme of at least two years duration. In order for an applicant to qualify as an EU student he or she must be a national of an EU member state and satisfy the conditions of the Nationality test. In addition, certain categories of applicant, such as those who have refugee status in Ireland or who have permission to remain in the State as the spouse or the dependent relative of an Irish national, etc., will qualify for EU status. Any applicant who does not satisfy the Nationality test will be liable to pay the non-EU fee for the course of study for which they are applying. International students pay substantially higher course fees than home/EU students.

Maintenance grants are available to eligible students who are attending courses of further and higher education approved by the Department of Education and Science. These are means tested and will depend on the annual income earned by a student's parents. Information on eligibility requirements, and application forms for grants are available from local authorities.

Some banks are prepared to provide Student Loans in special circumstances and applications for details of these loans will need to be made direct to the banks. There are, in addition a number of scholarships available, details of which can be obtained from individual institutions.

MEDIA

Newspapers

Newspapers have been published in Ireland for over 300 years and around 5 million national papers are sold in Ireland every week. There are five daily newspapers: *The Irish Times, The Irish Examiner, The Irish Independent, The Star* and *The Irish News*. *The Irish Times* is politically and religiously non-aligned and is considered to have the most comprehensive news and culture coverage of all the newspapers. *The Times* was founded in 1859 and has its headquarters in Dublin. It has a circulation of approximately 113,835 and contains more foreign news than the majority of the others. *The Irish Independent* is the most popular of the newspapers and has the highest circulation (165,365); it is more partisan in its news coverage than *The Irish Times*. Its sister paper, *The Sunday Independent*, contains plenty of salacious news stories about celebrities of the sporting, TV and film world. *The Irish Examiner*, formerly *The Cork Examiner*, is published in Cork, has a circulation of about 62,413 and is widely read by the farming and business community of south-west Ireland. *The Star* is a tabloid published in Dublin.

There are several evening newspapers available including *The Evening Echo* (published by the Cork-based *Examiner* group) and *The Evening Herald* (nationwide and published by the *Independent* group) along with six Sunday newspapers: *Ireland on Sunday, The Sunday Independent, The Sunday Tribune, The Sunday World, The Sunday Life* and the *Sunday Business Post*. About 60 regional weekly newspapers are to be found in almost every county of Ireland and British newspapers and magazines are widely available in the country, with some titles (such as *The Sun* and *The Mirror*) publishing Irish editions. There are also a wide variety of magazines dealing with current affairs, economic issues and leisure interests – both home-grown Irish publications and imports from the UK and the USA. A daily broadsheet newspaper costs in the region of €1.50; tabloids charge a cover price of around 80 cents.

Useful Addresses

The Irish Times, 10-16 D'Olier Street, Dublin 2; ☎01-679 2022; fax 01-679 3910; www.irish-times.com.

The Irish Independent, Middle Abbey Street, Dublin 1; ☎01-705 5333; fax 01-872 0304; www.independent.ie.

The Evening Herald, Middle Abbey Street, Dublin 1; ☎01-705 5333; fax 01-872 0304; www.unison.ie.

The Irish Examiner, 1-6 Academy Street, Cork; ☎021-427 2722; fax 021-427 3846; www.irishexaminer.ie.

Evening Echo, 1-6 Academy Street, Cork; ☎021-427 2722; fax 021-427 5112; www.eveningecho.com.

The Star, 62A Terenure Road North, Dublin 6W; ☎01-490 1228; fax 01-490 2193.

Sunday Independent, Middle Abbey Street, Dublin 1; ☎01-705 5333; fax 01-705 5779; www.independent.ie.

Sunday Tribune, 15 Lower Baggot Street, Dublin 2; ☎01-661 5555; fax 01-661 5302; www.tribune.ie.

Ireland on Sunday, 50 City Quay, Dublin 2; ☎01-671 8255; fax 01-671 8882; www.irelandonsunday.com.

Sunday World, 18 Rathfarnham Road, Dublin 6; ☎01-490 1980; fax 01-490 1838; www.sundayworld.com.

Magazines. Ireland's media companies produce a wide range of magazines covering all kinds of passions and hobbies and topics of general interest. The biggest-selling Irish women's monthly magazine, *Image*, features articles on fashion, beauty, home and food, along with horoscopes, diaries and real life stories. International English-language magazines such as *Time*, *Newsweek* and *New Scientist* are widely available at newsagents throughout the country. Glossy magazines cost in the region of €3-€4.

Television and Radio

National television and radio services in Ireland are operated by *Radió Telefís Éireann* (RTÉ), the public broadcasting company, which transmits on two television and five radio channels. RTÉ was set up in 1961 and derives its revenue from licence fees and the sale of advertising time. *RTÉ 1* broadcasts a mix of news and documentaries, while *Network 2*'s programming schedule has more feature films and light entertainment shows. A national independent commercial television station, *TV3*, was launched in September 1998 to provide an alternative to the sometimes-staid programming schedules of RTÉ. *TnaG* (Telifís na Gaelige), or *TG4*, is a dedicated Irish language channel and offers an average of 12 hours of programming a day. British radio and television programming can be picked up over much of the country and satellite and cable channels are widely available.

Radio has been around in Ireland for far longer than television; the first radio programme was broadcast from Dublin in 1926 and from Cork in 1927. Most of the country was receiving programming from the national channel by the 1930s. In recent years, quite a number of independent regional and community radio stations have emerged all over the country and have gained a substantial audience.

There are three 24-hour national radio stations. *Radio 1* features news, current affairs and drama programming while *Radio 2FM* is dedicated to pop music. *Lyric* is a relatively new station, which broadcasts classical music and features programming covering opera, jazz, traditional & world music, cinema and theatre. Irish speakers are served by RTÉ's dedicated 24-hour radio station, *Radió na Gaeltachta*, which was set up in 1972. In addition, *RTÉ Radio Ceolnet* (www.rte.ie/radio/ceolnet/index.html) is a traditional music Internet broadcast service which allows listeners over the web access to a number of music programmes broadcast over the years as well as a vast back catalogue of folk music recordings. There is also a national independent radio station, *Today FM*

RTÉ Radio Frequencies		
Radio 1	88-89FM	www.radio1.ie
2FM	90-92FM	www.2fm.ie
RnaG	93FM	www.rnag.ie
Lyric	96-99FM	www.lyricfm.ie

The *RTÉ Guide* and *TV Now* magazines have listings of all television and radio and satellite programmes, as do the daily newspapers. The *RTÉ Guide* is also available online at www.rteguide.ie. Another useful source of information is Aertel – a teletext and internet service available 24 hours a day, seven days a week and one of the primary sources of information on everything from news to cinema listings, football scores or flight times.

Useful Addresses

Radio Telefís Éireann (Radio and Television), Donnybrook, Dublin 4; ☎01-208 3111; fax 01-208 3080; www.rte.ie.

Today FM, 124 Upper Abbey Street, Dublin 1; ☎01-804 9000; fax 01-804 9099; www.todayfm.com.

TV3 Television Network, Westgate Business Park, Ballymount, Dublin 24; ☎01-419 3333; fax 01-419 3330; www.tv3.ie.

Satellite & Cable Television

Cable television provision began in Ireland after local programmes were first transmitted via cable in Dublin in 1976. Satellite television programmes began to be transmitted in 1986. The Multipoint Microwave Distribution System (MMDS) was launched in 1989. Today most houses in Ireland are either covered by a cable system or are within the reach of an MMDS transmitter.

Digital Satellite Television allows subscribers the choice of up to 100 broadcast TV channels as well as pay-per-view films, 44 music channels and around 35 television stations. Sky Digital is the sole provider of digital satellite television services in Ireland.

Due to the low density of housing in rural areas MMDS has proved to be more practical to implement than cable. Sound and pictures are transmitted as low-power microwaves, which a rooftop mini-dish decodes and then sends to a Set Top Box, which converts the signals to UHF. Three cable companies – Casey Cablevision, Chorus Communication and ntl Ireland – are licenced to provide digital and analogue services in Ireland. ntl, with 430,000 subscribers, is by far the largest cable company and as well as being able to offer multiple TV channels, also offers telephone and high speed Internet services. ntl Ireland holds franchises for Counties Dublin, Waterford, and Galway while Chorus Communication holds franchises for the other 22 counties in the Republic. A standard digital connection fee with ntl costs €65; with a standard viewing package starting at around €12 per month.

Useful Addresses
Chorus Communication, ☎LoCall 1890-202 029; www.chorus.ie.
ntl Ireland, Building P2, East Point Business Park, Dublin 3; ☎01-245 8000; www.ntl.com.
Casey Cablevision, 8 Main Street, Dungarvan, Co. Waterford; ☎058-41845; fax 058-45243; info@cablesurf.com.

Television Licences

Households, businesses or institutions with one or more television set must, by law, be in possession of a current TV licence. *An Post*, which collects TV licence fees on behalf of the Minister for Communications, Marine and Natural Resources, maintains a database containing records of every premises requiring a television licence. Shops that sell or rent TVs must inform *An Post* of a buyer's name and address. TV licence inspectors are employed to track down those without a licence and should you be found in possession of an unlicensed set, you could be prosecuted and face a fine in excess of €1,000. Since January 2003 the cost of a TV licence has been €150 (which works out at less than 42 cents per day. The licence for black and white television sets has been abolished. TV licences can be bought from any of the 1,000+ post offices across the country, by phoning LoCall number 1890 228 528 and giving debit or credit card details, through the Internet at www.billpay.ie or by post from Licence Services, 3rd Floor, GPO, Freepost, Dublin 1.

COMMUNICATIONS

Post

Ireland's postal services are provided by *An Post*, which is obliged to deliver mail to the home or premises of every person in Ireland each working day (i.e., Monday-Friday) and not less than five days a week. The service is reliable and fast. Airmail sent from Ireland should reach Great Britain in two to three days, the rest of Europe within three to four days, America within six days and the rest of the world within a week or two. Surface mail to Britain can take about five days, to the rest of Europe up to two weeks, to the USA up to a month and to Australia or New Zealand considerably longer.

Letter Post, the core division of *An Post*, looks after the nationwide collection, processing and distribution of mail, together with the processing of outgoing and incoming international mail. It delivers over 780 million letters a year and the Dublin Mails Centre, an automated sorting facility opened in 1994, processes over 1.6 million items of mail every day.

Dublin is the only place in the Republic that has, or needs, postal codes – even-numbered codes signify places south of the River Liffey; odd numbers refer to places north of the River. Northern Ireland has postal codes similar to those in the rest of the UK. Mail can be held for collection at any post office free of charge for up to three months. It should be sent to the recipient 'c/o Poste Restante' at the address of the post office where the mail is to be collected. Identification will need to be shown when collecting items from Poste Restante.

There are over 1,900 post offices in Ireland offering standard post office services such as the collection and the delivery of letter and parcel post, the facility to pay certain household utility bills (for telephone, gas, cable television, television licence, local authority rents, etc.) and, at designated post offices, the payment of social welfare benefits (pensions, household benefits, etc.). In addition, some of the larger post offices offer banking and bureau de change services. Post boxes in the Republic are green.

Main post offices (known as branch offices) are usually open 9am-5.30pm Monday to Friday and 9am-1pm on Saturdays. Smaller country sub-post offices often close at lunchtime and at 1pm one day a week. Some of the larger urban post offices are open longer hours and may trade on Sundays, for example the General Post Office in O'Connell Street in Dublin is open from 8am-8pm Monday to Saturday and 10.30am-6.30pm on Sundays and public holidays. There are three types of letter post services in Ireland:

- First Class mail service aims to deliver mail by the next working day throughout Ireland for items posted before the latest time of

posting. There is no Second Class mail service in Ireland.
- International Priority letter service delivers time-sensitive mail by airmail to over 200 countries.
- International Economy letter service is provided to over 200 countries by purchasing the postage stamps available in post offices and various retail outlets throughout Ireland.

An Post can redirect mail from your old address to your new address for a period of up to 12 months and can hold your mail for you for up to 12 weeks if you are away from your property. At certain designated post offices you can apply for your passport and have it returned to you, by post, within ten working days.

For security reasons, larger items will need to bear a detailed description of the contents along with the name and address of the sender before being posted. The contents of such parcels destined for delivery outside the EU will also need to be declared on the appropriate customs declaration form (CN 22 and CN 23). The contents of parcels destined for delivery within the EU must be declared on the packaging of the parcel. Parcels destined for Northern Ireland are treated as internal deliveries and are excluded from these procedures.

Private post office boxes can be rented at delivery offices in Ireland. You can request delivery of your PO Box contents for a fee or pick up your mail in person. Annual rental charges for a PO Box range from €220 for a letters only service to €440 for letters and parcels. The fee charged for delivery of PO Box contents depends on your postal district.

Postage Rates. Rates vary according to factors including size, weight, destination and speed of delivery required. Rates for domestic post (mail originating from and being delivered within the 32 counties of Ireland, or 'Zone 1') sent first class begin at €0.41 for a letter or postcard weighing less than 50 grammes. The cost of sending letters to 'Zone 2' (Great Britain) depends on whether the mail is sent priority or economy and is also affected by the dimensions of the article to be sent. Rates for letters and postcards weighing less than 50 grammes begin at €0.41 for economy and €0.50 for priority. Rates for the rest of Europe ('Zone 3') begin at €0.57 for a letter or postcard weighing under 25 grammes increasing to €1.70 for a package to be sent priority with a combined length, width and depth not exceeding 900mm and weighing less than 25 grammes. Letters and postcards to be sent economy class to 'Zone 4' (Rest of the World) weighing less than 25 grammes with dimensions of a maximum of 235mm x 162mm x 5mm thickness will need a stamp of €0.44.

Swiftpost. The *Swiftpost National* service guarantees delivery of any items weighing up to 2kg, to any address in the Republic by the next working day and by 12.30pm to addresses in town centres, commercial centres or industrial estates. Postage rates start at €3.80 for a package weighing less than 100 grammes up to a maximum of €10.55 for a 2kg package. *Swiftpost Expres* guarantees priority (airmail) delivery for items weighing up to 2kg sent to Britain, Denmark, Finland, France, Germany, Iceland, Netherlands, Norway, Portugal, Sweden, Switzerland and Spain. The *Expres* service also allows customers to track their items and obtain confirmation of delivery. Rates start at €5 for a package weighing less than 100 grammes sent to Britain (€6.30 to the rest of Europe) up to a maximum of €21 for a 2kg package to Europe. Sending mail by *Swiftpost International* ensures a faster delivery time than by sending items Priority (Air Mail). *Swiftpost International* covers those countries not covered by *Swiftpost Expres* (200 countries worldwide). The service is not a guaranteed service, however, and confirmation of delivery is not possible on items sent using *Swiftpost International*. There is a fee of €3.60 to pay for the service, in addition to the price of priority postage.

Registered Post. Registered Post is very useful when sending important correspondence or valuable items by post. It is a secure service providing the mailer with proof of delivery (a signature is obtained on delivery of the item sent) and items – within Ireland and Britain – are monitored using a bar code tracking system. Items sent by registered post receive priority and are insured up to the replacement value stated on the customer receipt. Rates for sending mail by registered post vary depending on size, weight, destination and amount of compensation required should an item get lost in transit.

Telephones

eircom, formerly known as *Telecom Éireann*, is now a privately owned company and controls much of the telephone, Internet and data industry in Ireland. Competition is slowly being introduced as the telecommunications market is deregulated, bringing benefits to consumers in the form of lower charges. There are over 1.6 million telephone lines in Ireland. Ireland's phone system uses US standard – RJ11 – plugs, which means that should you have a telephone or a modem bought in the USA it can be plugged directly into the Irish telephone system. Telecommunications networks in Ireland are regulated by the *Commission for Telecommunications Regulation (ComReg)*, Abbey Court, Lower Abbey Street, Dublin 1; ☎01-804 9600; fax 01-804 9680; www.comreg.ie.

There are three types of public telephone in Ireland: coin phones, card phones and privately owned coin phones. Public telephones are to be found all over Ireland – roadside booths as well as phones in pubs, shops, hotels and restaurants, and municipal buildings such as bus and railway stations and libraries. Local, national and international calls can all be dialled direct from these phones. The most commonly found public telephone is now the card phone. Telephone cards of 10, 20, 50 and 100 units can be bought in post offices and in most newsagents and work out at around €2.55 for 10 calls to €20.30 for 100 calls. The location of cardphones and Callcard Agents can be obtained by calling Freefone 1800 250 250.

Coin Phones. Some businesses provide their own coin phones instead of using an *eircom* provided payphone. In such cases charges imposed by the business owner apply, which may be higher than eircom payphones as the facility exists on private payphones to increase call charge rates. Additionally, in some cases calls to 1-800 numbers (Locall numbers) may be blocked and information calls may incur a charge or be blocked completely.

Dial Tones. The dial tone of telephones in Ireland is a continuous high-pitched tone; the ringing tone (the sound heard in the earpiece rather than the sound made by the phone set) is a repeated double beat tone (burr-burr). The engaged tone is signified by a high-pitched, broken tone (beep-beep-beep). If a number is unobtainable you will hear a continuous steady tone (burr).

Codes. The dialling code for Ireland from abroad is 353. The code for Dublin is 01. When calling Dublin from another country dial +353 then 1 (drop the zero in the Dublin code) and then the number you require. To call another country from the Republic dial 00 followed by the country code and then the area code (if there is a leading zero in the area code, drop it). International dialling codes from Ireland to the rest of the world are listed in the telephone directories available in post offices and offices run by *eircom*.

Charges. Local calls cost €0.25 – or one card phone unit – for three minutes, €1 for a national call. Cheap rates are available from 6pm to 8am on weekdays and all day on weekends and public holidays. Be aware that calls made from hotel rooms are more expensive than calls made from a public telephone and can often triple the cost of a call.

Text Messaging. Text messaging is available to all landline telephones as well as mobile networks. Text messages sent to landline telephones will be either displayed on the phone if there is a digital readout screen, or read to the customer using a text to speech server. The fixed network SMS centre numbers are 1740 9911 (outgoing) and 0818 365135 (incoming). These SMSC codes are normally pre-programmed into SMS capable phones purchased in Ireland.

Telephone Directories. In 1998 the responsibility of producing the *eircom* Phone Book was given over to Golden Pages Ltd. and in 1999 an online service, www.goldenpages.ie, was launched containing all six Golden Pages directories online. In 2000, in conjunction with *eircom's* 11811 directory enquiry service, Golden Pages Talking was launched which allows users calling 11811 to be put through to the Golden Pages Talking service in order to request service providers in their local area.

Mobile Phones. Ireland has one of the highest mobile phone ownership rates in the EU with over three million mobile phone users – about 75% of the population. The Irish system runs on the digital GSM network. Mobile phones in Ireland take the prefix 086 (Digifone/0_2), 087 (Eircell/Vodafone), 085 (Meteor) or 088. American mobiles – which are mostly analog – will not work in Ireland, however mobiles from Europe will work by tapping on to the local Eircell or Esat networks. Handsets can be hired. Contact Eircell (website: www.eircell.ie) for further information. Competition between the mobile phone companies has resulted in a drop in phone charges in the past few years. Coverage for mobile phones in Ireland is still uneven and you are advised to go with the mobile phone company that can provide the best quality in your area. In the cities coverage doesn't matter so much but in the smaller towns and countryside, the location of the nearest mast and transmitter is critical. A Bluetooth headset allows you to leave your mobile phone anywhere within a ten metre radius while you receive or make calls on your mobile.

Prepaid Versus Monthly Rental Plans. There are two types of mobile phone payment plans. Prepaid plans charge only for each phonecall made from a mobile, and tend to be more expensive than using a Monthly Rental plan. Top up cards – for €5 and upwards – are available at any phone shop, over the Internet or through the mobile phone company. With a Monthly Rental plan you have to pass a credit check and charges vary from €12.70 to €185 a month – the difference in price affects the number of free calls you are allowed in the package.

Emergency Numbers & Directory Enquiries. The number for the emergency services (Police (Gardaí), Fire Department, Ambulance, Coastguard, Mountain Rescue) is 999. Calls to this service are free of charge. You will be asked which service you need and for the address or location where assistance is required. A 112 emergency service number, which also operates in most other European states, is used in addition to 999. The operator for calls within Ireland and Northern Ireland can be contacted by dialling 11811. For directory enquiries for the rest of the world dial 11818 or 114. To report a fault on the line dial 1901.

The Internet

Most Internet service providers charge a flat monthly fee of between €12.70 and €20.32 in addition to a fee paid for the time you are on-line (charged at the local call rate). However, increadingly 'Anytime' packages are being offered. For example Esat BT now charges a flat rate of €29.99 for 180 hours of surftime any time of the day, any day of the week. Eircom offers several flat rate packages – their 'Anytime' package costs €20.99 a month for 150 hours of unlimited surftime.

Broadband is only available in a very limited number of areas in Ireland. ntl's cable modem Internet service, though limited to a few areas in Dublin at present (most of ntl's cable network is only capable of one-way transmission and not two-way – which is required for broadband) is pretty good value. The monthly charge for an uncapped 512k/128k service is €35 a month, with a connection charge of €92 if you choose to buy your own cable modem or you can hire a modem for €5 a month. Chorus also have cable broadband on offer in a limited number of areas in Kilkenny, Clonmel and Thurles – with a monthly charge of around €35.

Useful Addresses

eircom, Customer Services, eircom net, Unit 2B, Eastpoint Business Park, Fairview, Dublin 3; ☎01-701 0000; http://home.eircom.net.
Esat BT, Grand Canal Plaza, Upper Grand Canal Street, Dublin 4; ☎01-432 7007; www.iol.ie.

CARS & MOTORING

Roads & Signage

Ireland is still one of the least congested countries in Europe when it comes to driving but, due to the paucity of dual carriageways and stretches of motorway, getting from A to B along often narrow roads that rarely bypass towns and villages mean that travelling by road is not as fast as in other countries. Although a lot of investment has recently been put into improving roads, away from the major cities and above all in rural areas the quality of roads and signage can still be pretty bad, and frustrating. Place names on road signs are written in both Irish and English (except in some of the Gaeltacht) but more often than not you will find that signs are rare and/or misleading. In the Republic the old 'T' (Trunk) and 'L' (Link) routes have now been renumbered as 'N' (National) and 'R' (Regional) routes.

Brown and white signs denote tourism destinations, blue & white signs give motorway information while green signs are used on National primary and secondary routes; white signs are used on all other regional and local routes. Note that there is a difference between an English statute mile and an Irish mile. An Irish mile (still marked on some old milestones) measures 2,240 yards – 480 yards longer than an English mile. Older signage gives distances in English miles but these are gradually being replaced with modern green and white signage giving distances in the European kilometre. It is best to make sure that you know the name of the next town on your itinerary rather than to rely on following a route number as often the number won't be given on the signage and many locals will navigate by name only ('it's along the Westport road') rather than use the road number. Ireland used to be renowned for the advanced state of decay of many of the cars pootling along its more rural roads but increasingly, as the economy has picked up, more money has been spent on buying a new set of wheels. The National Car Test (see below) has also driven many of the more dilapidated cars from the Republic's roads. Beware of cattle and sheep on the roads and slow moving agricultural vehicles.

Tolls are payable at several points in the Dublin area – on the M50 ring road between the N4 and N3 interchanges, on the R131 east link bridge, and the Drogheda Bypass. In each case the toll charge is approximately €1.50 for cars, with higher tolls for vans and trucks. Tolls are also being introduced on some new motorways. Payment is by cash or with discount cards purchased from toll plazas. The traffic information of the motoring organizations is broadcast in English by RTÉ Radio 1 and 2 and most commercial radio stations.

Parking regulations are strictly enforced, particularly in Dublin. Tow trucks and vehicle clamping programs are in operation so be sure to check the signs for days and hours of chargeable parking specific to the location. Typical pay and display parking meter costs are €1 to €2.50 per hour. Multi-storey car parks (typical cost €1.50 to €2.50

per hour) are signposted along the parking routes with advance space availability indicators showing how many spaces are left in each park. Some car park payment machines accept payment by credit card. In Dublin's city centre you can also charge your on-street car parking to your mobile phone account or credit card by using mPark, a mobile parking payment service whereby, once you have registered (☎ 01-449 9000; www.mpark.ie), car parking charges can be rung through on your mobile phone, alleviating the need to carry change.

Driving Regulations

Speed limits are 30mph (48km/h) in the centre of towns and villages unless signs indicate otherwise. The general speed limit on most roads outside of built up areas is 60mph (96km/h) with the speed limit increasing to 70mph (110km/h) on motorways. When towing, vehicles travelling on non-urban roads and motorways are restricted to 80km/h. On the spot fines can be issued for speeding offences and be aware that drink driving laws are strict – don't attempt to drive with more than 80mg of alcohol per 100ml of blood coursing through your veins. Unfortunately it is not possible to tell how many whiskies or Guinnesses this represents with any degree of certainty since the amount will vary according to a person's gender and weight. Driving could well be affected after only one or two units of alcohol (one unit is equivalent to half a pint of ordinary strength beer or lager; one measure of spirits; one standard glass of wine; or one standard glass of sherry). It will take about one hour to get rid of each unit of alcohol imbibed and so if you have had a particularly heavy drinking session you could still be over the limit the following morning.

Drive on the left side of the road though be aware of the predilection for some locals to drive along the middle of the road. Those in the front seats of cars must wear seatbelts, as must those in the back if seatbelts are fitted. Children under 12 years old must travel in the back of a car. Motorcyclists and their passengers must wear crash helmets.

It is now illegal to use a mobile phone while driving in Ireland, unless you are using a hands-free loudspeaking device. Motorists who use hand-held mobile phones face a €435 fine, three months' jail and a six-month driving ban. The ban on mobile use also applies to truck and other heavy goods vehicle drivers. It is also illegal to use portable hands-free kits (i.e. an earpiece connected by wire to a handheld phone) or to use other radio devices – i.e. CB and other 2-way radio devices. If you are driving alone then it makes sense to either divert all calls to voicemail or change the phone settings to 'no answer', which will then allow you time to pull over to take the call.

Driving Tests

In order to take a driving test, you must be 'normally resident' in Ireland and have an Irish correspondence address. Normal residence is taken to be the place where the person usually lives, that is for at least 185 days in each calendar year. If you hold a current valid full driving licence issued by an EU member State you can exchange your licence for a full Irish Licence. Your local Motor Tax Office should be contacted for more details. US citizens are permitted to drive with a US driver's licence for the duration of a visit to Ireland; i.e., as long as their status is that of tourist and not resident. Once a US citizen decides to become resident in Ireland, regardless of how long he or she has been in the country, an Irish driver's licence must be applied for.

Appointments for driving tests are arranged in the order in which applications are received and the national average waiting time for a driving test is around 10 weeks, depending on the number of applications received by the Department of Transport. Waiting times for each centre can be found on the website, www.drivingtest.ie. You will normally be given an appointment notice four to five weeks in advance of your test indicating the time, date and venue for the test, together with conditions that will need to be met. Further information can be obtained from the Driver Testing Section of the Department of Transport (Government Buildings, Ballina, Co. Mayo; ☎ LoCall 1890-406 040; fax 096-24400; www.drivingtest.ie). The Department's website also has details of driving test centres throughout Ireland.

The average pass rate for those taking the test is 55.4% (as of April 2003). Fees vary from €38 for Categories A, A1, B, EB, M, W to €76 for categories EC, EC1, ED, ED1. Vehicles registered in the UK or Northern Ireland require a tax disc. Otherwise foreign registered vehicles do not need to display either an Irish insurance or tax disc. They should however comply with their own National regulations. You will be required to produce evidence from your insurer that you are insured for the purpose of the driving test.

Driving Licences

Upon passing the driving test, the tester will issue you with a Certificate of Competency, which you can then exchange for a full driving licence at your local Motor Tax Office. In Dublin contact the Motor Taxation Office at River House, Chancery Street, Dublin 7 (☎01-872 0077) or the Motor Taxation Office at Nutgrove Shopping Centre, Nutgrove, Dublin 14 (☎01-4933 411). If you have no driving licence from your home country then, to be eligible for a full licence, you must first obtain a provisional licence (learner's permit) and take the Irish driving test. All first time applicants for a provisional licence must take an eye examination. This test must be given by an optician practising in Ireland.

Endorsements & Disqualification

In 2002 a penalty points system was introduced into Ireland so that any motorist found guilty of speeding, or driving an uninsured vehicle or drving without wearing a seatbelt now has penalty points imposed on his or her licence, in addition to being fined. Any driver receiving 12 penalty points in any three-year period will face an automatic six-month disqualification from driving. Penalty points remain on a driver's licence for a period of three years. An endorsement on your license is likely to increase motor insurance premiums.

If you are disqualified from driving you must not drive any motor vehicle over the period of disqualification unless you decide to lodge an appeal against the conviction, which you must do within 14 days of the judgement. The more serious driving offences (serial drink driving, dangerous driving, etc) can carry the penalty of being disqualified from driving for life.

Insurance

Ireland has a bad track record of road safety and is among the worst in the EU when it comes to road accidents. Insurance premiums in Ireland have always been pretty high compared to the UK.

The law requires that vehicles using public and private roads in Ireland must be covered by insurance. The minimum cover a driver must have is third party insurance, which includes cover for injury to other people. For many, taking out comprehensive insurance – which covers all risks such as fire and theft or damage to your car and pays personal accident benefits and medical expenses where necessary – is considered worth paying the extra premiums on.

The cost of car insurance varies greatly because there are a number of factors to be taken into account, such as the age and sex of the driver, the type of vehicle to be insured, the age of the vehicle and the size of engine, the area in which the driver lives – be it town or country, etc. Discounts are awarded on premiums payable if the driver has not previously claimed on car insurance. This 'no claims bonus' is lost for succeeding years, however, should a driver make a claim. Drivers who have claimed more than once may end up having to pay heavier premiums in future years.

There is a lot of competition between insurance companies (such as Hibernian, Allianz, AXA and Royal & SunAlliance) for custom and so it is advisable to shop around for the best quote. Motoring organisations such as the AA (Automobile Association) and the RAC (Royal Automobile Club) have their own insurance schemes. If you don't want to shop around yourself, insurance brokers will be able to find a good insurance deal for you. The Irish Brokers Association (87 Merrion Square, Dublin 2; ☎ 01-661 3067; fax 01-661 9955; www.irishbrokers.com) carries lists of its members.

National Car Test (NCT)

In compliance with EU directives, compulsory car tests (similar to the UK's MOT) were introduced in Ireland in January 2000. The direct result of this was that Ireland's roads were swept clean of the decaying old crocks that pootled about all over the country, to be replaced by new vehicles.

The majority of vehicles over four years old now undergo the National Car Test every two years and any driver who cannot produce a car test certificate will not be able to tax his or her vehicle. Tests are carried out by an independent body – the National Car Testing Service Ltd – whose centres check the reliability and roadworthiness of a vehicle, looking at brakes; exhaust emission; wheels and tyres; lights; steering and suspension; chassis and underbody; electrical systems; glass and mirrors; transmission; interior and fuel system. It is advised to get your vehicle serviced before taking it to a test centre.

Certain vehicles are excluded from having to undergo the NCT, including cars that are taxed as 'vintage' and cars permanently based on islands not connected to mainland Ireland by road. Commerical vehicles that have their rear side windows blocked off and are commercially taxed are not required to undergo the NCT but must be tested by the Department of Environment, Heritage and Local Government.

Imported vehicles must undergo the NCT if they are over four years old, regardless of whether they have passed a similar test in their country of origin. Tests can be applied for through the booking department of the National Car Testing Service Ltd at Citywest Business Campus, Lakedrive 3026, Naas Road, Dublin 24 (☎1890-200 670; fax 01-4135 996; www.ncts.ie). There are 43 Test Centres throughout Ireland.

Motoring Organisations

Organisations such as the AA and RAC offer all or some of the following services to members: vehicle insurance cover, breakdown services with recovery anywhere in Ireland, free public transport or hire car, hotel charges, home start and legal advice and aid. The AA is the largest of these organisations and currently has in excess of 350,000 members in Ireland. Membership starts at around €105. The RAC's Roadside Recovery package costs €90 – the cost of a package depends on the services provided. If you are a member of a motoring organisation, you will have a contact number to ring if you break down and the organisa-

tion will then arrange for a repair person or recovery vehicle to assist you. If you do not belong to an organisation, other breakdown services are available from garages – though these may prove expensive. If your vehicle is less than reliable, and even if it is brand new, membership of a motoring organisation is a good investment.

Useful Addresses
AA Ireland, 23 Suffolk Street, Dublin 2; ☎01-6179 999; fax 01-6179 900; www.aaireland.ie.
RAC Motoring Services, RAC House, 232 Lower Rathmines Road, Dublin 6; ☎01-4125 500; fax 01-4125 555; www.rac.ie.

Car Rental

Car Rental firms can be found in all the larger towns and cities and at ferry terminals and airports. Addresses of firms can be found in the Golden Pages directory under *Car Hire*. It is advisable to ring round for a selection of quotes as prices can vary considerably depending on the size, make, type of vehicle required and period of rental. Hire charges are usually based on a daily or weekly rate with prices for weekend rentals often higher than for the same period of time during a working week. You will need to return the car with the same amount of fuel it had when you received it unless you want to incur a surcharge. There may be restrictions on the type of vehicle you can hire as well as an increased insurance charge if you are under 21 years of age. If you have endorsements on your licence for careless driving you may be refused car hire. Some car insurance policies include free car rental to cover any period that you are without a car as a result of an accident.

Irish Car Rentals (www.irishcarrentals.com) have offices in Dublin, Shannon, Cork, Limerick, Galway and Kerry; at the time of going to press they were offering sub-compact cars from €109 per week including unlimited mileage, cdw and theft loss insurance, taxes and VAT.

Fuel

Unleaded petrol, LRP (lead replacement petrol) and diesel fuel is available in Ireland. Although there are now plenty of 24-hour garages in Ireland, petrol stations in the more rural areas may close on Sundays and in the evenings. Note that due to the extra tax charged by the British government fuel is more expensive in Northern Ireland, so it makes sense to fill up in the Republic before a trip to the north.

Diesel used to be significantly cheaper than petrol, with many people in recent years switching to diesel-engine vehicles to take advantage of the savings. However, once scientists produced evidence that diesel is less environmentally-friendly than unleaded petrol, tax has increased on diesel so that there is now hardly any difference in price between petrol and diesel. Diesel-engine vehicles are generally less thirsty than petrol-engine vehicles though and work out to be more economical in the long run. Diesels also tend to be more reliable than petrol-engines.

The cost of fuel varies from place to place by as much as five cents a litre and you can expect to pay less in the towns and cities and more in more rural areas.

PETROL PRICES

Prices per litre at time of writing were in the region of

- €0.86 per litre for unleaded petrol
- €0.84 per litre for diesel
- €1.60 for Super Unleaded
- €105.5 for LRP

PUBLIC TRANSPORT

Rail

The train service in Ireland is run by *Iarnród Éireann* (Irish Rail) and has its main terminus at Connolly Station, Amiens Street in Dublin. The rail network is far from extensive but serves the main towns and cities of the country. However, if you want to get away into the scenic parts of the country you will need to either take a bus or hire a car. For travel around Dublin and its environs the Dublin Area Rapid Transit (DART) provides quick access to and from Malahide and Howth in the north, to Greystones, County Wicklow in the south. Minimum fares on the DART start at €1.05 up to a maximum of €3.35. Suburban rail services run as far north as Dundalk in County Louth, as far south as Arklow in County Wicklow, and inland to Mullingar in County Westmeath. Four-day Dublin Explorer tickets allowing travel around Dublin on DART and Dublin Bus services are available at DART stations. A light rail system linking Dublin and its suburbs, Luas, is planned and the first two rail lines: Tallaght to Connolly Station; and Sandyford to St Stephens Green are due to open in summer/autumn 2004.

Information on rail services and fares can be obtained from railway stations, travel agents, tourist offices and *Iarnród Éireann* (☎1850-366 222; www.irishrail.ie).

Bus & Coach Services

Bus Éireann (Irish Bus – Broadstone, Dublin 7; ☎01-8302 222; fax 01-8309 377; www.buseireann.ie) runs extensive services throughout the country. The cost of travelling by coach is much less than travelling by train and Bus Éireann also offers cheap day return and other discounted tickets. Tickets can be bought from bus stations and Bus Éireann offices throughout Ireland as well as on the bus or coach at point of departure. Within Dublin city and its suburbs bus services are operated by Dublin Bus (59 Upper O'Connell Street, Dublin 1; ☎01-8734 222; www.dublinbus.ie). Tickets for Dublin bus services can be bought from agents throughout Dublin – for example from Spar supermarkets, and newsagents – and many of the buses operate an 'autofare' system whereby passengers must have the correct change to board as drivers do not handle cash. The main bus station in Dublin is Busáras on Store Street.

Taxis & Minicabs

Taxis in the main cities of Dublin, Cork, Limerick and Galway are metered, but outside these centres taxis and minicabs are not. In the main centres you will find taxis waiting at ranks outside bus and train stations and at official ranks outside airport terminals. In the smaller towns and in more rural areas local taxi services may be few and far between but will be listed in the Golden Pages directory. Staff in the pubs and bars should also be able to put you on to a local taxi firm. The minimum fare for a taxi in Dublin is €2.75 between 8am and 10pm for the first 5/9th of a mile or 2.5 minutes, rising by €0.15 for every subsequent 1/9th of a mile or 30 seconds. There are extra charges payable for additional passengers, luggage, animals (other than guide dogs), the time of day, Sundays and public holidays.

BANKS & FINANCE

Choosing a Bank

If you know whereabouts in Ireland you will be living, a sensible move is to open an account with a bank that has a branch local to you. Many rural towns and villages will only have one bank, if they have one at all and in such locations your best choice will be to join the Allied Irish Bank (AIB) or the Bank of Ireland, which serve these the regions better than other banks.

Unlike in the UK, most personal accounts in Ireland carry service or transaction charges, although as long as you remain in credit, these charges are quite small. Bank charges can be reduced, or kept to a minimum by using ATM cards to withdraw cash instead of cheques, making purchases with a credit or debit card, paying regular bills by direct debit, and by using 24-hour banking and on-line services to pay bills, transfer funds from one account to another or check the balance and recent transactions on your account. Full-time students and those aged over 60 are entitled to free banking with some banks. If you need a business account, it is advisable to check charges made by different banks as they can vary widely. Details can be obtained from the banks or via their websites. The majority of banks now have 24-hour telephone banking services and on-line banking facilities.

Banks are open from 10am-4pm Monday to Friday, and on one day a week stay open until 5pm (days vary from place to place).

Useful Addresses

Allied Irish Bank, Bankcentre, Ballsbridge, Dublin 4; ☏01-660 0311; www.aib.ie.
Bank of Ireland, Lower Baggot Street, Dublin 2; ☏01-661 5933; www.bankofireland.ie.
National Irish Bank, 7-8 Wilton Terrace, Dublin 2; ☏01-638 5000; www.nib.ie.
Ulster Bank, 33 College Green, Dublin 2; ☏01-677 7623; www.ulsterbank.com.
Permanent TSB, 56-59 St. Stephen's Green, Dublin 2; ☏01-661 5577; www.permanenttsb.ie.
The Irish Bank's Information Service, Nassau House, Nassau Street, Dublin 2; ☏01-671 5299; fax 01-679 6680; www.ibis.ie.

Bank Accounts

Retail banks offer a wide range of services to both personal and business customers and there is a great deal of competition between the different banks to draw in customers. Accounts offered vary from bank to bank, but there are basically two kinds of account: the current account and the savings or deposit account. Individual banks will provide details of their range of accounts on request, and they are available in most cases on-line.

Current accounts generally pay a low rate of interest on credit balances, but this will vary depending on the type of account you hold. Chequebooks with a cheque guarantee card are available with this type of account. Cheque guarantee cards will, as their name suggests, guarantee funds to cover the value of any cheque that you present, up to a certain amount. The card will also usually allow you to withdraw cash, request a balance or a statement, order a chequebook or other services from cashpoints (ATMs) situated outside banks and in other outlets such as supermarkets and garages. Most of the main banks belong to a system that allows you to use your card in cash machines provided by a range of banks. There will be a daily limit on the amount of cash you can withdraw, which will vary depending on the type of account you have and the funds you normally have available.

Deposit accounts are savings accounts which pay a higher rate of interest, often on a sliding scale so that the larger your credit balance, the higher the rate of interest payable. A basic deposit account will allow withdrawals or money transfers on demand, and may offer a chequebook and cash card facility.

Opening an Account

Application forms for the various different accounts are available from branches or, increasingly, on-line. You will need to supply personal details of name, address, date of birth, occupation and so forth, together with proof of identity such as a driving licence or passport, and proof of address such as a utilities bill. You do not need to be a resident of Ireland to open a bank account in the country.

Plastic Money

Debit and credit cards are generally accepted in most of the larger retailers and outlets but some small businesses such as B&Bs, some pubs and smaller shops in more rural areas may not have the facilities required to deal with payment by these means. Either a credit or debit card is often required when reserving hotel rooms or hiring vehicles.

Debit Cards. A cheque guarantee card will usually be combined with a debit card such as PLUS or Cirrus. This allows money to be taken electronically from your card at point of sale, or from an ATM, as long as there are funds to cover it currently in the account. There is no cost for the service and no interest payable. Debit cards are taking over from cheques as a form of payment at many outlets due to their ease of use and because they eliminate the need for cheque guarantee limits. However, there is often a limit imposed on the amount of cash you can withdraw from an ATM using a debit card over a period of 24 hours. Increasingly, mail order companies and e-commerce websites will take payment by debit card as well as by credit card. Many shops now allow customers to obtain cash, known as cashback, on their debit cards when paying for goods with a debit card – a useful facility in areas where there is no bank ATM cashpoint nearby.

Credit Cards. Credit cards are issued by most financial institutions including all banks and building societies and a range of other organisations such as car manufacturers, chain stores and charities. Charities find issuing credit cards a useful fund-raising tool as they pledge a certain percentage of the profits from their credit card services will go towards their charitable works.

The most widely accepted credit cards in Ireland are Visa and MasterCard. Most cards issued by banks, building societies and other organisations will have their brand name attached to a Visa, MasterCard or other credit card service so that, although your card may be issued by a small institution, you can be assured that there is the guarantee of international financial backing to it. Credit cards allow the holder to spread repayments over a period of time, or indefinitely, with interest payable on the balance owed, unless the total balance repayable is paid off at the end of each month, in which case no interest is charged. There may be an annual fee charged in addition to the interest; and those credit card companies that issue cards where no annual fee is charged may charge a higher rate of interest. It is therefore advisable to compare interest rates/annual fees before deciding on a particular credit card.

Most credit cards are issued as ordinary, gold or platinum cards, with differing credit levels depending on the holder's annual salary or monthly payments paid into a bank or building society. Gold and platinum cards may also offer additional benefits, such as insurance, or emergency help to a holder.

Where credit cards are accepted abroad, they often offer the best exchange rate – sometimes as much as 5% better than the retail rate offered by banks and bureaux de change. Credit cards are also useful for cash advances as you can withdraw cash from ATMs and banks. When withdrawing money from an ATM using a credit card remember that all cash advances are subject to a 'transaction fee' so it is advisable to always take out larger amounts of cash rather than a number of smaller amounts, as you will be charged on each transaction.

Store cards are mainly intended for use against purchases in the shops of the company that have issued the card, and often incentives such as discounts or holidays are offered in order to encourage shoppers to use them. Store cards tend to charge a higher rate of interest than the average credit card company.

Useful Websites
American Express: www.americanexpress.com
MasterCard: www.mastercard.com
Visa: www.visa.com

Charge Cards. The main difference between credit cards and charge cards is that you must pay the total outstanding balance on the latter when it is due, otherwise a penalty will have to be paid. Charge cards include American Express and Diners Club cards. Charge cards are not as popular in Ireland as they are in the USA and to counteract this American Express introduced a credit card in 1995. International charge cards, if lost or stolen, can usually be replaced at short notice – something that may not be possible with a credit card. Gold and platinum cards may allow instant access to large amounts of cash or an unsecured overdraft facility at an advantageous rate.

Building Societies & the Post Office

In 1989, building society law was changed in Ireland to enable building societies to compete with banks. Since then, a number of building societies have opted to become banks by floating their shares on the stock market and consequently there are fewer building societies (*Mutuals*) than banks. EBS (Educational Building Society – Head Office, 2 Burlington Road, Dublin 4; ☎01-665 9000; fax 01-665 8118; www.ebs.ie) is the biggest building society in Ireland with 109 branches nationwide.

For those looking for an easy and accessible way to deposit and save money it is useful to know that *An Post*, Ireland's post office, offers a number of savings and investment options. These are available from its 1,200 branches nationwide. Good for those who decide to live in the more rural areas of the country.

Credit Unions

A credit union is a co-operative community-based organisation that allows people to save together and lend money to each other at affordable rates of interest. Credit unions are owned by their members, with each member having an equal say in the running of the organisation, irrespective of savings deposited. Members receive an annual dividend on savings up to €12,697. There are over 530 credit unions in operation throughout Ireland, and most are affiliated to the Irish League of Credit Unions (33-41 Lower Mount Street, Dublin 2; ☎01-614 6700; fax 01-614 6701; www.creditunion.ie).

The Euro

At present the euro area or eurozone is made up of twelve countries (Belgium, Germany, Greece, Spain, France, Ireland, Italy, Luxembourg, The Netherlands, Austria, Portugal, Finland) all of which have adopted the single currency. Although the European Union consists of 25 countries, Denmark and the United Kingdom have opt-out clauses and are not obliged to adopt the euro. Sweden will join the eurozone as soon as it has fulfilled all the conditions. The euro is also used in Andorra, Monaco, San Marino and Vatican City as well as several overseas territories of the twelve eurozone countries including the Canary Islands, Madeira, the Azores and the French Outre-Mer territories (Guyana, Martinique, Guadeloupe, Reunion and the collective territories of Mayotte and St Pierre and Miquelon).

Moneychangers throughout the eurozone are obliged to exchange money at the official, fixed rate at no commission (though they may well still charge a 'service fee'). Euro-denominated travellers' cheques allow the bearer to pay for goods and services in the eurozone at the official rate, commission-free.

The euro came into being in cashless form on 1 January 1999 when the eurozone member states formed an Economic and Monetary Union (EMU) and permanently locked the exchange rates of their countries against the euro. The Republic of Ireland changed its unit of currency from the Irish pound or punt (pronounced 'poont') to the euro (€) on 1 January 2002. Euro coins come in denominations of 1, 2, 5, 10 and

50 cents and €1 and €2. Euro notes come in denominations of 5, 10, 20, 50, 100, 200, and 500 euros. The one cent coin is slightly smaller than the old Irish 5p coin and the two euro coin is about the same size as the old Irish 2p coin. One side of the euro coins is the same in all Euro member states, while the other side shows the twelve stars of the EU flag, the year the coin was minted and a national emblem. In Ireland, the national emblem is the harp and the word 'Eire'. Euros can be used anywhere within the eurozone, regardless of country of issue.

Note that the unit of currency in Northern Ireland is still the British pound (£). Northern Ireland has its own bank notes, which are identical in value to those issued in England and Wales, Scotland and the Isle of Man. However, Northern Ireland notes are not accepted as legal tender in the rest of the UK.

Foreign Currency

Ireland has no currency restrictions, which means you may take in or out of the country as much money as you wish in most currencies. Banks will change most foreign bank notes, but will not exchange foreign coins. You are likely to get a better rate of exchange by drawing euros from your bank account direct, using a credit card or cash card at an ATM.

When buying or selling currency, shop around for the best deal. Exchange rates are posted by banks and bureaux de change, but often vary from place to place – bureaux de change at airports and ferry terminals tend to give lousy rates. In addition, there will be a commission charged on top, typically of around one or two percent with a minimum charge. Building societies and larger post offices will also buy and sell foreign currency. If you want to obtain travellers' cheques, you may need to order them two or three days in advance of collection. Take your passport with you when buying or selling foreign currency.

Transferring Funds

Money can be transferred to Ireland by banker's draft or a letter of credit, both of which may take up to two weeks to clear. Money can also be sent via a post office by international money order, a cashier's cheque or by telegraphic transfer by a company such as Western Union. You will need your passport to collect money transferred from abroad and to cash a banker's draft or other credit note. Another way of transferring funds is to send money direct from your bank to another, via an inter-bank transfer. Both the sending and receiving bank will charge a service charge or a percentage of the amount transferred, so it may be expensive to transfer small sums in this way. It is usually quicker to transfer money between two branches of the same bank than between different banks.

TAXATION

Income Tax

Tax is paid to the Revenue Service and is used by the government to pay for a range of services that benefit the general public, for example health and hospital care, education, welfare and care benefits, housing, roads, etc. Under the PAYE (Pay As You Earn) system your employer calculates any tax due and deducts it at source from your gross pay, together with any pay-related social insurance contributions (PRSI). As soon as you accept an offer of employment you will need to contact the PAYE tax office to obtain your Tax-Free Allowance certificate (TFA certificate). Tax is then deducted on your gross earnings less the amount of your Tax-Free Allowance. Irish nationals will need to complete form IT67, available from the tax office; non-nationals will need to complete form 12A. You will be asked to include details of your employer's PAYE Registration number and the address of their tax office. Until your employers receive your TFA certificate they will deduct tax at an emergency rate, but any excess tax taken from your salary will be repaid once the employer has the TFA certificate. If you are an Irish national you will have received a Personal Public Service number (PPS No.) from the Department of Social, Community and Family Affairs on your 16th birthday. If you do not have a PPS number you will need to contact the Department to receive one. Pay-related social insurance may be deducted from your salary if you earn over a certain amount and such contributions will entitle you to certain welfare benefits.

Generally you will be charged Irish tax on your worldwide income earned or arising in a tax year (the Irish tax year runs 1 January to 31 December) during which you are resident, ordinarily resident or domiciled in Ireland for tax purposes. For any tax year during which you are non-resident and not ordinarily resident in Ireland you will be charged tax on your income from Irish sources only. The extent of your liability to Irish tax may also be influenced by your domicile status and possibly by a double taxation agreement.

Your residence status for Irish tax purposes is determined by the number of days you are present in Ireland during a given tax year. A day for tax purposes is one on which you are present in Ireland at midnight. If you spend 183 days or more in Ireland for any purpose in a tax year you will be regarded as resident in Ireland for that particular tax year. If you spend 280 days or more in Ireland over a period of two consecutive tax years you will be regarded as resident in Ireland for the second tax year.

If you remain resident in Ireland for three consecutive years after your arrival, you will be classed as being ordinarily resident in Ireland from the beginning of the fourth year. If you are ordinarily resident with an Irish domicile (a permanent residence), your Irish and/or foreign sourced income will be taxable in full. However, income accruing from a trade, profession, office or employment, the duties of which are exercised outside Ireland, is exempt from tax. In addition, other foreign income, e.g. investment income, provided that it does not exceed €3,809 in the tax year in which it is earned, is also exempt.

Exceptions are made for incomes derived from employment for which all duties have been exercised outside Ireland. In addition other foreign income, for example, invested income, is also exempt, provided it does not exceed a set amount in the tax year in which it is earned. Ownership of property in Ireland will not necessarily make you resident in Ireland for tax purposes, but it could be a relevant factor in determining a single country of residence under a double taxation agreement.

If you are resident in Ireland and in receipt of a pension originating from outside Ireland your foreign pension will be liable to Irish tax unless it is relieved under the provisions of a double taxation agreement.

Electing to be Resident. Even if you have not spent the required total number of days to be classed as resident in Ireland, you can elect to be resident for that tax year on condition that you will be resident there over the following tax year for the required number of days. As a resident you will be liable to tax on any worldwide income earned or arising during the entire tax year of your arrival in Ireland. However, income from employment will be taxable only from the date of your arrival in Ireland.

Specific queries regarding residency and taxation should be addressed to the Residence Section, Revenue Commissioners Government Buildings, Nenagh, Co. Tipperary; ☎ 067-33533. Information leaflets on the Irish legal requirements for non nationals living in Ireland can be obtained from the Immigration Division of the Department of Justice, Equality and Law Reform, 72-76 St. Stephen's Green, Dublin 2; ☎ 01-678 9711; fax 01-662 0966; e-mail info@justice.ie.

How Irish Income Tax is Paid. The income tax due is payable either by a process of self-assessment or on a weekly or monthly basis, as appropriate. Under the PAYE (Pay As You Earn) system employers deduct tax at source from salary payments. Under the self-assessment system tax is paid by direct debit instalment or in a lump sum each year. Self-assessment is used by individuals who are either self-employed or who are in receipt of foreign sourced income. Further information can be found in *Leaflet IT 10 (A Guide to Self Assessment)* available from local tax offices.

Double Taxation Agreements

Ireland has concluded a number of double taxation agreements with other countries in order to avoid double taxation. Double taxation agreements exist between Ireland and the following countries: Australia, Austria, Belgium, Canada, Cyprus, Czech Republic, Denmark, Estonia, Finland, France, Germany, Hungary, Italy, Israel, Japan, Latvia, Lithuania, Malaysia, Mexico, Netherlands, New Zealand, Norway, Pakistan, Poland, Portugal, Russia, Slovak Republic, South Africa, Spain, Sweden, Switzerland, UK, USA, and Zambia.

Under double taxation agreements, if your income is deemed to be taxable in Ireland as well as in a country with which Ireland has a double taxation agreement, a double charge of tax is prevented either by exempting the income from tax in one of the countries, or by allowing credit in one country for the tax paid in the other country on the same income. However, the way this is handled will depend on the details of the particular agreement, the nature and source of your income and, in some cases, on your nationality. Income arising in a country with which Ireland does not have an agreement will still be subject to tax in Ireland. Tax will be deducted on the net amount you have received after paying tax in the country where the income originated.

National Insurance (PRSI)

In addition to income tax, national insurance (known as Pay-Related Social Insurance, or PRSI) and, where applicable, a 2% health contribution are also deducted at source by an employer or through self-assessment. PRSI contributions qualify you to contributory social welfare payments such as Unemployment Benefit, Disability Benefit and Old Age (Contributory) Pension. The amount of your contribution will depend on your category as an employee, which is dependent on your earnings.

PPS (Personal Public Service) Number

Before you can take up paid employment in Ireland you will require a Personal Public Service Number (PPS No.), formerly known as an RSI No., obtainable from your local social welfare office. If you are a non-Irish National, you will need your passport and supporting documentation such as household bills. Further information on how to obtain a PPS number is available from your local social welfare office and the Department of Social and Family Affairs Information Service, (Áras Mhic Dhiarmada, Store Street, Dublin 1; ☏01-874 8444).

Income Tax Rates

For each pay period you will pay tax at the standard rate of 20% up to your standard rate cut-off point. Any income above your standard rate cut-off point is taxed at 42%. Personal circumstances dictate the amount of tax credits (personal allowance, private health insurance premiums, mortgage interest, etc.) that you will be entitled to. Information about tax credits available are obtainable from local tax offices.

EXEMPTION LIMITS/PERSONAL ALLOWANCES

Single Earners
General Limit (under 65 years of age)	€5,210
65 years of age & over	€15,500

Married Earners
General Limit (under 65 years of age)	€10,420
65 years of age & over	€31,000

TAX RATES & BANDS 2004

Personal Status	Tax Rate
Single/Widowed without dependent children	€28,000@20%; balance@42%
Single/Widowed qualifying for One-Parent Family Tax Credit	€32,000@20%; balance@42%
Married Couple (one spouse with income)	€37,000@20%; balance@42%
Married Couple (both spouses with income)	€37,000@20%; (with increase of €19,000 max.); balance@42%

VAT

Value Added Tax (VAT) is payable on most goods and services at a standard rate of 21%. This rate applies to all goods and services that are not exempt or liable at zero or reduced rates. There is a reduced rate of 13.5% applying to certain fuels, buildings and building services, certain newspapers, and a further lower rate of 4.3% applicable to livestock, live greyhounds and the hire of horses. A zero-rate applies for certain goods and services including exports, certain food and drink, oral medicine and some books. Financial, medical and educational activities are exempt from VAT. For ratings of VAT on specific goods and services you will need to contact the local tax office.

Other Taxes

Capital Gains Tax. This tax is payable on profits made from the selling of assets such as land, property and businesses, though certain gains are exempt from tax and special tax reliefs and allowances apply to the disposal of a family business or a family home and to certain types of business share sales. The current rate of CGT is 20%. Taxation relating to Capital Gains is convoluted and there are numerous provisos, thresholds and exemptions to be considered when calculating rates. It is therefore highly probable that you will want to discuss any matters referring to CGT with a qualified accountant or lawyer.

Capital Acquisitions Tax. Capital Acquisitions Tax (or CAT) consists of an Inheritance Tax, which may apply when a person dies and leaves assets to another, and a Gift Tax, which may apply when a person during his/her lifetime gives a gift to another. Both taxes are payable by the person who receives the gift or inheritance and both taxes are subject to thresholds and exemptions. CAT is explained more fully in the *Retirement* chapter.

Further Information

If you have any queries on your tax position, you should contact the tax offices, both at home and in Ireland before leaving for Ireland. The Revenue Commissioners in Ireland produce a whole range of leaflets on tax matters, available free of charge on request. Contact them using the 24-hour telephone number (1890-306 706) or e-mail custform@revenue.ie. Alternatively, forms and leaflets are available from local tax offices and are downloadable from the Revenue website at www.revenue.ie.

Comhairle, the Citizens Advice Bureau of Ireland, can also help to clarify matters relating to taxation in Ireland. Comhairle runs 80 Citizens' Information Centres nationwide, providing free, impartial and confidential information; and a Citizens' Information Call Centre where information and advice can be imparted by telephone and e-mail. Comhairle can be contacted on 1890-777 121 (calls within Ireland are charged at local rates) or by e-mail at callcentre@comhairle.ie. Information Centres can be located by calling the above number or by using the search facility on Comhairle's website at www.comhairle.ie.

HEALTH

The Irish Health Service

The Department of Health and Children (formerly the Department of Health) has overall responsibility for the development of health policy and the maintaining of health services in Ireland. At a regional level these responsibilities are supervised by regional Health Boards, which were set up under the Health Act of 1970. In addition to these government-funded bodies, a number of voluntary agencies provide services – from hospitals to community care schemes. Anyone from an EEA member state or who is deemed to be ordinarily resident in Ireland is entitled to free or subsidised public health services. However, the level of free entitlement you will receive depends on your level of income – the higher your income the less free treatment and services you are entitled to.

The Department of Health and Children, Hawkins House, Hawkins Street, Dublin 2; ☎01-635 4000; fax 01-635 4001; www.doh.ie.

Non-EU Nationals. A non-EU national is regarded as a resident of Ireland by a Health Board if he or she can provide evidence of the intention to remain in the country for a minimum period of one year. Proof of intention includes:

- Proof of a property purchase or rental, and evidence that the property in question is the applicant's principal residence.
- Evidence of the transfer of funds, bank accounts, pensions into

Ireland.
- An Alien's Registration Book, or a residence permit.
- A work permit or visa, or a statement from an employer.

A student from a non-EU country attending a course of study of at least one academic year is regarded as being ordinarily resident in Ireland and will be eligible for the full range of medical services. Dependents of those who are eligible for the full medical services in Ireland will need to prove that they are also ordinarily resident in Ireland to have access to the same medical cover as their parents or guardians.

Medical Cards

Medical Cards, resembling credit cards, are issued by the regional health boards (contact details below). If you are issued with a medical card it will normally also cover a dependent spouse and dependent children if they are also deemed to be ordinarily resident in Ireland. Those over 70 years old are eligible for a Medical Card regardless of income if they are residents of Ireland. Full-time students aged 16-25 who are financially dependent on their parents are entitled to a Medical Card if their parents hold a Medical Card. Any student financially independent of his or her parents and who satisfies the means test may also be entitled to a Medical Card. Any student in receipt of Disability Allowance will normally be eligible for a Medical Card. Lone parents with dependants are assessed under the income limits for married persons. If you are a Medical Card holder you will be eligible for a number of services free of charge. These include:

- GP services (usually in a practice within seven miles of your home)
- Prescribed drugs and medicines
- Public hospital and outpatient services
- Dental treatment
- Optical services
- Aural services
- Maternity and infant care services (plus a maternity cash grant of €10.16 on the birth of each child)

- Community care and personal social services
- Exemption from paying the Health Contribution
- Possible exemption from paying school transport charges

Holders of Medical Cards can use them for a period of up to three months in another Health Board region and attend any surgery in that area participating in the Medical Card scheme. However, if you are a card holder and are going to be away from your own area for longer than three months you should apply to the health board for the area in which you are residing for a new Medical Card.

WEEKLY INCOME LIMIT FOR FREE MEDICAL CARD

	Aged under 66	Aged 66-69
Single person living alone	€138	€151
Single person living with family	€123	€130
Married couple*	€200	€224
Allowance for child aged under 16	€25	€25
Allowance for dependants aged over 16 (with no income)	€26	€26

In a marriage where one spouse is aged over 70 years and the other is under 70 years old, the spouse under 70 years old will be subject to the income guidelines

Health Boards

Health boards administer the health services in Ireland. There are currently ten health boards, with each health board responsible for the provision of health, community care and personal social services to the people in its area. In addition to looking after hospitals, doctors' surgeries, etc., health boards are also responsible for the provision of home nursing services, home helps, occupational therapy and social work services.

Contact Details for the Ten Health Boards of Ireland

East Coast Area Health Board, Southern Cross House, Boghall Road, Bray. Co. Wicklow; ☎01-201 4200; fax 01-201 4201.

Eastern Regional Health Board (ERHB), Mill Lane, Palmerstown, Dublin; ☎01-620 1600; fax 01-6201 60120; www.erha.ie. The ERHB oversees and plans health and personal social service strategies for over 1.5 million people in Counties Dublin, Wicklow and Kildare. The ERHB is subdivided into three area health boards: the Northern, the East Coast, and the South Western.

Midland Health Board, Arden Road, Tullamore, Co. Offaly; ☎0506-28986; fax 0506-26314; www.mhb.ie. The MHB provides care and social services for more than 203,000 people in Counties Laois, Longford, Offaly and Westmeath.

Mid-Western Health Board, 31/33 Catherine Street, Limerick; ☎061-483 286; fax 061-483 350; www.mwhb.ie. The MWHB provides health services for approximately 320,000 people in Counties Limerick, Clare and Tipperary North Riding.

North-Eastern Health Board, Navan Road Kells, Co. Meath; ☎046-80500; fax 046-41459; www.nehb.ie. The NEHB covers a region of 6,498 sq. km. looking after health services for around 345,000 people in the counties of Louth, Cavan, Meath and Monaghan.

Northern Area Health Board, Swords Business Campus, Balheary Road, Swords, Co. Dublin; ☎01-813 1800; fax 01-813 1870; e-mail nahb@erha.ie.

North-Western Health Board, Manorhamilton, Co. Leitrim; ☎072-55123; fax 074-55627; www.nwhb.ie. The NWHB holds responsibility for the administration and provision of health and personal social services in the counties of Donegal, Sligo and Leitrim for over 211,000 people.

South Western Area Health Board, Oak House, Millennium Park, Naas, Co. Kildare; ☎045-880 400; fax 045-880 482.

South-Eastern Health Board, Lacken, Dublin Road, Co. Kilkenny; ☎056-20400; fax 056-51702; www.sehb.ie. The SEHB looks after a total population of approximately 392, 000.

Southern Health Board, Cork Farm Centre, Dennehy's Cross, Wilton Road, Cork; ☎021-454 5011; fax 021-544709; www.shb.ie. The SHB looks after the population of Counties Cork and Kerry.

Western Health Board, Merlin Park Regional Hospital, Co. Galway; ☎091-751 131; fax 091-752 644; www.whb.ie. The WHB has responsibility for health, welfare and social services in Counties

Galway, Mayo and Roscommon and caters to around 330,000 inhabitants of western Ireland.

Private Health Care

BUPA Ireland and VHI (Voluntary Health Insurance Board) are the two providers of private medical health insurance in Ireland; the latter company is by far the larger of the two and has an 84% share of the Irish private medical insurance market. BUPA has offices in Fermoy, Co. Cork and in Dublin, and currently provides private health insurance to around 320,000 members throughout the country.

The services offered by both companies are relatively similar and tax relief can be claimed on subscriptions paid to private health insurers at 20%. Premiums are calculated on a 'community rating', which means that all adults pay the same amount for the same benefits, regardless of of age, sex or health status. Those over 65 may be declined insurance unless they already hold a policy or are transferring from another insurance company. Taking out private health insurance means that you will not have to join a waiting list for medical treatment and you can choose the level of care and luxury you get in hospital. Companies have agreements with certain hospitals to pay the hospital bills directly, or in certain circumstance you will need to pay the medical fees and then put in a claim with the insurance company.

Useful Addresses
VHI, IDA Business Park, Dublin Road, Kilkenny; ☎056-775 3200; fax 056-61741; www.vhi.ie.
BUPAIRELAND, 12 Fitzwilliam Square, Dublin 2; ☎01-662 7662; fax 01-662 7672; www.bupaireland.ie.

General Practitioners

All areas of Ireland are well served by local General Practitioners (GPs) running daily surgeries. Some GPs will also carry out house calls should the need arise. Doctors' surgeries are generally open from 8am-6pm Monday to Friday and operate on an appointment system. GPs who are in the General Medical Services Scheme will provide services free of charge to those patients who hold a Medical Card. Regional Health Boards provide lists of those GPs in an applicant's locality. Some GPs will only take on private patients who pay for consultation services, medicines and prescriptions.

Drugs & Medicines

If a GP gives a patient a prescription for drugs or medicines, this will need to be presented at the local pharmacy (chemist). Everyone in Ireland is entitled to either free or subsidised Government-approved prescribed drugs and medicines and certain medical and surgical aids and appliances. Medical Card holders receive such things free of charge; others will have to pay the full price unless they are registered for the Drugs Payment Scheme, by which an individual or family only pays a maximum of €78 for prescribed drugs, medicines and certain appliances bought in any one month. You can register for this scheme by completing forms available from pharmacies, GPs and health boards. Each person named on the registration form will then be issued with a plastic swipe card which is presented at the pharmacy whenever prescriptions are bought.

Most pharmacists are open from 9am-6pm, Monday to Saturday. In the larger towns and cities some stay open later on certain days or open on a Sunday morning on a rota system.

Dentists

Dental treatment in Ireland is provided by both private dentists and those who work for regional health boards. Free routine dental treatment (including examinations, extractions, fillings, scalings, polishing, the removal or amputation of roots, root treatment, x-rays, provision of dentures and emergency dental treatment for the relief of pain) is mainly available to Medical Card holders and their dependants, and children under the age of 16 through the Dental Treatment Services Scheme (DTSS). About two million patients are treated under this scheme every year. There are a number of treatments that are not provided free of charge to Card holders, such as crowns, veneers, orthodontics, bridgework, etc.

If you do not have a Medical Card and have to pay for dental treatment from a private dentist you may be able to claim tax relief for certain specialised dental treatments although routine treatments such as extractions, scaling and filling of teeth and provision and repairing of artificial teeth and dentures are excluded from tax relief. Further information on tax relief is available from the Revenue Forms & Leaflets Service (☎ 01-878 0100). Help with paying for dental treatment is available to those on a low income by applying to the Department of Social, Community and Family Affairs (St Oliver Plunkett Road, Letterkenny, Co. Donegal; ☎ 074-25566) or by completing forms available from dentists participating in the Dental Treatment Services Scheme.

If you are eligible for free dental treatment your regional health board will decide whether you are to be treated by one of its own dentists or by a private dentist. If you are to be treated privately you will be able to choose from a list of local dentists who have agreements with the health board to provide services.

Dental services for pre-school children and children under 16 years of age attending state schools are referred from child and school health services and are provided free of charge in health board clinics and in primary schools.

There is a shortage of dentists in Ireland and health boards give priority to certain groups. The Irish Dental Association, (10 Richview Office Park, Clonskeagh Road, Dublin 14; ☎ 01-283 0499; fax 01-283 0515; www.dentist.ie) has an informative website where you can use a search facility to find a dentist in your local area.

Disability Benefit

Disability benefit is paid to those insured people under 66 years of age who are unable to work due to illness. To be able to claim disability benefit you will need to have paid at least 39 weeks PRSI since you first started work in the relevant tax year, or have 26 weeks PRSI paid in the relevant tax year plus 26 weeks PRSI paid in the tax year immediately preceding the relevant tax year. (The relevant tax year for a claim refers to the second last complete tax year before the start of the Benefit Year – the first Monday in January).

If you have 260 weeks PRSI paid since you first started work you may be entitled to Disability Benefit for as long as you are unfit to work until you reach 66 years of age. If you have between 39 and 259 weeks' PRSI paid you may be entitles to claim Disability Benefit for up to 52 weeks.

If you are living in Ireland but your last employment was in an EEA country (Austria, Belgium, Denmark, Finland, France, Germany, Greece, Iceland, Ireland, Italy, Liechtenstein, Luxembourg, Norway, Portugal, Spain, Sweden, Switzerland, the Netherlands, the UK) you will need to send your claim for Disability Benefit to the Department of Social and Family Affairs who will arrange to send it on to the country concerned. Under European Community regulations the country in which you last paid insurance contributions is generally responsible for payment of Disability Benefit.

Disability Benefit is made up of a personal rate of €124.80 for yourself, with additional sums paid for dependants (€16.80 for each child; €82.80 for each adult dependant). It is normally not payable if you leave Ireland to stay in a country not covered by EC regulations unless your absence from Ireland is for medical treatment. During the course of a claim for Disability Payment you may be asked to attend a medical assessment carried out by a doctor employed by the Department of Social and Family Affairs. More information on Disability Benefit can be obtained from your local social welfare office and the Information Services Department of the Department of Social and Family Affairs (Áras Mhic Dhiarmada, Store Street, Dublin 1; ☎ 01-704 3000; www.welfare.ie).

LOCAL GOVERNMENT

There are 29 County Councils in Ireland and 753 directly elected councillors. Councillors do not receive a salary, although they can claim certain expenses when on Council business. The number of councillors elected to each council within Ireland depends on the size of the county. There is at least one Council for each County, with the exception of Dublin, which has three – South Dublin, Dun Laoghaire-Rathdown, and Fingall; and Tipperary, which has two – North Tipperary and South Tipperary. Local elections take place every five years.

In addition, there are five City Councils in Ireland (Cork City, Dublin City, Galway City, Limerick City, and Waterford City), five Borough Councils (Clonmel, Drogheda, Kilkenny, Sligo, and Wexford) and 75 Town Councils.

A County Council has jurisdiction or control throughout its administrative area and represents the local community at a national level as well as carrying out its responsibilities, such as providing public services, at a local level. Broadly, local authorities look after the following areas of responsibility within their jurisdiction:

- Agriculture, education, health, and welfare
- Development incentives and controls
- Environmental protection (including rivers, lakes, air and noise)
- Housing
- Planning
- Recreation facilities and amenities
- Roads
- Water supply and sewerage

Contact details for county, borough and city councils in Ireland can be found in the *Starting a Business* Chapter.

The Vote & Elections

Those who are resident in Ireland but are not Irish citizens have the right to vote in some, but not all, of the elections. For example, British citizens may vote at Dáil elections, European elections and local elections; other EU citizens may vote at European and local elections; non-EU citizens may vote at local elections only.

A new electoral register is compiled each year and published on 1 November, followed by the issuing of an amended register on 15 February. Registers or draft registers can be inspected at the offices of county councils or county registrars and public libraries, post offices and Garda stations. Prospective voters have until 25 November each year to make a correction to their entry in an electoral register or to have their name included in one. Documentation such as a birth certificate or a certificate of naturalisation may be asked for in order to prove an applicant's eligibility to vote.

Should you find that you are qualified to vote but have missed the deadline to have your name included on a register, you have up to 13 working days before polling day to apply to be included in a supplement to the register, which will then allow you to vote at any election or referendum held during the year. You must be registered at one address only, and you must live at that address on the first of September before the Electoral Register comes into force. If you leave the address where you are registered as living, but plan to return there within eighteen months, you can continue to be registered there, as long as you do not register at any other address.

You will normally be required to vote in person at an official polling station, but postal voting is acceptable in some cases depending on your place of work. You can also vote by post if you cannot get to a polling station through illness or disability or if you are studying at an educational institution that necessitates you living away from the address where you are registered. If registered as a postal voter, you are obliged to vote by post only – you will not be allowed to turn up at a polling station to vote. A list of voters who live in hospitals, nursing homes or similar institutions and who wish to vote at these locations is also kept. Application forms for inclusion on the electoral register, special voters list, postal voters list and correction of the draft electoral register are available from all county councils, post offices and public libraries.

CRIME & THE POLICE

Ireland's crime rate is among the lowest in the EU and especially in the more rural areas you are unlikely to be affected by criminal activity. The highest levels of crime occur in the urban areas of the country, as would be expected, and certain rougher areas of Dublin, Cork and Limerick are to be avoided. Elsewhere you shouldn't feel afraid to wander about after dark. Much of the crime in the more rural areas is drink-related.

The Police (Gardaí)

The *Garda Síochána* ('Guardians of the Peace') is the police service of the Republic. In addition to providing State security services and criminal law enforcement functions, the Gardaí are also responsible for dealing with traffic violations.

The first organised police force in Ireland began with the foundation in 1822 of the Irish Constabulary. With the foundation of the Irish Free State in 1922 the Constabulary was disbanded and the Garda Síochána was created to take its place. Three years later the Dublin Metropolitan Police, which had originally been founded in 1836, was amalgamated with the Garda Síochána. An Garda Síochána has its headquarters in Phoenix Park in Dublin and employs a force of 11,230 with an additional 500 civilian support staff. Uniformed members of the Garda Síochána do not carry firearms and continue to be equipped only with a wooden truncheon, though firearms are carried by the 1,700 detectives employed by the force.

The general direction, management and control of An Garda Síochána is the responsibility of a Commissioner, appointed by the Government, responsible to the Minister for Justice, Equality & Law Reform – who in turn is accountable to the Dáil (the Irish Legislature). The Commissioner is responsible for the running of the Gardaí on a day-to-day basis, aided by two Deputy Commissioners and ten Assistant Commissioners. The Deputy Commissioners advise the Commissioner of policy matters and Deputy Commissioners co-ordinate the activities of the Assistant Commissioners. In descending order from Assistant Commissioner, Garda rank structure is as follows: Chief Superintendent, Superintendent, Inspector, Sergeant, Garda.

For policing purposes the Republic is divided into six regions, each commanded by a Regional Assistant Commissioner whose duties are mainly operational and who is responsible for ensuring the operational efficiency of his respective region. Each Region is divided into Divisions, commanded by a Chief Superintendent. Each Division is in turn divided into Districts, commanded by a Superintendent (known as a District Officer), who is assisted by a number of Inspectors. Districts are divided into sub-districts, each normally the responsibility of a Sergeant. Each sub-District usually has only one police station, the strength of which may vary from 3-100 Gardaí. In some areas there may also be several sub-stations, occupied by one member of the Garda. Throughout Ireland there are 703 Garda Stations.

District Officers deal with matters of the law such as the licensing of hotels and bars and the issuing of firearms certificates. As well as the provision of normal police services, each Division operates a Traffic Unit responsible for dealing with the enforcement of traffic regulations. Throughout the country, and in the Dublin Metropolitan Region, each District has a number of plain-clothes officers who make up local Detective Units.

The Prison Service

A General Prisons Board was first established in Ireland in 1878. Its functions were absorbed by the Department of Justice in 1928 following the foundation of the Irish Free State in 1922. Today the Irish Prison Service has a staff of approximately 3,400 administering 17 custodial institutions and has an annual budget in excess of €300 million.

The Irish Prison Service is in transition – from being an office of the Department of Justice, Equality and Law Reform to becoming an independent executive agency. Over the past two years the Service has commissioned three new prisons, including Ireland's first purpose-built women's prison, its first-ever dedicated facility for remand prisoners; and a new state-of-the-art facility for adult male prisoners with will place strong emphasis on education, work and training. Over the past five years in Ireland there have been roughly 2,600 to 3,200 people held in custody in Ireland.

Irish Prison Service, Monastery Road, Clondalkin, Dublin 22; ☎01-461 6000; fax 01-461 6027; www.irishprisons.ie.

Emergency Services

The numbers to call in the event of a life-threatening emergency are 999, or 112. Calls are free and an operator will be put through to the emergency service you require: fire, Gardaí, ambulance, lifeboat or mountain rescue. For non life-threatening emergencies you should telephone the local branch of the service that you require – numbers are to be found in the Golden Pages, or by dialling 1190 for Directory Enquiries.

ENTERTAINMENT & CULTURE

Food & Drink

Ireland is not generally known as a culinary hotspot yet things are changing in the area of food provision as in everything else in Ireland. Seafood is obviously plentiful in a land surrounded by some of the most unpolluted waters in Europe – scallops, oysters and Dublin Bay prawns – and because of the lush pasture, lamb and beef is plentiful (Irish stew anyone?). The image of Ireland as a place of pubs, smokey bars and Guinness drinkers is also changing – has changed – with the advent of the nationwide no smoking ban in public places from April 2004. Drink is still drunk, and Guinness is so thoroughly Irish that the company even use an image of a Harp as their logo. You'll still find the blousy drinking establishments down certain side streets, but increasingly the bars are bright and well, like Ireland, rich.

Arts & Culture

Ireland has an impressive cast of giants in the arts field (U2, James Joyce, Oscar Wilde, the list goes on…) and has always embraced the new while retaining its cultural integrity. Dublin remains at the centre of a lot of what is on offer but theatre groups tour the nation and because of the relatively small size of the country, access to 'culture and the arts' is not too much of a problem.

The Arts Council (*An Chomhairle Ealaíon*, 70 Merrion Square, Dublin 2; ☏ 01-618 0200; fax 01-676 1302; www.artscouncil.ie), established in 1951, supports all aspects of the arts, in both the Irish and English languages – architecture, dance, drama, film, literature, music, opera and visual arts. The Council annually funds over 350 arts and non-arts organisations in Ireland and supports over 450 professional artists though grants and bursaries. The Arts Council also supports arts centres, festivals and community arts.

A useful place to find out what is going on in the Irish arts world is the website, WOW! (www.wow.ie). It's a very impressive and thorough website with listings and interviews and articles on all aspects of the arts including theatre, cinema, music and festivals.

Music & Dancing

Irish music and the sessions that take place in the pubs and bars up and down the country are a tradition that is appreciated by many who travel to Ireland and to those who live and work there. Traditional Irish instruments such as the Harp, the Uilleann pipes and the Bodhran (the percussion instrument consisting of a goatskin stretched over a round frame played with a double ended baton) are still played with verve by many musicians. Ireland is very proud of its musical heritage and many of the Irish are naturally musically inclined.

There has been a resurgence and an increased interest in Irish dancing since the Riverdance and Lord of the Dance phenomena. Step dancing, the traditional Irish dance involving the dancer dancing on the spot keeping the arms by the sides and the legs together while striking the floor with impressive displays of footwork is beautiful to watch. The *Fleadh Cheoil* takes place every year in August and features ten days of music and dancing.

Comhaltas Ceoltóirí Éireann (CCÉ), formed in order to promote Irish traditional music and culture, now has more than 400 branches all over the world. In Ireland, branches of the CCÉ run classes teaching traditional music and organise informal gatherings of musicians. More information about the activities organised by CCÉ can be obtained from 32 Belgrave Square, Monkstown, Co. Dublin; ☎ 01-280 0295; fax 01-280 3759;www.comhaltas.com.

Museums, Galleries & Historical Monuments

As befitting such an interesting and ancient country, there are a number of art galleries, museums and monuments to visit in Ireland. Some of the largest and best galleries and museums, such as the National Gallery, the Museum of Modern Art and the National Museum are located in Dublin. Other museums celebrate a more localised artistic and cultural history of Ireland – some charge an admission fee; others do not. Historic buildings and monument are located all across the country and the Irish Tourist Office or a good guidebook will be able to introduce you to those.

Many of the sites, museums and galleries are run by *Dúchas* – The Heritage Service – and admission to these sites is free to those who have bought a Heritage Card. These cards are available from Dúchas sites at a cost of €7.50 for a child or student, €20 for an adult, €15 for a senior citizen and €50 for a family. Cards are valid for a year.

Sport

There is plenty on offer in Ireland for those who like to watch or participate in sports. Horse riding and horse racing are massive in Ireland and many of the population like a flutter on a race, especially the bigger races such as the Irish Derby or the Irish Grand National. Ireland is famous as a place for breeding horses and there are tax incentives for those that do. There are 28 racecourses in Ireland and racing takes place all year round.

Traditional Irish sports such as Gaelic football, hurling and *camogie* attract huge crowds of supporters and the All-Ireland Gaelic Football final at Croke Park in Dublin is the great event in the sporting calendar, attracting massive crowds. Gaelic sports are a passion in Ireland and heavily supported nationwide. Football (soccer) has a following, but more of spectators than participators.

Ireland has some of the cleanest and most lightly-fished waters in Europe and salmon, trout and sea trout are native species to the country. With the numerous lakes and over 11,000 km of riverbank on offer many people take up course fishing. The 5,600 km of coastline and the hundreds of lakes and rivers also make an excellent playground for those who like watersports – sailing, subaqua, surfing, windsurfing, sailing and canoeing are all popular outdoor pursuits in Ireland.

Another important sport to Ireland is Golf – big business in a country that boasts around four hundred courses – and many people go on holiday to Ireland just to play the links courses. The K Club

(The Kildare Hotel & Golf Club), an hour's drive west of Dublin near the village of Straffan, has the finest parkland golf course in Ireland and will host the Ryder Cup in 2006. Membership, however, doesn't come cheap – first-year membership in the K Club costs more than £60,000; a 50-year membership package can sell for as much as £150,000.

Health clubs and leisure centres are becoming increasingly common in Ireland and most of the larger towns have a public swimming pool. Addresses and telephone numbers for local recreation centres, sports and leisure complexes, and clubs and associations can all be found in the Golden Pages.

RELIGION

Since the foundation of the Republic of Ireland, the Catholic Church has always had a position of great power in the social and political life of the country, and the Church has been established in Ireland for far, far longer than the State. The Constitution of 1938 was co-written by the first Taoiseach, Eamon de Valera and the Catholic Archbishop of Dublin, Charles McQuaid, which explains the articles of the Constitution outlawing abortion and divorce and the special clause decreeing that a woman's place is in the home rearing children. Religion is deeply embedded in the national psyche of Ireland but over the last decade or so the grip of the Church on the state has loosened a huge amount. Secularisation has been speeded along by scandals among clerics, which have weakened the traditional moral authority of the Church.

According to the 1991 census 92% of the population of the Republic were Roman Catholics, 2.5% were Church of Ireland (Anglican), 0.5% Presbyterians, 0.1% Methodists and less than 0.1% Jewish. About 3% of the population belonged to other religious groupings or have no specific religious beliefs. The Census of 2002 showed that there were just over 3.4 million Roman Catholics in Ireland

Ireland is one of the most religiously observant countries in Europe. Mass on Sundays still attracts large congregations and the parish priest is considered a figure of far more importance than an Anglican vicar is in Britain. The Catholic Church has been the leading provider of education within Ireland, establishing schools, hospitals and universities controlled by nuns and monks, until very recently. The majority of marriages take place in church rather than registry offices and although divorce has been legalised, abortion is still illegal, except in cases where a woman's life is in danger. Pilgrimages are an important feature of the lives of the Irish faithful and several are observed every year.

Discrimination based on religion is now almost non-existent in Ireland and in 1992 a Muslim was elected to the Daíl. In the 1992-97 Daíl three Jews were elected as representatives despite the fact that both religious communities total only around one thousand members each.

SHOPS & SHOPPING

You will be able to find pretty much everything you require in Ireland's shops and certainly any goods that you can buy in other European countries you will be able to find the equivalent of in Irish high street stores. Shopping centres, both in and out of town, are becoming an increasingly common sight all over Ireland while in the smaller towns and villages mini-markets and family-owned businesses are the norm. There are plenty of bookshops for both new and second hand books in the larger towns and newspapers and magazines can be bought from supermarkets. Mail order and on-line shopping has arrived in Ireland and goods and services can now be bought 'from the comfort of your own home' and delivered straight to your front door. Remember to keep receipts in case you need to return faulty goods.

Complaints regarding goods and services should in the first instance be directed to the manager of the business in question and in the final instance to the Office of the Director of Consumer Affairs (4/5 Harcourt Road, Dublin 2; ☎ 01-402 5555; fax 01-402 5501; e-mail odca@entemp.ie) or the Consumer Advice Shop at the European Consumer Centre (ECC) in Dublin (13a Upper O'Connell Street, Dublin 1; ☎ 01-809 0600; fax 01-809 0601; www.eccdublin.ie).

Opening Times

Shops are generally open from 9am-5.30pm Monday to Saturday, though often in the smaller towns and villages shops will close for an hour for lunch and on one afternoon each week – usually on a Wednesday or Thursday. In the cities you will find shops such as supermarkets, small grocers and newsagents that stay open late into the nights and some of the larger stores operate late night shopping on a Thursday or Friday evening. Sunday trading is becoming increasingly common and stores in the shopping centres that have been springing up in the outskirts of towns and cities stay open for longer hours that you may find on the high streets.

Banks are open 10am-4pm Monday to Friday; some stay open until 5pm on Thursdays.

PUBLIC HOLIDAYS

If any of the following public holidays fall on a Saturday or Sunday, then the following Monday is given in lieu and banks, schools, shops and most other businesses are likely to be closed. Although Good Friday (the Friday before Easter Monday) is not an official public holiday it is observed in most parts of Ireland.

PUBLIC HOLIDAYS

1 January	New Year's Day
17 March	St Patrick's Day
March/April	Good Friday (not a statutory public holiday)
March/April	Easter Monday
First Monday in May	May Day
First Monday in June	Bank Holiday
First Monday in August	Summer Bank Holiday
Last Monday in October	Autumn Bank Holiday
25 December	Christmas Day
26 December	St Stephen's Day

Local Fairs and Festivals

Many of the counties of Ireland put on local fairs, shows and festivals throughout the year. Listed below are a number of them:

Ballinasloe Horse Fair, September/October, Ballinasloe, County Galway; www.ballinasloe.com.
Bloomsday Festival, June, Dalkey, Sandycove, Dublin; www.jamesjoyce.ie.
Clarenbridge Oyster Festival, September, Clarenbridge, County Galway; www.clarenbridge.com.
Coleman Traditional Festival, August, Gurteen, County Sligo; www.colemanirishmusic.com.
Cork International Film Festival, October, Cork City; www.corkfilmfest.org.
Cork Jazz Festival, October, Cork City; www.corkjazzfestival.com.
Dublin Horse Show, August, Dublin; www.rds.ie.
Dublin Theatre Festival, September/October, Dublin; www.dublintheatrefestival.com.
ESB Dublin Jazz Festival, July, Dublin; www.esb.ie.
Fleadh Cheoil na hEireann, August, Clonmel, County Tipperary; www.comhaltas.com.
Galway International Arts Festival, July, Galway City; www.galwayartsfestival.ie.
Galway Oyster Festival, September, Galway City; www.galwayoysterfest.com.
Galway Races Summer Festival, August, Galway City; www.hri.ie.
Irish Coffee Festival, July, Foynes, County Limerick; www.irishcoffeefestival.com.
Killarney Summer Festival, June/July, Killarney, County Kerry; www.killarneysummerfest.com.
Kinsale International Festival of Fine Food, October, Kinsale, County Cork.
Lady of the Lake Festival, July, Enniskillen, County Fermanagh; www.operaannalivia.com.
Lisdoonvarna Matchmaking Festival, August/October, Lisdoonvarna, County Clare; www.matchmakerireland.com.

Mary from Dungloe International Festival, July/August, Dungloe, County Donegal; www.maryfromdungloe.info.
National Ploughing Championships, September, Kinnegad, County Meath; www.npa.ie.
Puck Fair, August, Killorglin, County Kerry; www.puckfair.ie.
Rose of Tralee, August, Tralee, County Kerry; www.roseoftralee.ie.
Waterford International Festival of Light Opera, September/October, Waterford City; www.waterfordfestival.com.
Waterford Spraoi, August, Waterford City; www.spraoi.com.
West Cork Chamber Music Festival, June/6 July, Bantry, County Cork; www.westcorkmusic.ie.
Wexford Festival of Opera, October/November, Wexford; www.wexfordopera.com.

In addition to these festivals in the Republic there are a number of festivals throughout Northern Ireland. These can be found through the Northern Ireland Tourist Board (59 North Street, Belfast BT1 1NB; ☎028-9023 1221; fax 028 90240960; www.discovernorthernireland.com).

TIME

Ireland follows Greenwich Mean Time (or UT – Universal Time – as it has now become known). In late March the clocks are moved forward by one hour to bring in British Summer Time (BST) in order to give extra daylight in the evenings. In late October the clocks are moved back again to GMT/UT. The USA is between 5 and 12 hours behind Ireland, depending on the State; Australia is between 7½ and 11 hours ahead.

METRICATION

The metric system of weights and measures is in the process of being introduced in Ireland to bring the country into line with the rest of Europe, but the old imperial pounds and ounces system is still widely used, though to a lesser extent than in the UK. Speed limit signs will all be in metric (km/h) by 31 December 2004.

Car speedometers usually show speed in both miles per hour and km/h. The older road signs give distances in miles but all will show distances in kilometres by the end of 2005. Food and fruit and vegetables are now priced and weighed in metric and fuel is sold in litres. Beer continues to be served in pints rather than litres in pubs and bars.

CONVERSION CHART

LENGTH (NB 12 inches 1 foot, 10 mm 1 cm, 100 cm 1 metre)

inches	1	2	3	4	5	6	9	12	
cm	2.5	5	7.5	10	12.5	15.2	23	30	

cm	1	2	3	5	10	20	25	50	75	100
inches	0.4	0.8	1.2	2	4	8	10	20	30	39

WEIGHT (NB 14 lb = 1 stone, 2240 lb = 1 ton, 1,000 kg = 1 metric tonne)

lb	1	2	3	5	10	14	44	100	2246
kg	0.45	0.9	1.4	2.3	4.5	6.4	20	45	1016

kg	1	2	3	5	10	25	50	100	1000
lb	2.2	4.4	6.6	11	22	55	110	220	2204

DISTANCE

mile	1	5	10	20	30	40	50	75	100	150
km	1.6	8	16	32	48	64	80	120	161	241

km	1	5	10	20	30	40	50	100	150	200
mile	0.6	3.1	6.2	12	19	25	31	62	93	124

VOLUME

1 litre = 0.2 UK gallons   1 UK gallon = 4.5 litres
1 litre = 0.26 US gallons   1 US gallon = 3.8 litres

CLOTHES

UK	8	10	12	14	16	18	20
Europe	36	38	40	42	44	46	48
USA	6	8	10	12	14	18	

SHOES

UK	3	4	5	6	7	8	9	10	11
Europe	36	37	38	39	40	41/42	43	44	45
USA	2.5	3.3	4.5	5.5	6.5	7.5	8.5	9.5	10.5

RETIREMENT

CHAPTER SUMMARY

- Capital Acquisitions Tax in Ireland includes a tax on assets inherited, and a tax on gifts given by one person to another, payable by the person who has received the gift or inheritance.
- Less than 5% of senior citizens live in long-term care institutions or nursing homes in Ireland.
- There are approximately 110 clubs, with approximately 11,000 members, open to men and women over 55 in Ireland.
- **Residence Permit.** If you are a national of the EU or the EEA, you have the right to reside in Ireland, regardless of your economic circumstances, and may apply for a residence permit.
- **Pensions.** Ireland has social security agreements with all EU and EEA countries, in addition to Austria, Canada, Australia, the United States of America and New Zealand.
  - If you have not paid enough social insurance contributions in your home country and/or in Ireland, you may still qualify for an assistance-based pension.
  - Depending on your circumstances, once residing in Ireland you may be able to claim a contributory pension or a non-contributory pension.

Background Information

Although Ireland isn't often thought of as a popular destination for retirees, the laid back atmosphere of the countryside, the views, and the companionability of the Irish make for a desirable place to live for those who have had their fill of the cut and thrust of business and the working life. The aged and elderly in Ireland are also generally treated with more respect by the younger generation than in the rest of the EU. Ireland has a very high proportion of young people within its shores and the numbers of those aged 65 years or older is only expected to rise to around 11% of the total population by 2011.

The shock that many people feel after the drastic change of going from working all their adult life to suddenly having nothing that they *have* to go and do, day after day, can be traumatic. Between 1970 and 1990 participation in Ireland by men aged 55-64 in the labour force dropped from over 80% to around 60%. With advertisements for jobs with upper age limits of 40 becoming more widespread in the EU, retirement – and early retirement at that – is something that we are all going to get more used to. Everyone needs a project to keep them ticking over, rather than merely rusting away to an early grave. Moving house may be one of the most stressful times on one's life, but finding a new place to decorate, furnish with the accoutrements of one's life and travels, a plot of land to maintain and shape as you wish, is also invigorating and challenging. To remain in a house in which you have lived throughout the period of bringing up a family will always remind you of the past – of both the good and the bad and sometimes it is better to make a break with the past and move into a whole new world.

The problem of isolation can affect you as you get older and less active, especially if you choose to move to a remote rural area. Although it will always depend upon your need to take part in the lives of others and the social side of life, you need to appreciate that, however many committees you get involved in, however many rounds of golf you play or hills you walk, winter evenings are long and the weather can conspire to keep you in the house for long stretches at a time. The result of this is that you are almost certain to find yourself spending more time in close proximity to your partner, or alone.

With modern communications and transport it is no longer necessary to be as self-sufficient as was once the case, but out in the remoter areas of Ireland you may need to be emotionally self-sufficient. If you are used to having a strong family support network close to hand, moving out of driving distance from you daughter, son, sister or brother could leave you feeling vulnerable and adrift – at least until you have found new friends locally.

Less than 5% of the Irish over 65 live in residential care and four out of every five seniors living in the community are completely independent in daily living; over 85% of these own their own homes. Only about one in four live alone. It is expected that the North-Western and Western regions of Ireland will continue to have the highest number of seniors over 65 in the country, with Leinster having the lowest.

Residence & Entry Regulations

If you are an EU national or a national of the EEA, you have the right to reside in Ireland, regardless of your economic circumstances, and may apply for a residence permit. If you are coming from a non-EU/EEA country and moving to Ireland to retire, or you intend to move there without the promise of employment, you will be asked by the authorities for evidence of sufficient funds to support yourself, and any dependents if they are with you, during your residence. If you are arriving from a country covered by EU regulations, you are entitled to apply for the same benefits and services as those provided to an Irish citizen. For full details on entry regulations see the *Residence & Entry Regulations* chapter.

PENSIONS

Because you are likely to rely to a greater or lesser extent on a pension as your main source of income after you retire, you should find out all you can, preferably before you retire. For example, can you increase the amount you will receive by paying extra contributions? Will your pension be guaranteed? Is there any tax relief allowed? You will need to contact the Pensions Office in your home country to find out what the situation is for your own personal circumstances.

State Pensions

Ireland has social security agreements with all EU/EEA countries in addition to Austria, Canada, Australia, the United States of America and New Zealand. These Bilateral Social Security Agreements allow a person from Ireland or any of the participating countries to protect his or her pension entitlements while residing in another of the participating countries. You may even be able to combine any insurance payments made in Ireland and a participating country in order to qualify for a pension. If you are coming from a country covered by EU regulations you will need to complete forms E301 and E104, which provide details of your social insurance record, and take them with you to Ireland. These forms are available from social security agencies.

If you have not paid enough social insurance contributions in your home country and/or in Ireland, you may still qualify for an assistance-based pension. Assistance-based pensions do not relate to your social insurance record and are means tested. The Department of Social and Family Affairs in Ireland will examine all your sources of income and if your income is below a certain amount, you may qualify for a payment.

Contributory Pension

Depending on your circumstances, once residing in Ireland you may be able to claim a contributory pension (e.g. invalidity pension, retirement pension, old age contributory pension or widow/widower's contributory pension). Since January 2003 you will receive a full means-tested pension if you or your spouse or partner have savings or investments below €20,315.80 (as a single person) or €40,631.60 (for a married or cohabiting couple), and no other means. There are also several non-contributory pensions available (e.g. blind pension, widow/widower's non-contributory pension, and old age non-contributory pension). The amount received from a non-contributory pension is calculated using a sliding scale that takes into consideration any income, savings and investments you or your spouse may have. At the time of writing, savings and investments of less than €1,269.76 (for a single person) or less than €2,539.48 (for a married or cohabiting couple) were not assessed, while anything over this amount will affect the amount of benefits you may receive.

Old Age Non-Contributory Pension

This is a means tested payment for those aged 66 years and over who do not qualify for a retirement pension or an Old Age Contributory Pension. The payment is made up of a personal rate for yourself, with extra amounts payable for dependents. To receive an Old Age Non-Contributory Pension you will need to satisfy a means test, which takes into consideration any income that you earn, the value of any property you may own (excluding your own home) and the value of any savings and investments you have. If you are living with a partner or spouse their income will also be taken into account. There are a number of items that are not counted as income including the value of your home, any social welfare payments and supplementary welfare allowances or rent allowances paid to you. In addition, if you decide to sell your house at age 66 or over in order to move to more suitable accommodation, the proceeds of the sale up to €190,460.71 may be disregarded if you:

- Buy alternative accommodation
- Move into a registered private nursing home or into sheltered housing
- Move into accommodation with someone who is caring for you and who is in receipt of a carer's payment

Widow's and Widower's Pension

Non-Contributory. This is a means-tested payment for widows and widowers who do not have dependent children. To qualify for the pension you must be a widow or a widower and not living with another person as man or wife. The maximum rate of this non-contributory pension is payable if your weekly means are €7.62 or less. For each €2.54 increase in means thereafter the rate of pension payable reduces by €2.54.

RATES OF NON-CONTRIBUTORY WIDOW'S & WIDOWER'S PENSION

Age (Years)	Pension (€)
Under 66	€134.80
66-79	€154
80+	€160.40

Contributory. A Widow's and Widower's Pension may be payable if a deceased person or the spouse has enough PRSI (insurance) contributions. In order to qualify you must be a widow or widower and not living with another person as man or wife. You automatically qualify for this payment if your late spouse was receiving either a Retirement Pension or an Old Age Contributory Pension.

Contributions paid in other EU member states and in EEA countries may be used to help you qualify for a pension, as may contributions paid in countries with which Ireland has bilateral social security agreements. Anyone in receipt of a contributory pension may earn any amount of money from any other source and still remain entitled to a pension. It is taxable, though if it is your only source of income you are unlikely to have to pay tax. A Widow's and Widower's Pension remains payable while you remain widowed. If you remarry or cohabit, it is no longer payable.

RATES OF CONTRIBUTORY WIDOW'S & WIDOWER'S PENSION

Age (Years)	Pension (€)
Under 66	€140.30
66-79	€167.30
80+	€173.70

Further information on all matters relating to pensions in Ireland can be obtained from the Pension Services Office, College Road, Sligo (☎071-69800).

TAXATION

You will be charged Irish tax on any worldwide income earned or arising in a tax year during which you are resident, ordinarily resident and domiciled in Ireland for tax purposes. For any tax year during which you are deemed to be non-resident or not ordinarily resident in Ireland you will only be charged tax on your income from Irish sources. Irish tax liabilities may also be influenced by domicile status and any double taxation agreements in place with your country of usual residence. Note that the ownership of property in Ireland will not make you resident for Irish tax purposes. If you are aged 65 or over and remain in paid employment while in Ireland, you will be liable to pay income tax in the normal way. However, in such cases tax exemption limits are much higher and some extra tax credits are avaiable. See the section on Taxation in the *Daily Life* chapter.

Double Taxation Agreements

Because some income may be taxable in both the country where it is sourced and in the country in which the recipient is resident, many countries have entered into agreements to avoid double taxation. To date Ireland has concluded agreements with: Australia, Austria, Belgium, Canada, Cyprus, Czech Republic, Denmark, Estonia, Finland, France, Germany, Hungary, Italy, Israel, Japan, Latvia, Lithuania, Malaysia, Mexico, Netherlands, New Zealand, Norway, Pakistan, Poland, Portugal, Russia, Slovak Republic, South Africa, Spain, Sweden, Switzerland, UK, USA, and Zambia.

If your income is taxable in Ireland and in a country with which Ireland has a Double Taxation Agreement, tax is prevented from being charged under the agreement by either exempting the income from tax in one of the countries, or allowing credit in one country for the tax paid in the other country on the same income. The precise treatment of your income will depend on the details of the particular agreement, the nature and source of your income and, in some cases, on your nationality.

If you have income arising in a country with which Ireland does not have a Double Taxation Agreement then the amount of tax charged in

Ireland will be the net amount received by you after the deduction of the foreign tax has been paid.

Capital Acquisitions Tax

Capital Acquisitions Tax (CAT) in Ireland includes a tax on assets inherited, and a tax on gifts given by one person to another. Both taxes are payable by the person who has received the gift or inheritance. The executor of a will may be legally held responsible if CAT is not paid.

The amount of inheritance tax payable on a bequeathal from the deceased's will depends on the degree of relationship between the beneficiary and the deceased. Spouses of the deceased are exempt from inheritance tax, while children of any age and grandchildren under 18 may inherit up to €441,198 before a demand for Capital Acquisitions Tax will be made. Brothers, sisters, uncles, aunts, nephews, nieces and grandchildren over 18 may inherit €44,140 tax-free while any others included in the deceased's will may receive €22,060 tax-free. CAT is payable at a rate of 20% on the balance over the thresholds above. Additionally, the family home is exempt from Capital Acquisitions Tax if the person who inherits it has lived there for at least three years prior to the deceased's death, has no other house, and continues to own and reside in the house for the ensuing six years.

There are various exemptions relating to the valuation of gifts and more detailed information can be obtained from the Revenue Commissioners at the Capital Taxes Office, Dublin Castle, Dublin 2 (☎ 01-647 5000; www.revenue.ie), who also publish the guide: *What to do about tax when someone dies*.

LEAVING ONE'S FAMILY

Many retired people experience the 'empty-nest syndrome' most keenly when offspring have moved not just away from home, but hundreds of miles away to another part of the country, or even abroad. Yet if you decide to move to Ireland, with cut-price airfares on flights between Ireland and the rest of Europe, and the availability of ferries across the Irish Sea, together with the comparatively small size of Ireland, you needn't feel so cut off from family and friends back home. You will have the convenience of living in a beautiful country where everyone speaks your language, yet the exoticness of living in a foreign country that is daily becoming more European in outlook and style. Many people who have retired to Ireland discover that their children and grandchildren like to combine a holiday in Ireland with an extended family visit, so you may end up seeing more of your family than if they were to come for a fleeting visit – fitting you in on their way to somewhere else.

Of course, you may not find yourself living away from family and friends for long; one feature of moving to Ireland is that, once people come to visit you and realise what a beautiful country it is, and what a pleasing way of life can be had there, some will feel inspired to make the move themselves. So, if you are thinking of retiring to Ireland to get away from your old social circle, you might in fact end up disappointed!

HEALTH CONSIDERATIONS & SOCIAL SERVICES

The state of your health, both now and in the future, is an important thing to bear in mind when deciding to relocate on retirement. In Ireland public health services (GP services, prescribed drug and medicine provision, hospital services, dental, optical and aural Services, and certain community care services) are free to those aged 70 or over. Medical Cards, issued by the local health boards, which give you the right to free treatment and services are issued automatically to anyone aged 70. If you are younger than 70 you may be entitled to a Medical Card if you pass a means test or you have an entitlement to one under EU rules. If you receive a social security pension from another EU member state and have no other source of income in Ireland you may also be entitled to a Medical Card. If you do not qualify, you will still be able to obtain health services in Ireland but you will have to pay for many of them. Even in the most remote areas of Ireland you should have reasonably easy access to health care and health services.

There are a wide range of social security benefits and allowances to which elderly people may be entitled, depending on their circumstances, such as the Medical Card, allowances for gas, electricity and telephone and free television licences. Those over 70 years of age receive such things regardless of the amount or source of their income. Additional allowances may be payable if you are living alone, have dependents (aged up to 18, or aged 22 and in full-time education) residing with you, if you are aged 80 or over, or ordinarily resident on an island of the coast of Ireland or if you are co-habiting with a person who is not getting a social welfare payment in his or her own right. If you are aged 66 or over you will also be eligible for a free travel pass.

BUYING A RETIREMENT HOME

Access to health care and other services is just one thing to bear in mind when moving to a new area and buying a home for your retirement. The other aspects of social infrastructure, such as the distance needed to travel to shops and garages, the availability of public transport and the nearness of neighbours are also important. If you are a sociable person, you may find it important to have local clubs and associations to join and social events to attend. Before buying anywhere, ask local residents about these things and get hold of the local newspapers to see what events are coming up in that particular area.

Climate too is important. If you suffer from aches and pains exacerbated by cold and damp conditions, Ireland – and especially the west coast of Ireland – may not be the best place to retire to. On the other hand, of course, if you suffer from breathing difficulties exacerbated by a polluted atmosphere, the clean air could improve your health no end.

If you choose to settle in an area of Ireland on the basis of having spent many summer holidays there, it is wise to make sure that you find it as amenable at other times of the year. It is a good idea, before you take the big step of buying a house, to take an extended holiday of three to six months during the winter months in your chosen area. Rain and Ireland go together like hand and glove and even the most stoical of individuals can find continuous downpours depressing.

Sheltered Housing, Residential & Nursing Homes

Less than 5% of senior citizens live in long-term care institutions or nursing homes in Ireland; most remain living in the family home or live independently. However, local authorities and the private sector do provide sheltered housing for elderly people. This type of housing, whether rented or bought, is especially designed for elderly people who are capable of living alone but may also need some day-to-day help. Sheltered housing is usually built in small complexes, and often has a resident warden on hand to look after the complex and the residents.

Most houses of this type are self-contained units with one or two bedrooms. Most sheltered housing will have some communal facilities – perhaps for laundry services or for group meals and activities – onsite or are built near existing day centres where additional support services can be accessed.

A project like St Brendan's Village in Mulranny, Co Mayo (☎ 098-36287; fax 098-36287; www.saint-brendans.com) is a good example of such housing, where seniors are able to continue to live in their own community with the minimum of support, but with the added advantage of having carers available when needed. Such projects are helping to stem depopulation in the more rural areas of Ireland by providing employment and hope for the local elderly population.

There are also a number of State-run and privately-run nursing homes in Ireland. Demand for places and fees charged are very high. Where ongoing medical care is required for an elderly person unable to care for him or herself, there may be a requirement for the person to be admitted to a local authority or private nursing home. Charges for stays in nursing homes are made according to a means test and if a resident cannot afford to pay the fees, costs will be met by the local authority. The Federation of Irish Nursing Homes (193 New Cabra Road, Dublin 7; ☎ 01-8690918; fax 01-8681615; www.finh.ie) can provide a list of all of its members.

DAILY LIFE, HOBBIES & INTERESTS

In Ireland the average retired man finds that he has 91 hours of leisure time available each week; the average retired woman has 72 hours a week. The worst way to see out your retirement years to sit about gently rusting away, and in Ireland especially there is no need for the socially inclined to become reclusive. The Irish are approachable and warm people and the stigma of 'being old' is not felt so keenly as it is in other places in Northern Europe. Even in the more remote rural communities there will be clubs and groups, which meet regularly and a number of charities work specifically on behalf of older people to provide social and educational facilities of various kinds.

In addition, Sports facilities of all kinds are available throughout Ireland and private or local authority leisure centres offer a range of facilities and courses, some specifically aimed at older people. Golf especially, and swimming, are popular sports in Ireland and can be enjoyed even when other physical pursuits are becoming too onerous. Local groups meet all over the country to enjoy all manner of pastimes, from singing or learning an instrument to art classes and more esoteric activities such as yoga or t'ai chi. Getting involved in charity or voluntary work will also bring you into closer contact with your local community.

For those less keen on organised activities, retirement is an ideal time to take up pastimes such as photography or rambling – and Ireland offers some fabulous landscapes. If you enjoy travelling and sightseeing, you will be in a country of such varied terrain and so much historical heritage that you could spend several years exploring its rural, urban and historical treasures. Many historical monuments and museums have discounts for retired people and, depending on your age, you will also be eligible for discounts on public transport. Most entertainment events and educational facilities also offer discounts on admission or enrolment fees for retired people – both in town and country.

There are approximately 110 active retirement clubs open to men and women over 55 and run on a voluntary basis around Ireland, with approximately 11,000 members. The Federation of Active Retirement Associations (FARA – 1-2 Eustace Street, Dublin 2; ☎ 01-679 2142; e-mail fara@eircom.net) can put you in touch with your local association or give you advice on setting up a new group. Age & Opportunity (Marino Institute of Education, Griffith Avenue, Dublin 9; ☎ 01-805 7709; fax 01-853 5117; www.olderinireland.ie) is an Irish national agency working on behalf of seniors to promote the greater participation of older people in Irish society. The agency works in a broad range of areas, from the arts to physical activity, and publishes *Opportunities in Retirement,* which details sport facilities available to seniors. An Age & Opportunity initiative funded by the Irish Sports Council is *Go for Life* – which has enlisted the services of physical fitness professionals to work exclusively with older people. The National Council on Ageing and Older People has its offices at 22 Clanwilliam Square, Grand Canal Quay, Dublin (☎ 01-676 6484; fax 01-676 5754; www.ncaop.ie).

WILLS & LEGAL CONSIDERATIONS

A will sets out how the writer wishes to dispose of his or her property and also often includes a clause stating how property not effectively dealt with in the will should be disposed of. It is not necessary that a will be in set format, but it is standard practice for a will to include the testator's (writer's) name and address, a clause revoking all earlier wills or codicils followed by a clause appointing executors and giving their addresses. If the testator subsequently wants to change his or her will this may be done by adding a codicil – a separate document added to the end of the will – signed by the testator and witnesses in the margin opposite the changes. A will is always revocable by the testator (unless he or she becomes mentally incompetent) and a will is revoked automatically by a subsequent marriage (unless the will was made in contemplation of that marriage) by another will being made, or by burning, tearing or destruction of the will by the testator or someone in the testator's presence on his or her direction. It is relatively inexpensive to have a straightforward will drawn up by a solicitor and it is also now possible to draw up a will electronically.

It is also possible to draw up your own will, and such a deed will be valid if certain legal requirements are met: these are that the will must be in writing, you must be over 18 years old or have been or be married, be of sound mind and sign the will in the presence of two witnesses – who must be present simultaneously and who must see you sign the will. Such witnesses do not have to see the contents of the will. However, if you have substantial assets it will always be preferable to consult a solicitor.

The person named as the executor of a will is responsible for dealing with the terms of the will and taking out probate. If there is no will then the next of kin can apply to the Probate Office for a grant of representation. If the terms of a will are quite straightforward, the person appointed as executor can make a personal application to the Probate Office in Dublin (Probate Personal Application Section, 1st Floor, 14-24 Phoenix Street, Smithfield, Dublin 17; ☎ 01-888 6174) or to one of the 14 District Probate Offices in Ireland. The Probate Office will then certify that the will is valid and that all legal, financial and tax matters are in order so that the executor can distribute the estate. No assets of the deceased can be sold or distributed until the will has been 'proven'. Note that in Ireland Probate Tax has now been abolished. If the estate is in any way complex, then the next of kin should consult a solicitor – whose fee will usually be around 3% of the value of the estate.

A testator may leave his or her estate in any way he or she wishes, subject to the minimum requirements for the family. These state that where there are no children, a spouse is entitled to one half of the estate; and if there are children, a spouse is entitled to one third of the estate; though any children are not necessarily entitled to the rest of the estate. These requirements are known in law as the 'legal right share'. If there is no will, where there are no children, a spouse is entitled to the entire estate. If there are children, the spouse is entitled to two thirds of the estate; the remaining third is then divided between the children (if one of the children has died then his or her children take a share).

If a married couple jointly owned the family house then, on the death of one, the other automatically becomes the owner. If the deceased was the sole owner of the house then the spouse may require that it be given as part of the share of the estate, depending on the value of the house in relation to that of the estate. Non-married partners have no automatic legal rights to each other's estates, and though they may make wills in favour of each other, the terms will not negate the legal right share of a spouse.

Any debts must be paid out of the estate before distribution among beneficiaries. Where there is not enough money to repay all debts, then debts concerning the funeral and the administration of the estate take priority above all others.

The National Irish Register of Wills and Testaments (Room 13, Upper Mall, Terryland Retail Park, Headford Road, Galway; ☎ 091-568844) was set up in order to help ensure that wills can be located after death and to minimise the incidences of apparent intestacy through wills being untraceable. The Register publishes a useful explanatory leaflet, *Thy Will be Done if Thy Will be Found*.

DEATH

Death is not always a surprise when it comes. The death of a family member is something that we try to turn away from, hoping that it won't involve us doing more than grieving. Unfortunately there is a surprising amount of red tape surrounding this often unmentionable but inevitable end to life

If a death occurs at home, the GP and the next of kin of the deceased, along with the Registrar of Births, Deaths and Marriages, must be contacted as soon as possible. If the death occurs at night and is sudden and unexpected the deceased's GP should be notified at once or, if unavailable, first thing in the morning. The doctor will issue a Medical Certificate of cause of death. This will then need to be taken by the nearest relative of the deceased to the appropriate Registrar of Births, Deaths and Marriages (determined by where the death occurred) within five days, whereupon the Death Certificate will be issued for a fee of €6.98. In addition to the Medical Certificate, the Registrar will require the following information about the deceased:

- Full name
- PPS (Personal Public Service) Number
- Sex, marital status, occupation and age
- Date and place of birth
- Occupation of spouse (if deceased was married or widowed)
- Occupation of father, or mother (if the deceased is a child)

The address of the Registrar will be given by the GP, undertaker or hospital, or may be found in the local telephone directory. The Registrar of Births, Deaths and Marriages in Dublin is located in Joyce House, 8-11 Lombard Street East, Dublin 2 (☎ 01-634 4000;

www.groireland.ie). If the death took place in hospital, the hospital usually registers the death and arranges the laying out of the body. Most hospitals have mortuaries where the body of the deceased is held until the funeral arrangements have been made, but you can also decide to take the body home, or take it to a funeral home, or have it embalmed if there is likely to be a delay in organising the funeral. If a GP or hospital cannot determine the cause of death then the Gardai and the coroner may be called out and a post mortem performed on the body. It is usual to ask permission from the next kin if this is to occur. If the deceased wished to donate their organs, held a donor card, and died in hospital, the hospital will contact the next of kin before arranging the removal of the organs.

Undertakers will be able to deal with the organisation of the burial or cremation of the deceased. They will help the next of kin to obtain the necessary documentation, arrange a burial plot, put death notices in newspapers and organise religious services. They can also arrange transportation of the deceased and mourners to the funeral service and deal with local florists, etc. The Irish Association of Funeral Directors (Strand Road, Portmarnock, Co. Dublin; ☎ 01-846 4900; fax 01-846 4904; www.funeralnet.ie) have a code of practice explaining what help you can expect to receive from any one of its members.

All burials will need to be registered with the local authority and the location of the graveyard noted. In Ireland cremation facilities are at present only available in Dublin. Before a cremation is carried out, forms will need to be signed stating that there is no reason why the body should not be cremated.

A bereavement grant from the Department of Social and Family Affairs of approximately €635 may be payable if the deceased paid the relevant PRSI contributions or if the next of kin is insured and the deceased is his or her dependent child or spouse. Further information about financial help with funeral arrangements can be obtained from local post offices, Citizens' Information Centres and from the Bereavement Grant Section of the Social Welfare Services Office (Government Buildings, Ballinalee Road, Longford; ☎ 043-45211; www.welfare.ie). If the deceased had a Medical Card, this will need to be returned to the issuing Health Board.

Complete guides to life abroad from Vacation Work

Live & Work Abroad

Live & Work in Australia & New Zealand	£10.99
Live & Work in Belgium, The Netherlands & Luxembourg	£10.99
Live & Work in China	£11.95
Live & Work in France	£10.99
Live & Work in Germany	£10.99
Live & Work in Ireland	£10.99
Live & Work in Italy	£10.99
Live & Work in Japan	£10.99
Live & Work in Russia & Eastern Europe	£10.99
Live & Work in Saudi & the Gulf	£10.99
Live & Work in Scandinavia	£10.99
Live & Work in Scotland	£10.99
Live & Work in Spain & Portugal	£10.99
Live & Work in the USA & Canada	£10.99

Buying a House Abroad

Buying a House in France	£11.95
Buying a House in Italy	£11.95
Buying a House in Portugal	£11.95
Buying a House in Spain	£11.95
Buying a House on the Mediterranean	£12.95

Starting a Business Abroad

Starting a Business in France	£12.95
Starting a Business in Spain	£12.95

Available from good bookshops or direct from the publishers
Vacation Work, 9 Park End Street, Oxford OX1 1HJ
Tel 01865-241978 * Fax 01865-790885 * www.vacationwork.co.uk

In the US: available at bookstores everywhere
or from The Globe Pequot Press (www.GlobePequot.com)

Section II

WORKING IN IRELAND

EMPLOYMENT

STARTING A BUSINESS

EMPLOYMENT

CHAPTER SUMMARY

- **The Employment Situation.** Employment rates among older women in Ireland are well below the EU average.
  - Some employers operate a 'flexi-time' system.
- **The Economy.** Ireland continues to be among the world's most attractive business locations.
  - Ireland is rated as the fifth most liberal economy in the world.
- **Wages.** The highest earners in Ireland, apart from Managing Directors and General Managers, are Directors of Sales and Directors of Information Technology.
  - The national minimum wage in Ireland is €7 (approx. £4.66/US $8.27) per hour, which is the third highest rate among the EU member states.
  - Employees can expect a pay review at their place of work on a yearly basis and a small percentage increase in salary each year.
- **Employment Prospects.** There are labour shortages in a number of employment sectors in Ireland – especially in IT, nursing and the construction industry.
  - Only 7% of the available workforce in Ireland is employed to work the land.
- **Trade Unions.** *The Irish Congress of Trade Unions* represents the interests of employees of both the Republic of Ireland and Northern Ireland.
  - More than one out of every five part-time employees in Ireland is a member of a union.

THE EMPLOYMENT SCENE

For much of the twentieth century Ireland was synonymous with high unemployment and a poverty-stricken economy based mainly on agriculture; it was also a country of mass emigration. However, such a picture bears no relation to the Ireland of the latter part of the twentieth and early twenty-first century. Since the boom in the Irish economy that has come with the information age, Ireland has become something of a back office for Europe due to the rapid rise in telemarketing and technical services, software development companies and call centres that have sprung up all over the country. While the production of foodstuffs, especially wheat, barley and butter, remains a vital mainstay of the Irish economy it may come as a surprise to some that Ireland is now one of the world's largest exporters of computer software. Not for nothing has Ireland become known as 'the Celtic Tiger'.

Ireland these days sees more immigrants than emigrants and there are labour shortages in a number of employment sectors – especially in IT, nursing and the construction industry. With one of the lowest corporate tax rates in the world, Ireland has managed to attract businesses from all over the globe to locate their European operations there, and the Irish working population are now involved in a wide range of activities and sectors such as pharmaceuticals, medical and engineering technologies, e-commerce, information communications technologies and financial and international services.

According to the 2004 Index of Economic Freedom, the result of research by the Heritage Foundation and The Wall Street Journal, Ireland is now ranked as the fifth most liberal economy in the world after Hong Kong, Singapore, New Zealand and Luxembourg. The USA was ranked 10th in the Index, which takes into consideration a nation's economy, the fiscal burden of government, the government's intervention in the economy, its monetary policy, capital flows and foreign investment, banking and finance, wages and prices, property rights, regulation and informal market activity. Those countries such as Ireland, which scored highest in the Index, have the highest standards of living as well as the highest per capita incomes.

In 2002 the Irish unemployment rate of 4.4% was 3.4 percentage points below the EU average of 7.8% and if performance in the market is measured purely on the comparison of unemployment rates then the Irish labour market is in good shape, relative to the rest of the EU. Over the 1994-2001 period the Irish long-term unemployment rate fell from 9.2% (almost twice the EU average of 4.9%) to only 1.3% (against an EU average of 3.1%). However, while unemployment in Ireland is still extremely low by EU standards, the employment rate is only slightly above the EU average. The difference between the employment rates in Ireland and the rest of the EU is much less pronounced than the difference in unemployment rates (65.7% and 64.1% respectively), while the female employment rates for Ireland and the EU are virtually identical. High employment rates among younger women have pushed up the overall average but employment rates among older women are still well below the EU average. However, the number of people employed in agriculture continues to fall, with just 7% employed in Ireland to work the land.

In relation to the EU Labour Market Index (which takes into consideration the unemployment rate, the long-term unemployment rate, the employment rate, the female employment rate, the older worker employment rate (aged 55-64), the effective average exit age, labour productivity, labour costs growth, tax rate on low-wage earners, early school-leavers and life-long learning) Ireland is in fourth position, behind the Netherlands, Denmark and Sweden.

According to the Economist Business Intelligence Unit's 'Business Environment Rankings', Ireland will continue to be among the world's most attractive business locations, at least until 2005. Continued growth and development in certain areas, especially in high tech industries, is expected and companies such as Google, Overture and eBay have all announced their intention to establish centres in Ireland. Other companies that have strong links with Ireland include Cape Technologies, DigiSoft.tv, Vistamed, Diageo, Pfizer, Ingersoll Rand and ABB – all of which have either established production facilities or operation centres in the country, or are involved in setting up Research and Development projects there. Forfás estimates that some 80% of those who will make up the workforce of the knowledge-based Irish economy of ten year's time are already at work, which means that Ireland is still calling out for employees with the skill levels necessary to keep the economy thriving on its R&D-driven manufacturing industries. The ICT, biotechnology, financial services, engineering and food processing sectors are all primed for significant growth from 2005. This means that priority will need to be given to the ongoing training and education of workers and those coming into the workforce. It is also good news for those with the necessary skill sets who want to live and work in Ireland.

RESIDENCE & WORK REGULATIONS

If you enter Ireland as an employee you may need a work permit in addition to an entry visa. There are, however, a number of groups of people who do not require a permit to take up employment in Ireland.

Permit-Free Employment

A work permit is unnecessary in the following circumstances:

- For citizens of the European Economic Area (the EU member states plus Norway, Iceland and Liechtenstein).
- For Swiss citizens (in accordance with the term of the European Communities and Swiss Confederation Act of 2001).
- For those who have been granted refugee status, and for postgraduate students if employment is an integral part of the course of study being undertaken.
- For the spouses or parents of an Irish citizen, and those who have been granted leave to remain in the country on humanitarian grounds.
- For those posted to Ireland on a corporate transfer or secondment for a maximum period of four years to an establishment or undertaking in Ireland that is owned by a company or group that operates in more than one state.
- For those coming to Ireland from an overseas company for a maximum period of three years for training, whether or not it entails paid work, at an Irish-based company.

From 1st May 2004 Accession State nationals (those from Poland, Lithuania, Latvia, Estonia, Czech Republic, Hungary, Slovakia, Slovenia, Malta and Cyprus who will be joining the European Union) will no longer require work permits to work in Ireland.

If you are an EU national and in receipt of unemployment benefit from your home country, you can stay in Ireland and transfer your unemployment benefit from your country of origin. Benefit will be paid to you in Ireland for up to three months, after which time you may qualify for unemployment assistance – a means tested payment – if you satisfy the conditions.

Working Holidaymakers

Ireland has bilateral agreements with Australia and New Zealand whereby nationals aged between eighteen and thirty years of age from these two countries can apply to spend time in Ireland working and travelling. The Working Holidaymaker permit is valid for an overall period of one year (or becomes invalid on the day the holder turns thirty), and the holder must not engage in work with any one employer for a period in excess of three months. Applications from Australians should normally be made in Canberra so that permits can be issued prior to departure for Ireland, however, for those who fail to apply for a permit before departure, the Department of Foreign Affairs in Dublin offers a 'postbox' service and can issue application forms and explanatory leaflets, accept completed application forms and supporting documents, check passports, forward applications to Canberra for a decision, and then convey the decision and permit to applicant in due course. Applicants will need proof of a return ticket to their country of origin and evidence of sufficient funds to be able to support themselves through a substantial part of their working holiday. There is a processing fee involved and decisions on permits can take about six weeks. Additional details about working holidaymaker permits can be found at the Irish Department of Foreign Affairs' website at www.gov.ie/iveagh.

Students and recent graduates in the US can take advantage of a number of reciprocal exchange programmes that permit short-term work in Ireland. Those interested should contact CIEE (the Council on International Education Exchange) at 7 Custom House Street, 3rd Floor, Portland, ME 04101, USA; ☎1-800-40-Study (Toll-Free) or

1-207-553-7600; fax 1-207-553-7699; www.ciee.org. Canadians who are full-time post secondary students, or who have recently graduated, can apply for a one-year work visa through SWAP (Student Work Abroad Programme). Run by Travel CUTS/Voyages Campus, SWAP is Canada's largest international exchange programme and has associated offices throughout Canada, details of which can be found on the SWAP website at www.swap.ca and from their Toronto office at Suite 100, 45 Charles Street East, Toronto, ON M4Y 1S2; ☎416-966 2887).

Useful Addresses

The Embassy of Ireland in Australia, 20 Arkana Street, Yarralumla, Canberra, ACT 2600; ☎02-6273 3022; fax 02-6273 3741, e-mail irishemb@cyberone.com.au.

The Consulate General of Ireland in New Zealand, 6th Floor, 18 Shortland Street (PO Box 279), Auckland 1001, New Zealand; ☎09-977 2252; fax 09-977 2256; www.ireland.co.nz.

Department of Foreign Affairs, 80 St Stephen's Green, Dublin 2; ☎01-478 0822; www.gov.ie/iveagh/.

Au Pairs

Prospective au pairs must be citizens of an EU or EEA member state and aged between 17 and 30 years of age. An au pair will need to register with the Irish police on arrival but does not need to apply for a work permit. Because the Au Pair programme is classed as a cultural exchange for young European people who are single with no dependants and who want to improve their level of English whilst living as part of a host family, an au pair is not strictly an employee and is therefore not liable to pay tax or national insurance contributions. However, as a consequence, au pairs are not paid a salary but are expected to receive a minimum pocket money of €65-€75 per week from the host family. An au pair generally can expect to work around 30 hours a week and baby-sit a couple of evenings per week. In exchange for their services, au pairs will have their meals provided, have their own bedroom, and two days free a week to pursue cultural and linguistic pursuits.

Prospective au pairs from countries requiring a visa may be able to obtain a student visa if they are registered to study English at an approved language school, as students are permitted to take up a part-time job of less than 25 hours a week to support themselves whilst studying.

Work Permits

For nationals of non-EEA member states, work visas are normally only granted to those who have a specific skill that fits with a shortage of such in the existing labour market, i.e. for nurses or IT professionals. Applications for work permits can take up to eight weeks to process and have to be arranged by the employer in advance of the arrival in Ireland of the prospective employee. Work permits are valid for a period not exceeding one year and applications for renewal should be made 25 working days before the expiry of a current permit. The Work Permits Section of the Department of Enterprise, Trade & Employment (Davitt House, 65a Adelaide Road, Dublin 2; ☎01-631 3333/631 3308; Lo-Call Number 1890-201-616; fax 01-631 3268; www.entemp.ie) publishes a list of all occupations that are ineligible for work permit applications (i.e., occupations in which any vacancies occurring must be filled by nationals from the EEA only). Office hours for enquiries are 9.30am-1.00pm and 2-5pm; Monday to Friday. Note that staff at the Department of Enterprise, Trade and Employment are prohibited from answering queries from prospective employees named on any work permit application and therefore all queries from potential employees should be directed through their prospective employers.

Non-EEA member state nationals may be granted work permits without the need to establish that there is no suitable Irish/EEA/Swiss national available to do the job applied for if they are one of the following:

- A doctor who has been offered a position in a hospital recognised by the Irish Medical Council and who has full medical registration from the Irish Medical Council, or a doctor with temporary registration from the Irish Medical Council.
- An entertainer who is travelling to Ireland to perform at a

particular event – this category includes performers and their back up crews and film crews.
- A professional sportsperson.
- A participant in an exchange programme recognised by the Minister for Enterprise, Trade and Employment.
- Anyone entitled to take up employment in Ireland under the terms of any international bilateral agreement ratified by Ireland.

An employee who holds a work permit may only take up employment with a different employer after the new employer has obtained a work permit on their behalf. In such cases the existing work permit would need to be returned with a covering letter from the former employer to the Department of Enterprise, Trade & Employment.

Work Authorisation Scheme/Fast Track Visa Programme

Due to the rapid growth in the Irish economy in recent years there are shortages of skilled employees in certain sectors of the employment market such as ICT, construction and nursing. In order to relieve these shortages the Department of Enterprise, Trade and Employment has initiated the Work Authorisation Scheme to speed up the recruitment of suitably qualified people from non-EEA member countries for those sectors where skill shortages are particularly acute. The Scheme applies only to those persons who already have an offer of employment in Ireland. Before the introduction of the Scheme, work permits could take up to six weeks to be granted. Under the new Scheme permits are usually issued from the Consulate General of Ireland in the country of the applicant in fifteen days. Up to date information on sectors of employment and countries included in the Work Authorisation Scheme can be obtained from the Visa Office of the Department of Foreign Affairs, Hainault House, 69-71 St Stephen's Green, Dublin 2; ☎01-633 1006; www.iveagh.gov.ie.

SKILLS & QUALIFICATIONS

On moving to Ireland to take up a specific job where a work permit is required, you will need proof that you have the skills and qualifications appropriate for that job. Although the qualifications that you already possess may be recognised by the official bodies in your home country, they may not necessarily be recognised in Ireland. Therefore, you and your potential employer in Ireland will need to find out whether your qualifications are acceptable or whether further examinations or training periods need be taken. Because there is such a wide range of courses and diplomas available throughout the world – academic, professional and vocational – qualifications obtained outside of Ireland will be looked at on a case-by-case basis to see how they compare with such qualifications obtained in Ireland.

EU/EEA Nationals

Within the European Union, academic qualifications are assessed by National Academic Recognition Information Centres (NARICs), which were established in all EU member states to co-ordinate the drawing up of certificates for the academic recognition of diplomas. In Ireland, the National Academic Recognition Information Centre is administered within the Higher Education Authority (3rd Floor, Marine House, Clanwilliam Court, Dublin 2; ☎01-661 2748; fax 01-661 0492; www.hea.ie).

In relation to professional and vocational training, the EU has passed directives ensuring that qualifications and practical experience gained in an EU member state are deemed to be valid throughout the EU and EEA. This is achieved through a system of compensatory measures to take into account the differences in length and content of the courses. What this means in practice, is that if your training was much shorter or the content of your course was very different to that required in Ireland, you would be asked to pass an aptitude test or to undergo a period of supervised practice. For a number of professionals, however, including GPs, dental practitioners, nurses, midwives, veterinary surgeons, architects, pharmacists and lawyers, training requirements in all EU member states have been standardised.

The mutual recognition of other professional qualifications within the EU is also made in respect of 'regulated' professions (i.e. those whose practice is regulated by law, Government regulations, private chartered bodies or professional associations) which require the completion of a higher education course of at least three years, or the equivalent part-time duration, at a university or other higher education establishment. Any professional training required in addition to the education course should also have been completed. Anybody working in a trade or profession that has a regulatory body should in the first instance contact the relevant professional body in their home country to enquire as to the need for specific qualifications in order to take up employment in Ireland.

Further details on these matters can be found in a fact sheet, *Working in Another Country of the European Union* published by the European Commission. A catalogue of publications can be obtained from the Publications Department of the European Commission (8 Storey's Gate, London SW1P 3AT). Alternatively, fact sheets can be downloaded from www.cec.org.uk/info/pubs/catalog.htm. A series of guides about working in Ireland, and elsewhere in the EU, is available from *Dialogue with Citizens*, a programme established by the aforementioned European Commission. These guides can be obtained in the UK via a freephone hotline number (0800-581 591) or from Citizens' Advice Bureaux, and from the Dialogue website at http://citizens.eu.int – an excellent resource containing a wide range of information in many European languages on all aspects of living, working and studying in other EU countries.

Nationals of Other Countries

There are no international standard agreements between Ireland and non-EU member states, so each case will be looked at on an individual basis. For non-EU/EEA citizens wishing to work in Ireland your prospective employer will have to apply for a work permit on your behalf and you will need to prove that you have particular skills or qualifications required by your employer.

If you are looking for a list of regulated professions and details of the relevant regulatory authority in the UK, contact the Department of Trade & Industry Enquiry Unit (1 Victoria Street, London SW1H 0ET; ☎ 020-7215 5000; www.dti.gov.uk).

TRADE & PROFESSIONAL BODIES IN IRELAND

Advice on the requirements of specific professions may be obtained from the relevant Professional Associations, many of which are listed below. Trade Unions may also be able to provide useful information. *The Irish Congress of Trade Unions* is the umbrella organisation for trade unions in Ireland and represents the interests of employees, both in the Republic of Ireland and in Northern Ireland. *The Irish Congress of Trade Unions* has its office in Dublin at 31-32 Parnell Square, Dublin 1 (☎01-889 7777; fax 01-887 2012; www.ictu.ie).

Useful Addresses
Architectural Association of Ireland, 8 Merrion Square, Dublin 2; ☎01-661 4100; www.archeire.com.
Association of Advertisers in Ireland, Rock House, Main Street, Blackrock, Co. Dublin; ☎01-278 0499; fax 01-278 0488; www.aai.ie.
Association of Chartered Certified Accountants, Ireland, 9 Leeson Park, Dublin 6; ☎01-498 8900; fax 01-496 3615; http://ireland.accaglobal.com.
Association of Consulting Engineers of Ireland, 51 Northumberland Road, Ballsbridge, Dublin 4; ☎01-660 0374; fax 01-668 2595; www.acei.ie.
Association of Electrical Contractors Ireland, McKinley House, 16 Main Street, Blackrock, Co. Dublin; ☎01-288 6499; fax 01-288 5870; www. aeci.ie.
Association of General Practitioners, Monang, Abbeyside, Dungarvan, Co. Waterford; 058-41106; www.agp.ie.
Association of Optometrists Ireland, 18 Greenmount House, Harold's Cross Road, Dublin 6; ☎01-453 8850; fax 01-453 8867; www.optometrists.ie.
Chartered Institute of Management Accountants, 44 Upper Mount Street, Dublin 2; ☎01-676 1721; fax 01-676 1796; www.cimaglobal.com.

Chartered Institution of Building Services Engineers, CIBSE Secretary, c/o Homan O'Brien Associates, 89 Booterstown Avenue, Blackrock, Co. Dublin; ☎01-205 6300; fax 01-205 6301; www.cibseireland.org.

Consumers' Association of Ireland Limited, 45 Upper Mount Street, Dublin 2; ☎01-661 2466; fax 01-661 2464; www.consumerassociation.ie.

Crafts Council of Ireland, Powerscourt Townhouse Centre, South William Street, Dublin 2; ☎01-679 7368; fax 01-679 9197; www.ccoi.ie.

Dublin City Centre Business Association, 40 Dawson Street, Dublin 2; ☎01-679 1599; fax 01-679 7393; www.dcba.ie.

Electrical Contractors Association, Federation House, Canal Road, Dublin 6; ☎01-497 7487; fax 01-496 6953.

Institute of Bankers in Ireland, 1 North Wall Quay, Dublin 1; ☎01-611 6500; fax 01-611 6565; www.bankers.ie.

Institute of Designers in Ireland, 8 Merrion Square, Dublin 2; ☎01-716 7885; fax 01-716 8736; www.idi-ireland.com.

Institution of Engineers of Ireland, 22 Clyde Road, Dublin 4; ☎01-668 4341; fax 01-668 5508; www.iei.ie.

Irish Association of Social Workers, 114 Pearse Street 2, Dublin 2; ☎01-677 4838; www. iasw.eire.org.

Irish Book Publishers' Association (Clé), 43/44 Temple Bar, Dublin 2; ☎01-6707 642; fax 01-6707 393; www.irelandseye.com.

Irish Business & Employers Confederation (IBEC), Head Office: Confederation House, 84/86 Lower Baggot Street, Dublin 2; ☎01-605 1500; fax 01-638 1500; www.ibec.ie.

Irish Farmers' Association, Irish Farm Centre, Bluebell, Dublin 12; ☎01-450 0266; fax 01-455 1043; www.ifa.ie.

Irish Hotel and Catering Institute, Goatstown House, 1-2 Goatstown Cross, Dublin 14; ☎01-298 8850; fax 01-298 8855; www.ihci.ie.

Irish Hotels Federation, 13 Northbrook Road, Dublin 6; ☎01-976 459; fax 01-974 613; www.ihf.ie.

Irish Management Institute, Sandyford Road, Dublin 16; ☎01-207 8400; fax 01-295 5150; www.imi.ie.

Irish Medical Association, 10 Fitzwilliam Place, Dublin 2; ☎01-676 7273; fax 01-661 2758; www.imo.ie.

Irish Nurses Organisation, 11 Fitzwilliam Place, Dublin 2; ☎01-676 0137; fax 01-661 0466; www.ino.ie

Irish Nursing Board (An Bord Altranais), 31/32 Fitzwilliam Square, Dublin 2; ☎01-639 8500; fax 01-676 3348; www.nursingboard.ie.
Irish Organic Farmers and Growers Association Ltd, Harbour Building, Harbour Road, Kilbeggan, Co. Westmeath; ☎0506-32563; fax 0506-32063; www.irishorganic.ie.
Irish Small & Medium Enterprise Association (ISME), 17 Kildare Street, Dublin 2; ☎01-662 2755; fax 01-661 2157; www.isme.ie.
Irish Tourist Industry Council (ITIC), 17 Longford Terrace, Monkstown, Co. Dublin; ☎01-284 4222; fax 01-280 4218; www.itic.ie.
Irish Translators' & Interpreters' Association, Irish Writer's Centre, 19 Parnell Square, Dublin 1; ☎01-872 1302; fax 01-872 6282.
Law Society of Ireland, Blackhall Place, Dublin 7; ☎01-672 4800; fax 01-672 4801; www.lawsociety.ie.
Licensed Vintners' Association, Anglesea House, Anglesea Road, Ballsbridge, Dublin 4; ☎01-668 0215; fax 01-668 0448; www.lva.ie
Marketing Institute, Marketing House, South County Business Park, Leopardstown, Dublin 18; ☎01-295 2355; fax 01-295 2453; www.mii.ie.
National Union of Journalists, Liberty Hall, Dublin 1; ☎01-805 3258; fax 01-874 9250; www.nuj.ie.
Periodical Publishers Association, 18 Upper Grand Canal Street, Dublin 4; ☎01-668 2056; www.ppa.ie.
Pharmaceutical Society of Ireland, 18 Shrewsbury Road, Dublin 4; ☎01-218 4000; fax 01-283 7678; www.pharmaceuticalsociety.ie.
Restaurants Association of Ireland, 11 Bridge Court, City Gate, St Augustine Street, Dublin 8; ☎01-6779901; fax 01-6718414; www.rai.ie.
Royal Academy of Medicine in Ireland, 6 Kildare Street, Dublin 2; ☎01-676 7650; fax 01-661 1684; www.rami.ie.
Royal College of Surgeons in Ireland, 123 St Stephens Green, Dublin 2; ☎01-402 2100; www. rcsi.ie.
Royal Institute of the Architects of Ireland, 8 Merrion Square, Dublin 2; ☎01-676 1703; fax 01-661 0948; www.riai.ie.
Services, Industrial, Professional and Technical Union (SIPTU), Liberty Hall, Dublin 1; ☎01-874 9731; fax 01-874 9466; www.siptu.ie.
Society of Chartered Surveyors, 5 Wilton Place, Dublin 2; ☎01-676

5500; fax 01-676 1412; wwwscs.ie.
Teachers' Union of Ireland, 73 Orwell Road, Rathgar, Dublin 6; ☎01-492 2588; fax 01-492 2953; www.tui.ie.
Technical, Engineering & Electrical Union, 5 Cavendish Row, Dublin 1; ☎01-874 7047; fax 01-874 7048; www.teeu.ie.
Veterinary Ireland, 13 Kilcarbery Park, Nangor Road, Dublin 22; ☎01-457 7976; fax 01-457 7998; www.vetinary-ireland.org.
Vintners' Federation of Ireland, VFI House, Castleside Drive, Rathfarnham, Dublin 14; ☎01-492 3400; fax 01-492 3577; www.vfi.ie.

SOURCES OF JOBS

There are a number of ways to look for work in Ireland before actually arriving there. To begin with, depending on your occupation, you should get in contact with the relevant professional or trade body in Ireland. You can also look for any relevant job offers posted on the EURES system (see below) and post your own CV on the database as well as talking to the EURES adviser at your local jobcentre. Check for vacancies in the national newspapers and professional journals at home and, if you can get hold of them, from Ireland as this is a good way of discovering which industries and firms are hiring staff. International publications such as the *Economist, New Scientist, International Herald Tribune*, etc. contain sections listing job vacancies with international firms. Public libraries contain a number of professional journals and reference books and it is worth asking friends and family for any contacts they may have in Ireland who might be able to help you with 'on the ground' information and advice. It is always worthwhile to apply 'on spec' to firms and organizations that interest you, and you should sign up with the privately-owned employment agencies, the majority of which are listed in the Golden Pages telephone directory and usually concentrate on office and temporary jobs. It is also a good idea to register with FÁS, the national employment service, and EURES.

Seasonal or casual work is also often quite easy to find, especially during the summer when the tourist industry is in full swing. It is easier to apply for such work in person once in Ireland as word of mouth and casual recruiting is not uncommon. There are also a number of books you may find it useful to consult on finding casual employment, including several published by Vacation Work (www.vacationwork.co.uk).

The Employment Service

FÁS, (Foras Áiseanna Soathair), (PO Box 456/27-33 Upper Baggot Street, Dublin 4; ☎01-607 0500; fax 01-607 0600; www.fas.ie) is Ireland's national training and employment authority and reports to the Department of Enterprise and Employment and provides information, advice and support for jobseekers, whether they are from Ireland or another country within the EEA. The 63 FÁS employment service offices located throughout the Republic can help out with finding temporary or permanent employment as well as advising on training courses, employee placement schemes, apprenticeships and community employment programmes. Once in Ireland it is a good idea to register with your local FÁS office (see below for addresses) and arrange an interview with one of the FÁS officers. By doing so you will improve your chances of finding work and will gain access to local, national and international job-hunting information, training, and employment programmes and services. It is not necessary to be registered, however, to obtain information and advice. FÁS also has a job bank where jobseekers can post their CV online, as well as search a database for work by specifying personal preferences such as location, hours per week wanted and occupation.

FÁS Employment Offices and services are divided into eight regions:

FÁS Offices in the Dublin Area

27/33 Upper Baggot Street, Dublin 4; ☎01-607 0500; fax 01-607 0611.

FÁS Baldoyle Training Centre, Baldoyle Industrial Estate, Baldoyle, Dublin 13; ☎01-816 7400; fax 01-816 7401.

Ballyfermot, Ballyfermot Hill, Dublin 10; ☎01-605 5900; fax 01-605 5960.

Enterprise House, 6 Bridge Street, Balbriggan, County Dublin; ☎01-

841 5141; fax 01-841 1010.
West End House, Smugboro Rd. Extension, West End Retail Park, Blanchardstown, Dublin 15; ☎01-826 2629; fax 01-824 9145.
Main Street, Clondalkin, Dublin 22; ☎01-459 1766; fax 01-457 2878.
Unit 1A, Northside Shopping Centre, Coolock, Dublin 17; ☎01-847 5911; fax 01-847 5770.
235 Crumlin Road, Crumlin, Dublin 12; ☎01-456 3000; fax 01-456 3018.
D'Olier House, D'Olier Street, Dublin 2; ☎01-612 4800; fax 01-679 9092.
18/21 Cumberland Street, Dun Laoghaire, County Dublin; ☎01-280 8476; fax 01-280 8476.
Unit 14C, Finglas Shopping Centre, Main Street, Finglas Village, Dublin 11; ☎01-834 6222; fax 01-834 6386.
FÁS Training Centre, Poppintree Industrial Estate, Jamestown Road, Finglas, Dublin 11; ☎01-8140 200; fax 01-834 6336.
FÁS Training Centre, Wyattville Road, Louglinstown, Dun Laoghaire, County Dublin; ☎01-204 3600; fax 01-282 1168.
FÁS Training Centre, Enterprise Park, Nutgrove Way, Rathfarnham, Dublin 14; ☎01-495 1414; fax 01-495 1415.
34 Main Street, Swords, County Dublin; ☎01-840 5252; fax 01-840 3751.
Social Services Centre, Square Complex, Tallaght, Dublin 24; ☎01-452 5111; fax 01-452 5591.

FÁS Offices in the South-East

Government Buildings, Castlepark, Arklow; ☎0402-39509; fax 0402-39413.
The Boulevarde, Quinnsborough Road, Bray, County Wicklow; ☎01-286 7912; fax 01-286 4170.
Carlow Shopping Centre, Kennedy Avenue, Carlow; ☎0503-42605; fax 0503-41759.
6 Mary Street, Clonmel, County Tipperary; ☎052-24422; fax 052-24565.
2/3 Emmet Street, Clonmel, County Tipperary; ☎052-23486; fax 052-26214.

Bridgepoint, Enniscorthy, County Wexford; ☎054-39300; fax 054-39309.
Irishtown, County Kilkenny; ☎056-65514; fax 056-64451.
56 Parnell St, Waterford, ☎051-862900; fax 051-862916.
Crescent Mall, Henrietta Street, Wexford; ☎053-23126; fax 053-22785.

FÁS Offices in the South-West

Government Buildings, Sullivan's Quay, Cork; ☎021-485 6200; fax 021-496 8389.
Rossa Avenue, Bishopstown, Cork; ☎021-485 6200; fax 021-454 1789.
30/31 Shandon Street, Cork; ☎021-494 6162; fax 021-494 6169.
Warner Centre, Barrack Street, Bantry, County Cork; ☎027-50464; fax 027-50203.
Unit 1, Kenmare Place, Killarney, County Kerry; ☎064-32466; fax 064-32759.
103/104 Davis Street, Mallow, County Cork; ☎022-21900; fax 022-22582.
17 Lower Castle Street, Tralee, County Kerry; ☎O66-712 3065; fax 066-712 2954.

FÁS Offices in the Mid-West

42 Parnell Street, Ennis, County Clare; ☎065-682 9213; fax 065-682 8502.
18 Davis Street, Limerick; ☎061-487 915; fax 061-412 326.
Perry Court, Upper Mallow Street, Limerick; ☎061-487 944; fax 061-412 977.
79 Connolly Street, Nenagh, County Tipperary; ☎067-31879; fax 067-31167.
Government Buildings, Gortboy, Newcastlewest, County Limerick; ☎069-62411; fax 069-61561.
FÁS Training Centre, Shannon Industrial Estate, Shannon, County Clare; ☎061-471 133; fax 053-23177.
Friar Street, Thurles, County Tipperary; ☎0504-22188; fax 0504-23574.

FÁS Offices in the Midlands

Townhouse Centre, St. Mary's Square, Athlone, County Westmeath; ☎0902-75291; fax 0902-78288.

7 Market Square, Longford; ☎043-46820; fax 043-45702.

Church Avenue, Mullingar, County Westmeath; ☎044-48805; fax 044-43978.

Georges Street, Newbridge, County Kildare; ☎045-431 372; fax 045-434 446.

4 Meehan House, James Fintan Lawlor Avenue, Portlaoise, County Laois; ☎0502-21462; fax 0502-20945.

Church Street, Tullamore, County Offaly; ☎0506-51176; fax 0506-21964.

FÁS Offices in the West

'Riverside', Church Road, Ballina, County Mayo; ☎096-24017; fax 096-70608.

Unit 7 & 8, Humbert Mall, Main Street, Castlebar, County Mayo; ☎094-34300; fax 094-22832.

Island House, Cathedral Square, Galway; ☎091-534400; fax 091-562718.

FÁS Training Centre, Industrial Estate, Mervue, Galway; ☎091-706 208; fax 091-753 590.

Lanesboro Street, Roscommon, ☎0903-26802; fax 0903-25399.

High Street, Tuam, County Galway; ☎0903-28066; fax 0903-28068.

FÁS Offices in the North-East

49 Church Street, Cavan, County Cavan; ☎049-433 1767; fax 049-433 2527.

14 North Quay, Drogheda, County Louth; ☎041-983 7646; fax 041-983 8120.

79 Park Street, Dundalk, County Louth; ☎042-933 1608; fax 042-933 6311.

Market Street, Monaghan, County Monaghan; ☎047-81511; fax 047-83441.

Tara Mall, Trimgate Street, Navan, County Meath; ☎046-23630; fax 046-21903.

FÁS Offices in the North-West

Mainstreet, Ballybofey, County Donegal; ☎074-30384; fax 074-31466.

Government Buildings, Shannon Lodge, Carrick-on-Shannon, County Leitrim; ☎078-20503; fax 078-20505.

Government Buildings, Cranmore, Sligo; ☎071-43 390; fax 071-44120.

FÁS Training Centre, Ballyraine Industrial Estate, Ramelton Road, Letterkenny, County Donegal; ☎074-20500; fax 074-24840.

The European Employment Service (EURES)

The European Employment Service was set up in order to advise on job opportunities and the living and working conditions in the 17 countries of the European Economic Area (EEA) through its network of more than 500 EURES advisors. The Service aims to facilitate the free movement of workers within the EEA and to assist employers in recruiting these potential employees by providing advice and guidance to workers and employers alike. EURES – which is co-ordinated by the European Commission – includes public employment services, trade unions and employer organisations.

EURES advisors are located throughout the EEA and have at their disposal databases of job vacancies throughout Europe. Advisors can also provide up to date information on a number of important issues that need to be addressed when seeking work abroad, such as comparability of qualifications, the cost of living, training opportunities, education, welfare and employment legislation and taxation. In Ireland the EURES advisers can be contacted through offices of FÁS, Ireland's national training and employment authority.

Employers in Ireland are able to advertise vacancies in the EURES databases through the FÁS Services to Business website (www.fas.ie/jbframe.htm). Jobseekers in Ireland looking to work elsewhere in Europe are able to post their CV on the EURES website (http://europa.eu.int/eures) where it can be accessed by employers from all over the EEA.

Newspapers

You will find a number of job vacancies in Ireland advertised in the local and national newspapers. Libraries in Ireland stock copies of the most recent editions of these, as well as those of the previous week or so. If you are searching for work in Ireland while still abroad, check at the nearest Irish embassy, consulate or tourist office to see if they hold copies of Irish newspapers. Alternatively, you could take out a subscription (see the media section in the *Daily Life* chapter for addresses). A few of the newspapers in Ireland publish a 'situations vacant' supplement once a week, in some cases these supplements relate to specific professions. The *Irish Times*' 'Business This Week' supplement is published every Friday and is linked electronically with the www.nicemove.ie website, while the *Sunday Tribune*, the *Sunday Independent* and the *Sunday Business Post* all include 'situations vacant' advertisements. Edition of the *Irish Examiner* on Friday's, Thursday's *Irish Independent*, and *Ireland on Sunday* are all good places to look for jobs and business information. Another approach to the hunt for employment is to place your own advertisement in the local Irish press of the area or areas in which you hope to live and work, detailing your qualifications, work experience and the type of employment that you are seeking.

Professional & Trade Publications

Job opportunities in specific fields are often advertised in the journals, newsletters and magazines published by trade, technical and professional organisations and governing bodies. If you are a member of such an institution in your own country, you may be able to acquire the magazine or journal of the Irish chapter of the trade organisation, or you can find relevant contact details in the Associations and Institutions section of Golden Pages directory service (www.goldenpages.ie). Some trade associations may allow you to place an advertisement in the their journal or newsletter. Note that some magazines and newspapers such as *New Scientist* and the *International Herald Tribune*, which have an international readership, sometimes carry 'situations vacant' advertisements for placements. Some in-house magazines of companies and organisations also carry advertisements and can be a good source of general industry information as well as employment opportunity.

The Internet

Although there are mixed reports as to the efficacy of online recruitment sites, there is no denying that there has been an explosion of such sites in recent years. Especially in the IT industry much of the business of recruitment and headhunting is carried out over the Internet. It is often possible to search for jobs by locale and specialisation and some sites allow you to post your own contact details and CV so that prospective employers can see who you are and what you can offer and email you directly should they require your expertise. Because of the nature of the business world it must be said that there will always be more opportunities for work via the Internet in the larger towns and cities of Ireland, where employers are likely to be more conversant with using the Internet as a tool for recruitment.

Most of the newspapers have sister websites which have designated 'situations vacant' areas, as do recruitment companies and employment agencies. Details of these can be found using a search engine directory such as google.com or yahoo.com. When look for recruitment sites, try and narrow down the search to specific areas of employment that directly relate to what you are looking for. There are billions of websites out there in cyberspace and it can be very frustrating trawling through endless websites that can offer you personally very little. A handful of general jobsearch websites relating specifically to Ireland, some of which carry useful information on the jobhunt and job prospects are: www.jobsinireland.ie; www.ireland.com/jobs; www.monster.ie; www.recruitireland.com; www.nixers.com; and www.irishjobs.ie. FÁS, the Irish training and employment agency, also has a comprehensive jobsearch database at its Job-Bank website, accessible at http://jobbank.fas.ie.

Employment Agencies

Private employment agencies take on the job of matching applicants with the relevant skills to the job vacancies that the agency has on its books. Some agencies deal with general long-term posts, others specialise in finding temporary workers ('temps') to provide cover at short notice during periods when full-time employees of a company are absent on holiday or maternity leave or through illness. Other agencies deal with recruitment in specific areas, such as in IT, catering, banking, clerical and secretarial, or recruit only those who can fill managerial and executive posts. The Irish Recruitment Agency industry is represented by the National Recruitment Federation (NRF, Cara House, Malahide Road Industrial Park, Malahide Road, Dublin 17; www.nrf.ie), which currently has a membership of over 120 agencies.

The agency IRC (11 Ely Place, Dublin 2; ☎ 01-661 0644; www.ircon.ie) has been operating since 1984 and offers a wide range of permanent and temporary positions. Areas of employment covered include banking, accountancy, IT, sales and marketing, office personnel, insurance, call centre, multilingual work, HR & Technical Engineering.

The agency Griffin Personnel (11 Ely Place, Dublin 2, ☎ 01-676 2719: www.griffinpersonnel.ie) have been meeting the recruitment needs of companies in Ireland since 1983. Griffin Personnel are a specialist agency who source specifically for secretarial & commercial roles. They have a wide range of permanent, contract and temporary positions available.

DB Recruitment (☎ 00353-1278 0450; e-mail jobs@dbrecruitment.ie; www.debrecruitment.ie) is a leading multilingual recruitment company. Its clients have constant requirements for multi-lingual candidates within customer service, telephone technical support and accounts positions in Dublin, Cork, Limerick and Belfast.

Reed has branches in Cork (1st Floor, 91 Patrick Street, Cork; ☎ 021-427 5433) and Dublin (47 Dawson Street, Dublin 2; 01-670 4466; www.reed.ie). Reed deals with general vacancies and also has dedicated consultants recruiting for the hospitality, computing and accountancy sectors.

There are many employment agencies that only deal with employment opportunities in their local area, and others that specialise in specific types of work only. Listed below is a selection from around the country:

Accountants Panel, 21 Northumberland Road, Dublin 4; ☎01-661 4771; www.thepanel.com.

Adecco Recruitment, 45 Grafton Street, Dublin 2; ☎01-677 8348; fax 01- 677 8349; www.adecco.ie.

Brightwater Selection, 36 Merrion Square, Dublin 2; ☎01-662 1000; fax 01-662 3900; www.brightwater.ie.

Careers Register, 26 Lower Baggot Street, Dublin 2; ☎01-679 8900; www.careers-register.com

Elan IT ReSource, 12/13 Temple Lane South, Temple Bar, Dublin; ☎01-670 5070; fax 01-670 5080; www.elanit.com.

Fastnet Recruitment, Penrose Wharf, Cork; ☎021-450 9200; fax 021-450 9095; www.fastnetrecruitment.com.

Grafton Recruitment, 1A South Mall, Cork; ☎021-422 3943; fax 021-422 3117; www.grafton-group.com.

Hays Accountancy Personnel, 1 Richmond Court, Mount Kenneth Place, Limerick; ☎061-440 771; fax 061-440 770; www.hayspersonnel.ie.

Hays Montrose, 62 Lower Baggot Street, Dublin 2; ☎01-661 2772; fax 01-661 2265; www.hays-montrose.ie.

Hennessey Recruitment, 98 Henry Street, Limerick; ☎061-430 950; fax 061-430 933; www.hennessyrecruitment.com.

Joslin Rowe Associates, 29 Lower Baggot Street, Dublin 2; ☎01-644 3737; fax 01-644 3738; www.joslinrowe.ie.

La Crème, 15 Lower Pembroke Street, Dublin 2; ☎01-4321 500; www.lacreme.ie. Also has offices in Cork, Limerick, Waterford and

Kilkenny.
NRC Recruitment, 37 College Green, Dublin 2; ☎01-677 6699; www.nrc.ie.
Parker Bridge, 8 Dawson Street, Dublin 2; ☎01-2409 303; fax 01-2409 327; www.parkerbridge.ie. Banking and Finance recruitment specialists.
Planet Recruitment, 21 Eden Quay, Dublin 1; ☎01-874 9901; fax 01-878 6492; www.planet-recruitment.com.
Premier Financial Recruitment, 15 Lower Pembroke Street, Dublin 2; ☎01-4321 555; www.premierjobs.ie. Also has offices in Cork, Limerick, Waterford and Kilkenny.
Richmond Recruitment, The Stables, Alfred Street, Cork; ☎021-500 355; fax 021-500 055; www.richmond.ie.
TMP/Hudson Global Resources, 10 Lower Mount Street, Dublin 2; ☎01-676 5000; http://ie.hudsonresourcing.com.
VanRath Financial Selection, 67 Middle Abbey Street, Dublin 1; ☎01-874 5100; www.vanrath.com.

Details of local and national agencies can be found in the Golden Pages or on the Internet – most agencies now have websites. You can search Golden Pages online at www.goldenpages.ie.

Company Transfers

Although companies seldom recruit with the idea of international transfer in mind, it may be worth applying for a job with a firm in your home country that has branches or subsidiaries in Ireland. If the idea of working in Ireland is one that you hope to pursue then it may be a good idea to bring this up at interview stage. Multinational companies with offices or subsidiaries in Ireland can be found in directories such as *Who Owns Whom* and *Europa* (Dunn & Bradstreet), *Kompass Ireland* (Kompass Ireland), *Hoover's Handbook of World Business* (Hoover's Inc.) and *Worldwide Branch Locations of Multinational Companies* (Gale Research), available in public libraries. A selection of such companies can also be found in the *Directory of Major Employers* at the end of this chapter.

APPLYING FOR A JOB

Application Forms & Letters

Generally, job advertisements will invite you to contact the company for further details, which should include a fuller description of the job advertised and the duties the successful applicant will be expected to perform. In addition, there should be details of the starting salary, any benefits and perks such as travel expenses, bonuses, company car, etc., and any personal and professional requirements necessary, for example trade qualifications, industry experience, etc.

Job ads should include instructions regarding how you are to submit your application and the last date upon which applications will be accepted. You may be sent a printed application form, which you will need to fill in exactly as requested – block capitals in black ink may be specified for example, or it may need to be typed. Alternatively, you may be asked to send your curriculum vitae together with a covering letter explaining why you want the job, why the firm should employ you and what you have to offer. It is very important to follow such instructions to the letter – prospective employers are not impressed by candidates who cannot follow simple instructions precisely. One area in which individual quirks of employers often display themselves is in the covering letter – some insisting on a hand-written letter, others only accepting a typed letter. If no preference is expressed it is always best to type the covering letter.

Until several years ago applications were only accepted if sent by post but with the speed of new technology in some cases applications may be faxed or send via the Internet. Advertisements often state the method by which the firm would like to receive applications, but if you are pressed for time it could be a good idea to telephone the firm to see if they will accept applications by fax or e-mail.

If you are sending an application by e-mail in response to an advert asking for a CV and a covering letter it is always preferable to send these in the main body of the text of an e-mail rather than as attachments. The software that you use on your computer may differ to that used by a particular employer and if they have problems receiving or reading your application then you are going to have a little less chance landing the job.

The Curriculum Vitae

A CV is the equivalent of a résumé, though it often contains a greater range of information. As well as including personal details such as name, address, date of birth and marital status, you should also include your educational qualifications and employment history with dates. The more recent and most relevant jobs and/or qualifications should be described in more detail than the others and should be listed chronologically with the most recent listed above the more ancient. In addition, a CV can contain information about your hobbies and interests, any volunteer or community work you have done, courses taken, skills acquired, membership of professional or other organisations. What you include or omit from your CV will depend on the type of job you are applying for, so although the basic biographical details will remain the same for most applications, to make your CV most effective you should consider the content for any particular application.

Ensure that everything included in the CV is relevant to the application and concisely stated while at the same time going into enough detail to impress upon the reader your experience and skills. Personnel officers or interviewers receive a vast number of CVs each week and will not wade through a mass of detail or waffle however brightly you may dress it up. A CV should at the most cover only two sides of A4 paper and any additional information that you believe relevant to the job application should be included in the covering letter.

It is perfectly acceptable to produce your own CV and computer software packages such as Microsoft Word make it easy with CV templates, which lead you through the process of creating your own CV step by step. There are also a number of books available which can advise you on how to write that 'sure-fire' CV. There are also CV writing services advertised in the press and on the Internet where, for a fee, a professional will create a good looking CV for you using the information you provide.

References

You will usually be asked to supply the names and contact details of several people known to you who can comment on your character in the work and/or social spheres. These 'referees' could be a former employer, teacher or lecturer, or a professional who has known you for some time and can write an informative paragraph or two on you. As a matter of courtesy you should ask whether a person wishes to be thought of as a referee before giving their details as such to a potential employer.

Generally, the referees will only be contacted as a final double-check on your character before you are offered the job. They will be required to write a letter or fill in a form giving their opinion of you and your suitability for the job.

Interview Procedure

Once your application has been received and processed, if a company is interested in what you have to offer (or what you have said you have to offer) you may be invited for an interview. This invitation will probably come in the form of a letter or e-mail, though it is possible that you may be telephoned, as a telephone call is a good way to try and sound out a prospective candidate, as well as allowing the personnel officer and yourself to arrange a mutually convenient time for an interview. At the application stage you may have been informed when interviews would be taking place, and if so you should ensure that you are available at that time. If you are not invited for interview you may be informed of the fact, although very often, particularly where there have been a large number of applications for a job, you will hear nothing further if you have been unsuccessful.

Interview procedure varies from firm to firm but usually it is a fairly formal affair with the candidate placed in a room with one or more interviewers whose job it is to draw out of the candidate their suitability and aptitude to do the work that will be required of them. Although the dress code in some industries is less strict than in others, it is always a good policy to dress formally for an interview – suit and a tie for men, and skirt and a blouse for women. Even if the general ethos of the company is to dress casually, you are not to know this and no one will fault you for dressing 'up' for an interview. As has been stated so often, first impressions count, and if you dress as though you are management material then you will, depending on how you wow the interviewers with your verbal skill, be taken as such.

It is always advisable to find out as much about a company as you can before an interview so that you can ask pertinent questions and be able to field any that may be lobbed your way. The Internet is an invaluable research tool and you can find out a great deal about a company and its activities by typing its name into a search engine such as google.com. It is also important that, when walking into an interview room, you take your enthusiasm for the job and the company with you. Enthusiasm and a generally informed demeanour in a prospective job candidate is an attractive quality to behold, and can help to dispel any doubts an interviewer may have about your suitability for a particular role in the firm. If you show that you have already given the firm and its activities some serious consideration then this will inspire a certain amount of confidence in your abilities.

Favoured questions at interviews are those along the lines of: 'Why do you want this job?', 'What are your strengths and weaknesses?' (a tricky question and you better have come up with some good comments for the latter part), 'Where do you see yourself in five years' time?', 'Is a Jaffa Cake a cake or a biscuit?' or 'Why should we employ you rather than another candidate?' It is as well to prepare answers to these, admittedly rather mean, questions and pause to consider before answering questions posed by the interviewers. Most questions are not asked in order to 'catch you out' but to probe and to discover how suitable you are for the job. At the end of an interview you may be asked whether you have any questions you wish to ask and it can create a positive impression if you have thought of some.

Often a decision will be made on the basis of your original application and an interview. If the interview of all candidates has taken place on the same day, you may be asked to wait for the successful candidate to be announced soon after the last interview has finished. Or you may be free to leave after your interview and then informed by telephone or in writing whether you have been successful or not.

If you performed well at the first interview and the firm is still undecided whether to take you on, then you may be invited back for a second interview. A second interview is often used as an occasion to show a candidate still under consideration around the premises and allow him or her to meet some of the other employees. In a less formal atmosphere a prospective employer will further be able to gauge how the candidate may fit in with the others in the firm, how they interact with relative strangers. If the interview process is an extended one, you may be asked to take part in a series of tests and selection procedures designed by recruitment specialists to measure candidates' strengths and weakness and even psychological profile. These include:

Group Discussion or Group Task. Candidates are asked to take part in a discussion or to perform a task or a problem-solving exercise whilst being observed by a member of the selection panel. Candidates may be given a discussion topic, or asked to choose from a number of topics. The way that individuals and the group as a whole interact during the process of decision and discussion allows the selection panel to gain an insight into the candidates' interpersonal and leadership skills.

Alternatively, candidates may be asked to carry out a task, such as to build a model using materials supplied by the selection panel, or to solve a problem by analysing given information, and then asked to decide on a course of action. Whether candidates succeed or fail at a task is less important than the way in which they tackle it and how they interact with the others in the group. As so many jobs these days stress the importance of being able to work as a team, recruiters are looking to employ team players and to find those who show leadership qualities within a group.

Oral Presentation. Each candidate is asked to prepare a talk to be delivered to the other candidates and/or members of staff. You may be asked to prepare the talk in advance, or within a set period of time on the day of the interview. The talk may be on a subject of your own choice, or on a topic supplied by the selection panel, and can vary in length from a few minutes to a quarter of an hour or more. The important thing here is to come across as being a fluent communicator and at ease when delivering the lecture, as well as being able to control and influence your audience.

Written Presentations. Candidates are given a number of facts and figures and asked to produce a written report with conclusions and a course of action to follow, if appropriate. The information may be given you in advance or on the day of the interview.

Psychometric Testing. Psychological tests designed to analyse a candidate's character, aptitudes and preferences have become very popular with personnel departments. These tests generally take the form of a written exam, where a candidate is required to work through a series of multiple-choice questions.

If asked to take a psychometric test as part of the selection process you should be briefed about its purpose before sitting it. You should also be given some sample questions to work through so that you can get an understanding of the kind of questions you will be answering and the kind of reasoning ability that the selection board are looking to test.

Useful Books & Websites

Build Your Own Rainbow: Workbook for Career and Life Management, Hopson, Scally & Barrie (Management Books, 2000).
How to Win Friends and Influence People, Dale Carnegie (Huchinon, 1994).
Jobcentre Plus, www.jobcentreplus.gov.uk. The Department for Work and Pension's employment service web pages offer advice and tips to assist those preparing for an interview, compiling a CV, etc.
Passing That Interview, Judith Johnstone (How To Books, 1999).
Résumé Writing Services, www.free-resume-tips.com. A US website relating to all things CV.
The Active Connection, www.activeconnection.co.uk. A recruitment website which includes a section on top interview and CV writing tips.
The Ultimate CV for Managers and Professionals, Rachel Bishop-Firth (How To Books, 2000).
What Color is Your Parachute?, Richard Nelson Bolles (Ten Speed Press, 2003). One of the best 'how to' books in the job-search market.
Writing a CV That Works, Paul McGee (How To Books, 1999).

ASPECTS OF EMPLOYMENT

The average employee in a small to medium sized firm in Ireland works between 37.5 and 39 hours per week and enjoys annual leave of 21 days. Four out of every five employees have an entitlement to sick pay and two-thirds of the workforce are in a company pension scheme. A recent survey conducted by the Irish Small Firms Association recorded that, on average, employees in Ireland earn 32% more than those working in similar positions in other EU countries.

A typical employee of a small firm earns between €20,000 (approx. £13,325/US $23,644) and €30,000 (approx. £19,984/US $35,465) per year. Around 45% of employees earn less than €25,000, 39% earn between €25,000 and €30,000; 16% receive more than €30,000. The biggest pay increases over 2003 were in software development, where salaries increased by between 10% and 23%.

Levels of salary and benefits packages are influenced on the whole by the size of a company – the larger the company and turnover the better the remuneration package. According to a 2003 survey by the Compensation and Benefits Research and Information Services, Inbucon, the highest earners in Ireland, apart from Managing Directors and General Managers, are Directors of Sales and Directors of Information Technology. Of the companies surveyed the average basic salary of an MD was €139,818, with senior management figures receiving a basic of €63,828. Middle management were being paid on average a €49,000 basic salary while those in the lower echelons were receiving around €30,000.

Salaries

Most wages and salaries in Ireland are paid monthly (12 times a year) or sometimes four-weekly (13 times a year), with payments generally being paid straight into an employee's bank or building society account. Employees should also receive a payslip itemising the amount of gross and net pay received along with deductions taken at source in relation to tax, pension and PRSI payments. Some manual labourers, employees in the hotel and shop trades, agricultural workers and casual and temporary workers may be paid weekly and in cash and in such cases a less detailed payslip may be enclosed with the wage.

Employees can expect a pay review at their place of work on a yearly basis and a small percentage increase in salary each year to take into account the increase in the cost of living index. Some firms will review the salary of a new employee after an initial six-month probationary period.

Minimum Wage. A national minimum wage was first introduced in Ireland in 2000 and the rate has risen over the years. As of 1 February 2004 the national minimum wage in Ireland is €7 (approx. £4.66/US $8.27) per hour, which is the third highest rate among the EU member states, behind Luxemburg and Holland. The minimum wage legislation has had some impact in terms of reducing the wage gap between genders but appears to have had little impact on overall trends in income and wealth distribution in Ireland. Unfortunately, the national minimum wage does not have to be paid to first time job entrants, those working as apprentices, or to a person employed by a close relative. Employees under the age of 18 are only guaranteed under the provision a wage of 70% of the national minimum. Once employees reach the age of 18 the entitlement is phased in by an increase of 10% a year. Special reduced rates also apply to those employees undergoing a course of accredited training or study.

Benefits & Perks

The value of employment packages, especially within the higher-paid and executive sectors of employment, is often increased by additional employee benefits such as the provision of a company car, annual bonuses, share options, reduced rate loans, free gym membership, etc. These 'perks' or perquisites come in addition to the regular salary and may be linked to the performance of the company as a whole, or the employee as an individual within the company, or to length of service. Not all perks are tax deductible, however, and although some lump sum bonuses may be payable tax-free other 'benefits-in-kind' are liable to income tax.

Sample Salaries

The following gives a sample of positions together with basis salaries offered (exclusive of bonuses and commissions and benefit packages) taken from a 2004 salary guide published by Manpower Ireland (54 Grafton Street, Dublin 2; ☎01-645 5200; www.manpower.ie). Salaries offered by companies will be highest in Dublin, with a secondary level in Limerick and Cork and lower levels offered elsewhere.

Job title	Salary (€000's) (if Dublin-based)	Salary (€000's) (outside Dublin)
Assistant Manager Retail	23-28	20-27
Bank Clerk	20-25	18-22
Civil Engineer	30-45	27-43
Financial Accountant	50-60	45-55
IT Director	80-150	70-120
Office Manager	25-35	23-30
Office Temp.	11-12.50/hour	10-11.50/hour
PA/Executive Assistant	28-35	25-32
PR Officer	25-30	20-27
Receptionist (<3 years experience)	18-24	16-23
Recruitment Consultant (agency)	23-38	18-27
Systems Analyst	30-55	27-50
Telesales Manager	38-50	30-45
Warehouse Operative	18-20	16-19
Web Developer	23-38	21-35

Working Hours, Overtime & Holidays

The standard working day for many of the Irish starts at 9am and finishes at 5.30pm, with an (unpaid) hour taken for lunch, usually sometime between noon and 2pm. European Directives govern the number of hours per week that an employee can work, which are at present set at an average of 48 hours in any four month period. Critically, this ruling does not mean that an employee **cannot** exceed the 48 hour limit, but that **on average** an employee may only work 48 hours in a week (not including breaks, annual leave, sick leave, maternity or adoptive leave, etc.). The ruling does not apply to the gardaí, the defence forces, those working at sea, trainee doctors, the self-employed, family employees, or transport employees.

Some employers operate a 'flexi-time' system whereby employees are not tied to a specific time schedule but may choose when they start and finish a working day, so long as they are present during a 'core' period of the day. Payment for weekend work, night work (over the period between midnight and 7am) and periods of overtime is usually at a higher rate than for regular working hours.

Holiday entitlement for full-time employees in Ireland is for a minimum of 20 days annual leave though many companies include additional leave as part of their benefits packages. The entitlement starts to accrue from the day you commence employment, but permission to take holidays is always at the employer's discretion. All companies have a 'leave year' and employees need to take their leave in that year or within the six months that follow. Holiday pay is paid in advance and if for any reason employment is terminated then outstanding leave will be payable by the employer. Annual leave is not affected by other types of leave such as maternity or parental leave.

Regular part-time workers – those who work at least six hours a week – are entitled to six hours' paid holiday for every 100 hours worked, and proportionally less for periods of less than 100 hours. Those who are employed and paid by an agency are paid holiday entitlement by the agency.

In addition to an annual holiday entitlement, there are nine public holidays in Ireland. Good Friday is not a public holiday, although many companies take this as a company holiday. Full-time employees who do not work on a bank holiday get a full day's pay, while those who do work on the day are entitled to paid leave and also to receive a paid day off within a month or an extra day's pay, or an additional day of leave entitlement. However, it is not unusual for companies to be a little more generous than that. If you are a regular part-timer and the day of a public holiday falls on one of your normal workdays, you should be paid your normal day's pay. Your employer is not obliged to pay any extra in this case. If you are a regular part-timer not working a bank holiday you will still get paid on a pro-rata basis. This is calculated by dividing the number of hours you work in a week by five, so if you normally work 20 hours per week, you should receive four hours' pay for the public holiday.

Employment Contracts

Employers are required by law to give a contract of employment to all employees paid a regular salary who work for more than eight hours a week and whose employment with a firm lasts more than a month. An employee should receive this contract within two months of the commencement of employment. A contract will set out the terms and conditions which exist between an employee and the employer and will include details of the name and address of the employee and employer, job title or brief job description, the commencement date of employment, and the date employment will end if it is for a fixed term. The contract will specify the salary to be paid and how this is calculated and when it will be paid. A contract should also list the hours of work, amount of holiday, sick pay, and paid leave entitlements, as well as any pension scheme included in the package. It should also list details of the employer's disciplinary rules and grievance procedures and the amount of notice required to terminate employment by both parties.

Employers must by law provide a contract stating the terms and conditions of their employment within two months of being requested to do so by an employee. If the employer is an employment agency then the agency, as the party paying the employee their wages, is deemed to be the employer, and must therefore provide the contract of employment.

Employees working on a fixed term or a specific purpose contract are required to sign a slightly different contract of employment which specifies the date of commencement and completion of employment and type of work to be entered into. The contract will also include a clause excluding the employee of the right to bring a claim against an employer under the Unfair Dismissals Act until they have completed at least one year's continuous service with the employer. However, it should be noted that employers are forbidden from issuing a series of short-term contracts to long-term employees in a bid to circumvent unfair dismissals legislation.

Termination of Employment

The length of notice an employer must give depends on the length of time an employee has been in continuous service with the company. The rules and regulations governing this period of notice, which are subject to rulings in Irish law, will be stated in the contract of employment. To qualify for the minimum period of notice an employee will need to have completed a probationary period of 13 weeks with a firm. Employees who work less than eight hours a week for an employee are also covered by the rulings of the various employee protection acts. Entitlements to notice are as follows: those who have completed 13 weeks' to two years' continuous service are entitled to notice of one week; two to five years' of service gives an entitlement of two weeks; five to ten years' gives four weeks; ten to fifteen years gives six weeks, and fifteen years' service or more entitles an employee to be given eight weeks' notice. Some contracts may require an employee to give a longer a period of notice and some may state that an employee may accept a payment in lieu of working out the notice period. Payment in this case will be equal to that which an employee would have received for working out his or her notice period.

An employer needs to give a good reason for terminating employment and should the employee feel that there has been an unfair dismissal then, as long as certain criteria are met, a claim can be made to the Rights Commissioner Service (Tom Johnson House, Beggar's Bush, Dublin 4; ☎ 01-613 6700) or to the Employment Appeals Tribunal (Davitt House, 65a Adelaide Road, Dublin 2; ☎ 01-631 3347; www.entemp.ie). Any claimant will generally need to have served one year's continuous service with the employer and will also need to make the appeal within six months of the dismissal. If an employee is found to have been unfairly dismissed then the usual consequence of the action is a settlement being paid by the employer as compensation for loss of earnings.

Redundancy

If an employer needs to make redundancies due to having to move the place of work, cutting staff numbers, changing the nature of the business or closing down operations, employees may be entitled to a lump sum redundancy payment. These payments are made to employees in jobs that are insurable for all benefits under the social welfare system, who are aged between 16 and 66 years of age, have 104 weeks' continuous service with the employer and who work for eight hours or more a week. The amount payable is calculated on two weeks' pay for every year of service, plus an additional one-week's pay. Redundancy payments are tax-free. If employees do not receive the redundancy pay that they believe they are entitled to then the matter may be referred to the Employment Appeals Tribunal at the address above.

Rights of Part-time, Temporary & Seasonal Workers

The rights of part-time employees are protected in Ireland by the 2001 Protection of Employees (Part-time) Act. The Act protects the interests of all those who, apart from working less hours than a full-time employee, are of comparable status in every other way. This includes anyone working under a contract of employment or apprenticeship, employed through an employment agency or holding office under or in the service of the State (i.e. civil servants, members of the defence forces, the gardai, etc.). Part-time workers are entitled to the same holidays, sick pay, overtime provision, pension schemes, etc., as full-time employee but on a pro rata basis.

Temporary and seasonal workers are often employed to help out during the busy times in agriculture and the tourism industry. Wages may be low, the hours long and the length of employment and terms of any contract short and kept to the minimum. By law, all those who carry out such work must have the right permits to work in Ireland.

TELEWORKING & E-WORKING

Personal home computer systems and the Internet has allowed more and more people to quit office life and to work from home instead where they can continue to perform the same duties as they would in the office. This 'e-working' tends to be in operation among the larger companies in Ireland that have a large number of staff and a high turnover – multinationals and their subsidiaries – especially in the financial and business services sector. By allowing employees to work from home, an employer can cut overheads while employees can fix the hours they work and cut out the daily commute to work from their day. The majority of e-workers do not work away from the office full-time but work at home for one or two days a week. Although many e-workers live and work in the cities of Ireland there are also a number of self-employed e-workers in the more remote areas who have set up their own businesses and work from home full-time.

Teleworking includes e-work, but also covers employment sectors such as telesales, call centres, mobile working and self-employed home workers. Call centres provide a number of services, including customer and technical support for computer systems, and sales and reservation services for transport and accommodation companies. Due to the large IT-literate labour force and the high levels of IT infrastructure in the country, Ireland is a leading European provider of call centre services. More than 65 companies have taken advantage of this fact and based their European call centres there. It is estimated that at present telework involves between 15,000 and 50,000 workers in Ireland – e-workers representing less than 10% of the total figure.

TRADE UNIONS & PROFESSIONAL ASSOCIATIONS

The Irish Congress of Trade Unions (ICTU) represents the interests of all Trade Unions in Ireland and total membership in the whole of Ireland (including Northern Ireland) amounts to around 750,000 workers, or 50% of the working population, of which 44% is female. More than one out of every five part-time employees in Ireland is a member of a union. There are 48 Trade Unions in the Republic of Ireland and a list of these is available from ICTU at 31/32 Parnell Square, Dublin 1 (☎01-889 7777; fax 01-887 2012; www.ictu.ie).

Under the Irish Constitution, all employees have the right to belong to a trade union and it is unconstitutional for an employer to dismiss or otherwise penalise an employee for trade union activity or membership. No-one is obliged by law to become a member of a union but in some sectors membership of a union is accepted as a condition of employment, though there may be a choice as to which union the employee joins. It is possible to claim a tax allowance for subscriptions paid to a trade union (usually at the rate of 0.5%-1.0% of gross annual salary). Trade union members may ask to be represented by their trade union in any grievance with their employer, though employers are not legally obliged to negotiate with a union on behalf of an individual employee.

In addition to the unions there are also a number of professional and trade associations that also represent the interests of members. These associations often act in a similar capacity to trade unions in that they are concerned with the rights and conditions of service of their members as well as representing the particular profession as a whole at government level. A number of trade and professional associations are affiliated to the Irish Business and Employers Confederation (IBEC), (Head Office: Confederation House, 84/86 Lower Baggot Street, Dublin 2; ☎ 01-605 1500; fax 01-638 1500; www.ibec.ie) which represents over 7,000 businesses and organisations and negotiates on their behalf to shape and influence policies relating to members' interests, both at a national and international level. Some of the main professional organisations in Ireland are listed together with contact details on page 185.

INCOME TAX & PAY RELATED SOCIAL INSURANCE (PRSI)

Employees are liable to pay income tax and PRSI (social security contributions), which are deducted at source so that salaries and wages will be paid net of these levies. Nationals of the European Economic Area (EEA) are not liable to pay PRSI if they are already paying social security contributions in their home country. Income tax exemption limits exist for senior citizens and those on a low income. For full details and rates, see the relevant sections in the *Daily Life* chapter.

Social Security & Unemployment Benefits

Low paid workers, those working part-time and those with family commitments may be entitled to social security benefits in addition to earnings from employment. The unemployed are entitled to claim Unemployment Benefit if they fulfil the criteria for such payments (and have paid enough PRSI contributions) set out by the Department of Social and Family Affairs. Those who fail to qualify for Unemployment Benefit because they do not have enough PRSI contributions should apply for Unemployment Assistance. For full details see the *Daily Life* chapter.

WOMEN IN WORK

The Catholic Church, which has always played a very strong role in Irish society, has been traditionally opposed to the notion of women working, teaching that a woman's main role in life was to marry, have children and stay in the home. Girls were asked to prepare for their future as wives and mothers and given little or no encouragement to continue in formal education. Well into the 1970s married women were barred from working in the civil service. Women were discouraged from going out to find paid employment. Although times have changed, there is still a fair amount of inequality between the genders in the workplace – most significantly, the gender pay gap which, at 15.5%, is one of the highest in the EU. Women are still earning less than their male colleagues in the same roles, and there are significantly less women holding office in the higher echelons of business.

The rate of employment among females in Ireland has increased by 15% since 1994 (from 54% to 78%). The Government continues to oppose the introduction of paid parental leave although it has committed itself to an EU target to place 60% of all women between the ages of 16 and 64 in employment by 2010. Equality in employment is also dependent on the Government increasing the amount of spending put into care work and until this happens, women will continue to have to balance paid employment with unpaid care work.

Maternity Leave

There are big differences in the amount of maternity leave given across Europe. Mothers in Sweden are given the most leave with 96 weeks, while women in Denmark, Italy and Finland may take up to 50, 47 and 44 weeks leave respectively. In Ireland the Maternity Protection Act of 1994 entitled mothers to a period of 14 weeks' maternity leave, with the option of taking an additional four weeks' leave. Changes were made to this ruling with the implementation of the Maternity Protection (Amendment) Bill in 2003 and the entitlement is now for a period of 18 weeks' leave, with the option of taking an additional eight weeks' leave. Of the 18 weeks, four are to be taken before the end of the week of the expected date of birth, and four after the baby has been born. A pregnant employee is entitled to take maternity leave irrespective of how long she has been working for her employer, as long as she gives the required notice.

Following a period of maternity leave, mothers are entitled to go back to their position at work, or a similar position offering the same terms and conditions. Those returning from maternity leave are entitled to any improvement in the terms and conditions of work implemented while they have been away. Should a mother decide to take the additional eight weeks' leave, her accumulated employment rights (except those of pay and superannuation contributions) will not be affected. An employee's entitlement to pay during maternity leave depends on the terms of the contract of employment and there is no obligation on employers to pay women on maternity leave. A recent survey by the Irish Small Firms Association found that only one business in six pays maternity benefits to employees on maternity leave.

Paternity leave is not recognised by employment law in Ireland and fathers will only be entitled to paternity leave in the tragic event of the mother dying while on maternity leave.

Maternity Benefit

Maternity Benefit is a social welfare payment paid to employed and self-employed women who satisfy certain PRSI contribution conditions and who are in recognised work up to the first day of their maternity leave. The last day of work can be within 14 weeks of the expected date of the arrival of the baby. It is payable for the first 18 weeks of maternity leave but not for the additional optional eight weeks' leave. Maternity Benefit is based on a rate of 70% of the employee's gross earnings, subject to a minimum and maximum payment.

Expectant mothers who work for an employer must have paid at least 39 weeks' PRSI contributions in the 12-month period before the first day of their maternity leave, at least 39 weeks' PRSI contributions since first starting work and at least 39 weeks PRSI contributions in the second last complete tax year before the year in which maternity leave commences. Self-employed women must have paid 52 weeks' PRSI contributions in the relevant tax year before the year in which the claim is made or 52 weeks' PRSI contributions in the tax year prior to the relevant tax year before the year in which the claim is made, or 52 weeks' PRSI contributions in the tax year later than the relevant tax year. Further information can be obtained from the Maternity Benefit Section of the Department of Social and Family Affairs (Social Welfare Services Office, Government Buildings Ballinalee Road, Longford; ☎ 043-45211 or 01-874 8444).

Parental Leave

Parental leave was introduced in 1998 as a result of an EU Directive and allows a parent (male or female) the option of taking up to 14 weeks' unpaid leave before his or her child is five years old. Employees wishing to take parental leave must normally have worked for their employer for a period of one year, however, if a parent has not completed a year's service before the child reaches the age of five but has completed three months' service, then he or she is still entitled to a reduced period of leave. This is calculated at a rate of one week for every month spent in continuous employment with the employer at the time leave commences. Leave can be taken in segments or in one continuous period at the discretion of the employer and is not transferable between the mother and father. Both parents are entitled to take parental leave, however, there is no entitlement to any social welfare payment equivalent to Maternity Benefit while on parental leave.

Childcare

In a recent report by the Organisation for Economic Co-operation and Development Ireland still suffers from a shortage of affordable childcare, which is directly responsible for the relatively low numbers of women in work. The cost of childcare (between €88 and €190 per week) in Ireland continues to increase with no corresponding increase in Child Benefit. Pre-school childcare remains inadequate and places are sought after. Playgroups exist, but the majority of these offer only morning or afternoon care for any one child, which doesn't allow a mother to take up full-time employment. The problem of finding childcare is doubly important in the case of single parents.

Useful Addresses & Websites

Centre for Early Childhood Development & Education (CECDE), Gate Lodge, St. Patrick's College, Drumcondra, Dublin 9; ☎01-884 2110; fax 01-884 2111; www.cecde.ie.

Childminding Ireland, The Enterprise Park, The Murrough, Wicklow Town; ☎0404-64007; www.childminding-irl.com.

IPPA-The Early Childhood Organisation, Unit 4 Broomhill Business Complex, Broomhill Road, Tallaght, Dublin 24; ☎01-463 0010; fax 01-463 0045; www.ippa.ie.

National Women's Council of Ireland, 16-20 Cumberland Street South, Dublin 2; ☎01-6615268; fax 01-676 0860; www.nwci.ie.

The National Children's Nurseries Association (NCNA), Unit 12c, Bluebell Business Park, Old Naas Road, Bluebell, Dublin 12; ☎01-460 1138; fax 01-460 1185; www.ncna.net.

COMPANY PENSION SCHEMES

The majority of companies in Ireland, especially those that employ a large staff, operate employee pension schemes, which provide a lump sum or a pension to an employee upon retirement, or to surviving dependents on the death of an employee. There is no obligation on employees to belong to such schemes, although generally they offer a better deal than a personal pension plan, especially for the employee who stays with the same company until retirement. It is permissible to be a member of an occupational pension scheme and pay earnings from other employment or from self-employment into a personal pension plan. Each scheme will have its own set of rules and contributions to approved occupational pension schemes may attract a certain amount of tax relief. Almost all pension schemes are regulated by the Pensions Board (Verschoyle House, 28-30 Lower Mount Street, Dublin 2; ☏01-613 1900; fax 01-631 8602; www.pensionsboard.ie).

There are two kinds of pension schemes operated by companies in Ireland: the majority operate the Defined Benefit Scheme, where the benefit entitlement is defined by reference to earnings, length of service and an index or a fixed amount. With these schemes the employee knows what his pension will be in advance, and contributions may vary periodically to ensure that the fund can meet the level of benefits. As a result such schemes often have provisions for the employer to top up the fund if necessary. A second scheme, the Defined Contribution Scheme, fixes the contribution to be paid by the employer and the benefits are decided on the value of these contributions and are not fixed in advance. With the Defined Contribution Scheme an employee will not know what level of pension they will eventually receive. Most occupational pension schemes are funded – which means that contributions are put into a designated fund from which all benefits are paid.

Occupational and personal pensions operate independently of the social welfare pension system, however, it is common for occupational pensions to take into account the level of social welfare pension received when calculating the level of benefit.

Under an occupational pension scheme, the maximum benefit that can be provided for a spouse or dependent has been increased from two thirds of the full pension to 100% of the provision. Tax relief and exemptions from PRSI and other levies are given 'at source' on money contributed to the scheme. There is an age related scale governing the maximum you can contribute to your main pension scheme for tax relief purposes, the maximum percentage of 30% of salary being permitted for those over 50 years of age. Note that tax has to be paid on a pension when you are in receipt of it.

Following the Pensions (Amendment) Act of 2002, if an employee leaves after paying into a company's scheme for at least two years, he or she will be entitled to the preservation of benefits. An employee cannot cash the benefits on leaving employment, but has several options, all of which will preserve the pension until retirement. An employee may opt to keep the benefits in the former employer's pension scheme or transfer them to another funded occupational pension scheme provided by a new employer. Alternatively the employee may transfer them to a Revenue-approved insurance policy or contract. If an employee has paid into a contributory scheme, but hasn't been in it long enough to qualify for the preservation of benefits, he or she may qualify for a refund of contributions, subject to a 20% tax charge.

PERMANENT WORK

PROFESSIONAL & EXECUTIVE

There are a wide variety of positions available for qualified professionals in all sectors of the economy in Ireland. As well as positions that arise within the smaller professional practices, large companies always need those trained in the professions – especially those with financial and legal expertise – to work 'in-house'. Local authorities have departments dedicated to dealing with legal and financial matters, planning departments need qualified surveyors and architects, other departments require engineers and scientists, etc.

Professional and executive positions are advertised in a number of places: professional associations have their own journals where 'situations vacant' advertisements may appear; local authorities advertise vacancies in the local and national press and on their websites; there are executive recruitment agencies, and recruitment newspapers and websites also advertise situations vacant. Many of the more high powered, high salary, high prestige jobs are advertised in the 'Appointments' sections of the broadsheet newspapers such as the *Irish Times* and the *Irish Independent*, and also appear on the electronic versions of these newspapers.

Remuneration packages are likely to be higher for those positions that are based in Dublin, and to a lesser extent for those in Cork and Limerick. Although theoretically professional qualifications should be transferable within the European Union, some trade and professional bodies may not recognise qualifications gained outside Ireland. Salaries for executive posts in marketing and sales tend to be the highest, followed by positions high up the ladder in financial and IT companies. The workforce in Ireland is a highly educated and highly motivated one, so be prepared to face tough competition for the top jobs.

IRISH CIVIL SERVICE

The Civil Service in Ireland continues to recruit regularly and it is the country's biggest single employer of staff with over 11,000 clerical staff, 8,000 executive and administrative staff, and 4,000 specialist professionals employed in a wide variety of disciplines.

The Civil Service Commission and the Local Appointments Commission provide recruitment and selection services for the various organisations within the Civil Service, including the local authorities (29 County Councils, 5 County Borough Corporations, 5 Borough Corporations and 49 Urban District Councils) and the 8 Health Boards. The Commission recruits personnel at all levels – for clerical and administrative posts to senior managerial appointments. It also recruits for some executive positions with the Harbour Authority, Fisheries Board and the Vocational Education Committees, as well as other public sector organisations such as the Garda and the Nurses Career Centre.

Anyone up to statutory retirement age (65 years old) may apply for positions in the Civil Service. The ability to speak Irish is not an entry requirement of the Service and a lack of proficiency in Irish will not put you at a disadvantage during the recruitment process, however, all posts carry nationality requirements. The Civil Service does not accept unsolicited 'on spec' CVs, but there is a facility on the Service's recruitment website (www.publicjobs.ie) for individuals to register an interest in a particular category of the Service. Positions vacant with the Civil Service can also be found in national newspapers, and on the recruitment website.

Selective, psychometric testing is used to sift candidates for posts in the Service and those who successfully past the tests will be invited to interview. These tests are designed to find those candidates with the right planning and organising skills necessary to effectively carry out work in the Civil Service. Before candidates take the tests they are sent a familiarisation booklet explaining the tests and including sample questions. Further details of current positions vacant, requirements and recruitment procedures are available direct from the Civil Service & Local Appointments Commission at Chapter House, 26/30 Abbey Street Upper, Dublin 1 (☎ 01-858 7400; fax 01-8587 500 for the Civil Service Commission enquiries or 01-858 7574 for Local Authority positions) and from the dedicated website at www.publicjobs.gov.ie.

FINANCIAL & BUSINESS SERVICES

The financial services sector in Ireland employs over 48,000 people with a further 25,000 employed in various auxiliary support services and the International Financial Services Centre (IFSC) at the Custom House Docks in Dublin is central to the industry. Established in 1987, this 16-hectare site is the location for 700 financial services companies dealing in all facets of the market including banking, fund management, futures and options trading and asset financing, among others. Another 450+ international companies are located around the Dublin area. According to the Irish Industrial Development Agency, Dublin is the world's fastest growing location for financial services and more than half the world's largest banks have operations there. Ireland's four main commercial banking groups are Allied Irish Banks, Bank of Ireland, the National Irish Bank, and the Ulster Bank (which has its head office in Belfast but has branches in and recruits staff in the Republic).

Within the accountancy sector the Big Five – PricewaterhouseCoopers, Deloitte & Touche, KPMG, Arthur Andersen and Ernst & Young – all recruit in Ireland. A survey published in 2003 by the Chartered Institute of Management Accountants indicated management accountants' salaries are around the €78,000 a year mark, with the average earnings for senior positions rising towards €130,000. Newly qualified management accountants (in their first five years) earn about €50,000.

ADMINISTRATIVE

Those with good secretarial and clerical skills should have no difficulty finding work in Ireland. Local authorities are among the biggest employers of administrative staff in the country and recruit through the Civil Service and Local Appointments Commission (see above). Administrative jobs are also advertised in the local and national press, in recruitment newspapers, in the 63 FÁS Employment Services Offices throughout the country, on local authority websites and those of general recruitment, executive search and employment agencies. Secretaries, PAs and clerks will always be in demand.

MEDICAL

There is a chronic shortage of nurses and junior doctors in Ireland. During the 1990s, despite an expanding health service, the number of student nurse places in colleges continued to drop, reaching a low of less than 1,000 by 1998. This failure of provision resulted in a serious shortage of nurses and midwives and matters further deteriorated as Irish nurses sought work and better terms and conditions and salaries in countries such as the UK and America. To bridge the gap, recruitment drives were carried out abroad and today there are over 5,000 nurses from non-EU countries (many coming from the Philippines) working in Ireland. However, increasingly these nurses are also being lost to institutions overseas.

To nurse in Ireland, you will need to register with *An Bord Altranais* (the Irish Nursing Board), the Government organisation regulating the nursing profession, preferably well in advance of your arrival in the Republic, as the process of registration can take up to six weeks. If you are from outside of the EU then you will also require a work permit, and this cannot be issued until registration with *An Bord Altranais* is complete. You will also need to provide a police clearance form, which is obtainable from the local police station in the country in which you have been residing for the previous five years.

Staff nurses earn in the region of €24,000-€35,000 per annum; senior staff nurses earning around €37,000 a year. Nurses work a basic 37.5-hour week, and shift work and overtime is common. Most nurses work in a Health Board (in hospitals and in the community) but are also employed by educational establishments, private healthcare providers, the prison service and in industry.

Agencies such as Alliance Nurses (59 Merrion Square, Dublin 2; ☎ 01-678 7333; fax 01-678 7281; www.alliancenurses.ie) and Kate Cowhig International Recruitment Ltd (41 Dawson Street, Dublin; ☎ 01-671 5557; fax 01-671 5965; www.kcr.ie) are able to place nurses, whatever their specialisation with clients needing midwifery, psychiatry, paediatric and learning disability skills, among others. Working through an agency allows you to choose to a greater extent when and where you work as well as being able to dictate the hours that suit you. Rates of pay are usually agreed with the Irish Nursing Organisation (the Irish nurses and midwives trade union). It is also a good idea to approach Health Boards and hospitals direct when searching for employment and contact details for the Regional Health Boards can to be found on page 136.

TEACHING

To register as a qualified teacher in Ireland you must hold a relevant third-level (university) qualification which in the opinion of the Teachers Registration Council enables you to teach at least one subject or area of study in a second-level (12-18 years) school together with a year's teaching experience. The usual qualifications that fulfil such requirements are: a relevant degree from a recognised third-level institution and a postgraduate qualification in education – such as the Higher Diploma in Education, or a degree awarded by a recognised third-level institution on the basis of a concurrent course of academic study and teacher training.

Qualifications obtained outside the EU must be acceptable to the Teachers Registration Council. Teachers whose qualifications were obtained within the EU are subject to special arrangements made under the EU mutual recognition of qualifications directive, for instance the UK's PGCE teaching qualification is recognised by the Department of Education in Ireland (though a qualification in Irish is also required).

There continues to be a demand in Ireland for teachers of secondary level maths, physics, chemistry, French, IT, religious studies and Irish, though for teachers in other subjects posts are not always easy to find. There is also currently a shortage of primary school teachers. ASTI (ASTI House, Winetavern Street, Dublin 8; ☎ 01-671 9144; fax 01-671 9280; www.asti.ie) is the main second-level teachers' trade union in Ireland and is a good place to begin enquiries into openings and employment opportunities. The Department of Education and Science (Marlborough Street, Dublin 1; ☎ 01-889 6400; www.education.ie) holds lists of primary and post primary schools in Ireland.

Starting salaries for new teachers in the state education sector vary depending on the academic qualifications held on entry, but as a guideline the minimum starting salary for a newly qualified teacher is roughly €26,000 a year. Salaries then rise on a scale to around €51,000 a year. In addition there are certain allowances payable in respect of special qualifications, with other premiums paid for the scale of responsibility held in a school (principal, deputy, special duties teacher, etc).

For those looking to teach English as a foreign language in Irish schools recognised by the Department of Education, regulations require that teachers have a primary degree and have also successfully completed a TEFL course of not less than 70 hours' duration. EFL training courses are available at universities, colleges of further education and independent language schools around the country and University College, Dublin offers a Higher Diploma in the Teaching of English as a Foreign Language (HDipTEFL).

Teachers of English as a Foreign Language are employed in independent universities, language schools, colleges of further education and adult education institutes. MEI-RELSA (107 South Circular Road, Dublin 8; ☎ 01-475 3122; fax 01-475 3088; www.mei.ie), the Recognised English Language Schools Association, is the trade and marketing body of the EFL industry in Ireland. The Advisory Council for English Language Schools (44 Leeson Place, Dublin 2; ☎ 01-676 7374; fax 01-676 3321; www.acels.ie) controls standards in EFL schools and organisations through an inspection and recognition scheme and holds a list of approved TEFL courses in Ireland together with a list of teaching organisations recognised by the Department of Education and Science. There is also a useful forum for EFL teachers in Ireland, which has a webpage at http://homepage.eircom.net/ciaranmac19/. Pay rates for TEFL teachers vary with the majority earning around €15-€21 per hour.

University posts for assistant lecturers and lecturers are advertised in the national press and subject to open competition. The number of posts for associate professor and professor are more limited. There is no specific time of year when recruitment takes place for such positions and the number of vacancies in any specific area of study is unpredictable. Temporary posts often arise when members of staff take sabbaticals. Pay for lecturers varies depending on the educational sector and type of educational establishment they work in – assistant lecturers earn around €28,000 to €35,00 per year; a lecturer earns around €38,000 to €60,000 per year.

COMPUTERS & IT

After North America Ireland is the second largest exporter of software in the world. Microsoft, Oracle, and Sun Microsystems have established operations in Ireland, as well as bluechip hardware manufacturers such as Dell, IBM, Gateway and Intel. IT job vacancies can be found in newspapers, trade magazines and the FÁS Employment Services Offices throughout the country, and on Internet recruitment sites and the websites of ITC companies.

Due to the nature of the work in the IT and computing sector there are also employment possibilities outside the larger cities and main areas of population as even in the remoter areas you will come across small businesses who need IT consultants and support staff. Software development companies are, increasingly, setting up operations outside the environs of Dublin. People who know how to fix, install and network computers will, like mechanics, always be in demand and can charge a premium for their (to many of us) esoteric knowledge.

Many people with sufficient industry knowledge and experience decide to enter the employment market as contractors, which can be very beneficial in terms of the variety of jobs on offer and of course the remuneration. Because of the short-term nature of contract work most employers pay substantially higher rates to contractors, and once one contract has been completed the contractor is free to take time out or to seek another contract. Contracts can be taken up all over the world and as a self-employed 'sole trader' tax will not be deducted at source, giving you the opportunity to seek ways to earn extra capital from your income. However, there are drawbacks to being self-employed in that you will have to deal with all your own paperwork (or employ an accountant and/or secretary) and you are not entitled to sick pay or holiday pay as you would if employed by a company.

POLICE (*AN GARDA SÍOCHÁNA*)

There are 11,747 members of *An Garda Síochána* ('The Guardians of the Peace') with, in addition, 1,747 civilian support staff. Recruitment takes place as and when necessary and details of recruitment drives are advertised in the national press, on the Garda website, and through the Civil Service and Local Appointments Commissioners.

Recruitment is by means of a three-stage process whereby applicants first of all sit three written exams to test verbal ability and analytical reasoning, together with a job simulation exercise. Those who successfully pass the tests are put forward to a second stage, which includes elements such as a written communication exercise and an interview. Those wishing to apply must be at least 18 years old and have obtained the minimum level of educational attainment required. There is no longer a specific height requirement for police officers, though candidates must pass a physical competency test and a medical examination. Candidates are barred from continuing the recruitment process if they are overweight, have defective hearing or severely defective vision. Candidates do not need to be Irish citizens but will need to have a firm understanding of the Irish language.

The majority of new recruits spend their first three years on normal uniformed policing duties, after which they can apply for any vacancies that arise in specialist areas. A university degree may assist an officer as his or her career develops and a relevant degree may be an advantage in sections dealing with computer crime, fraud and research, among others. There are also additional benefits and allowances for those with certain third-level educational qualifications. A police officer from outside Ireland cannot transfer internally but must go through the normal recruitment procedures. Rates of pay are on a sliding scale, beginning at around €24,000 per annum and increasing with length of service.

TOURISM

The tourism industry is very important to Ireland, with the 7.4 million visitors who visit the island each year bringing in revenue of approximately €3.7 billion. The majority (75%) of visitors to Ireland come from Britain, the USA, Germany and France, with a further 15% coming from Holland, Australia, Italy, Canada, Spain and Belgium. High profile marketing campaigns abroad, together with a nationwide investment in infrastructure, facilities and hotels brought huge increases in visitor numbers (and attendant revenues) during the 1990s. However, numbers of visitors have dipped since the heights of 2000 due to a number of factors including September 11, Foot and Mouth, the wars in Afghanistan and Iraq, inflation and the increasing cost of goods and services in the country. The adoption by Ireland of the euro, with its continuing strength against the dollar and sterling, means that the cost of a holiday in Ireland is not the cheap and cheerful option it once was.

The State's tourism development authority, *Fáilte Ireland*, provides information facilities for those wishing to participate in Ireland's tourism industry, whether through setting up in the accommodation provision business (hostels, B&Bs, hotels, etc) or investing in other businesses that attract and serve visitors to Ireland. During the summer season there remains almost 100% employment for workers in the tourism sector in bars, pubs, hotels and restaurants, with the industry employing around 140,000 people. Increasingly, visitors to Ireland are taking short break holidays (weekends, stag and hen parties, business trips), which mean that attractions and services remain busy for longer periods over the year, with implications for employment prospects. In December 2002 Ireland's Minister for Arts, Sport and Tourism appointed a Tourism Policy Review Group, which aims to double overseas visitor spend to €6 billion over a ten-year period to 2012 and increase visitor numbers to 10 million. Tourism will continue to play a very important role in the Irish economy and there will always be employment opportunities within this sector.

Useful Addresses

Tourism Ireland, Bishops Square, Redmonds Hill, Dublin 2; ☏01-476 3400; www.tourismireland.com.
Fáilte Ireland, Baggot Street Bridge, Dublin 2; ☏01-602 4000; fax 01-855 6821; www.failteireland.ie.

Regional Tourist Boards

Cork Kerry Tourism, Áras Fáilte, Grand Parade, Cork City; ☏021-425 5100; fax 021-425 5199; www.corkkerry.ie.
East Coast & Midlands Tourism, Dublin Road, Mullingar, Co. Westmeath; ☏044-48 650; fax 044-40 413; www.ecoast-midlands.travel.ie.
Ireland West Tourism, Forster Street, Galway; ☏091-537 700; fax 091-537 733; www.irelandwest.ie.
North West Tourism, Temple Street, Sligo; ☏071-61 201; fax 071-60 360; www.irelandnorthwest.ie.
Shannon Region Tourism, Town Centre, Shannon, Co. Clare; ☏061-361 555; fax 061-361 903; www.shannonregiontourism.ie.
South East Tourism, 41 The Quay, Waterford; ☏051-875 823; fax 051-877 388; www.southeastireland.com.

AGRICULTURAL & FISHING

The agri-food industry accounts for over 9.2% of Ireland's GDP, around 8.5% of exports and 10% of total employment (approximately 47,000 people). About 20% of the total area of Ireland is cultivated, with much of the rest let to pasture. The biggest earner for farmers is animal husbandry and dairy farming (accounting for over 50% of Irish food and drink exports); poultry production is also important. Principal field crops are wheat, barley, oats, and potatoes; hay, turnips, sugar beet and mushrooms are also important crops. The industry involves around 140,000 family-run farms (with an average farm size of 32 hectares) and 700 companies.

Currently the fastest growing sector of the agri-food industry is prepared consumer foods (ready meals), which account for 26% of total Irish food and drink exports. Ireland possesses the fastest and longest ready meals production lines in Europe and is one of Europe's leading suppliers of branded pizzas. It is also Europe's leading supplier of pizza cheese.

The Agriculture & Food Development Authority, Teagasc (19 Sandymount Avenue, Ballsbridge, Dublin 4; ☎01-637 6000; fax 01-668 8023; www.teagasc.ie), is the national body responsible for research, advisory and training services for the agriculture and food industry in Ireland. The Authority employs over 1,500 staff at 120 locations throughout Ireland and recruits permanent research staff and contract research scientists, as well as graduates with degrees in disciplines such as IT, nutrition, etc.

For up to the minute news about Irish farming the Irish Farmers' Journal (Irish Farm Centre, Bluebell, Dublin 12; ☎01-419 9504; fax 01-450 0669; www.farmersjournal.ie) is an invaluable publication and also contains classified advertisements. It is available in both print and online editions. Farm Relief Services Network (Derryvale, Roscrea, Co. Tipperary; ☎0505-22100; fax 0505-22088; www.frsnetwork.com) has 22 offices nationwide and provides assistance and personnel to farms in Ireland and also has a general recruitment division.

The fishing industry, which has traditionally been underdeveloped in Ireland, is expanding and the sea fishing industry now employs around 15,000 people. Deep-sea catches include herring, cod, mackerel, whiting, plaice, ray, skate and haddock. Crustaceans, particularly lobsters, crayfish and prawns, and molluscs such as oysters and periwinkles in coastal waters form the bulk of seafood exports. Aquaculture (fish farming) has also expanded, with salmon, trout, eels, mussels, lobsters, clams and scallops being the main species farmed.

Leading ports by value of catch landed include Killybegs, Dunmore East, Howth, Rossaveal and Castletownbere and these ports are therefore the best places to look for work in the industry. Apart from the core activities of sea fishing, aquaculture, processing and marketing, the industry generates additional employment opportunities in transport, equipment supplies, chandlery and net making.

The most significant employment areas in the industry are in seafood processing (especially of shellfish) followed by sea fishing operations. Employment figures in these sectors are fairly similar, though the geographical distribution of those employed in each sector differs enormously. For instance, County Donegal accounts for 61%

of employment in the sea fishing sector, whereas Cork accounts for 41% of employment in the shellfish sector.

The Irish Sea Fisheries Board, *Bord Iascaigh Mhara*, (PO Box 12, Crofton Road, Dun Laoghaire, Co. Dublin; ☎ 01-214 4100; fax 01-214 4254; www.bim.ie) is the Irish State agency with responsibility for developing the Irish Sea Fishing and Aquaculture industries and is a good source of information for those looking to work in the fishing industry.

Despite a reforestation programme aimed at reducing Ireland's dependence on timber imports and providing the raw material for paper mills and related industries, Ireland continues to be one of the least forested countries in Europe. The programme of reforestation has been ongoing over the past seventy years and during the past decade over 12,000 farmers have planted 250,000 hectares of forestry (planting by farmers now accounts for 90% of total afforestation). *Coillte Teoranta* (The Irish Forestry Board, Leeson Lane, Dublin 2; ☎ 01-663 5200; fax 01-678 9527; www.coillte.ie) acquired ownership of the State's forests in 1989 and looks after much of Ireland's forestry and forestry-related businesses and those looking to work in forestry should contact the Board for information on the industry and employment opportunities.

CONSTRUCTION

Around 190,000 people are employed in the construction industry in Ireland (this figure includes on- and off-site personnel) and all sectors of the industry are enjoying slow but steady growth. Tradesmen in the industry (electricians, carpenters, plumbers, painters, plasterers, etc) comprise over 75% of the industry's workforce and enjoy high salaries. However, most of these trades require a four-year, often poorly paid, apprenticeship involving a mixture of on-site training and specialised training courses. Almost 50% of architects in Ireland work on a self-employed basis, while others work for a practice or for the local authorities. Salaries for newly qualified architects are in the region of €25,000-€32,000 per annum. There are employment opportunities within each of the sectors of Main Contracting, Civil Engineers and Consultants, with Main Contracting perhaps the least active of the three. Civil Engineering, in particular, will continue to be quite buoyant due to the large infrastructural projects, such as road and bridge building, which are currently underway in Ireland.

The Expert Group on Future Skills Needs, a unit established by the Irish Government to develop national strategies to tackle the issue of training for business and education in Ireland, published its most recent report in October 2003. This Fourth Report found that project management; construction demolition and waste disposal, environmental management, and safety were all major areas of new and emerging skill needs. Other sectors of the industry generating employment opportunities are plant and equipment handling, prefabrication system building, materials technology, facilities management and energy efficiency services.

There are a number of employment agencies listed in the Golden Pages telephone directory, which specialise in placing professional construction staff and trades people with contractors and builders throughout the Republic and an online recruitment service, Construction Jobs, at www.construction-jobs.ie. Manpower Services (52-54 Grafton Street, Dublin 2; ☎ 01-6444 200; fax 01-6455 299; www.manpower.ie) also places construction personnel and has branches in the main urban centres of Ireland.

An industry magazine, Irish Construction Industry (Commercial Publications, Idrone Mews, 24 Idrone Lane, Blackrock, Co. Dublin; ☎ 01-283 3233; www.irishconstruction.com) contains information, articles and industry news, while CIF, the Construction Industry Federation (Construction House, Canal Road, Dublin 6; ☎ 01-406 6000; fax 01-4966953; www.cif.ie) represents businesses in all areas of the Irish construction industry and advises on training and careers in the construction industry.

THE ENVIRONMENT

Ireland is a beautiful country and its history, culture and landscape are a big draw for visitors for abroad. A number of organisations have been set up to ensure that the landscape and historical treasures are preserved for future generations and though many jobs working with the environment are either in the public sector – working either directly or indirectly with the Department of the Environment, Heritage and Local Government – there are also opportunities in the voluntary sector and with charities and educational trusts. The first stop for anyone looking to work in the environmental sector is ENFO, the national environmental information service set up by the Department of the Environment, Heritage and Local Government to provide information on the environment and sustainable development. ENFO (17 St. Andrew Street, Dublin 2; ☎ 01-888 2001; fax 01-888 3946; www.enfo.ie) has an extensive library open to the public six days a week at its headquarters in Dublin.

There are currently six national parks in Ireland: Killarney National Park in south-west Ireland covers over 10,000 hectares; Burren National Park, centred on the Mullaghmore limestone hills in County Clare covers 1,673 hectares; Connemara National Park encompasses some 2,957 hectares; Glenveagh National Park in north-west Donegal, Ireland's largest national park with a total area of over 16,500 hectares; Wicklow Mountains National Park covering an area of close to 20,000 hectares; and Ireland's newest National Park, Mayo National Park centred on the Nephin Beg mountain range. There are also a number of nature reserves and sites designated for nature conservation throughout Ireland. Dúchas, the Heritage Service, has its offices at 7 Ely Place, Dublin 2 (☎ 01-647 3000; fax 01-662 0283; www.duchas.ie) and through its Education and Visitor Services Division at 6 Ely Place Upper (☎ 01-647 3000) recruits and trains personnel to work in the National Parks. The guide service employs 22 supervisor guides and 20 head guides. In addition, around 300 guides are recruited seasonally. The six national parks are managed by the National Parks and Wildlife Service, a division of the Department of the Environment, Heritage and Local Government. Recruitment for clerical, administration and professional posts in the Department is arranged through the Civil Service Commission, the centralised recruitment and selection body for the Civil Service (see above for contact details).

Ireland's Environmental Protection Agency (EPA) is an independent authority established to protect the environment while ensuring that development is carried out in a sustainable manner. The Agency is divided into four divisions: Corporate Affairs, Environmental Management & Planning, Licensing & Control, and Environmental

Monitoring & Laboratory Services. EPA Headquarters is in Wexford (PO Box 3000, Johnstown Castle Estate, Co. Wexford; ☎ 053-60600; fax 053-60699; www.epa.ie) and there are also regional offices in Castlebar, Cork, Dublin, Kilkenny and Monaghan together with four sub-offices in Athlone, Letterkenny, Limerick and Mallow.

For those interested in becoming involved with volunteer work, Conservation Volunteers Ireland (The Steward's House, Rathfarnham Castle, Dublin 14; ☎ 01-495 2878; fax 01-495 2879; www.cvi.ie) organises projects, training courses and education to groups and individuals and offers opportunities to volunteers who wish to work in Ireland on projects protecting the island's natural and cultural heritage. The Irish Wildlife Trust (21 Northumberland Road, Dublin 4; ☎ 01-660 4530; fax 01-660 4571; www.iwt.ie) works to conserve Ireland's wildlife and habitats through various programmes campaigning and lobbying at both an international and local level, and working in co-operation with other environmental organisations. Through its volunteer arm, Groundwork (www.groundwork.ie), based at its Northumberland Road headquarters, the Trust organises summer work camps in Ireland's national parks.

TEMPORARY & SEASONAL WORK

TOURISM

Tourism in Ireland had for many years been a growth industry, but within the last few years there has been a dramatic drop in numbers. A survey of 767 tourism establishments by the Irish Tourist Board, *Bord Fáilte*, found that by the middle of June 2003 around 55% of hotel owners, 71% of B&Bs, 50% of caravan sites, and 49% of hostels had experienced a drop in custom from the previous year. Although the scarcity of Americans taking holidays abroad due to fears of the terrorist threat since September 11th 2001 will have heavily contributed to these figures, the replacement of the Irish Punt with the Euro as the nation's currency in January 2002 and the attendant rise in prices has also kept away visitors from Europe. Those living in the eurozone can now make immediate comparisons of the cost of living and many have decided to spend their holidays somewhere less expensive. That said, tourism is still big business in Ireland, especially in County Cork and County Kerry, and it is an industry that provides many temporary and seasonal jobs. Hotels, bars and restaurants need temporary workers over the summer period, especially in the areas that experience high numbers of tourists. Holiday camps, activity centres and theme parks are also fruitful areas for short-term work. Unless an employee can offer a specific skill or qualification (such as those gained by instructors, chefs, etc) wages are not spectacularly high for seasonal staff in such places. The annual publication *Summer Jobs Abroad*, (Vacation Work; www.vacationwork.co.uk), has good listings of seasonal work opportunities in Ireland. The Irish Tourist Board (Fáilte Ireland, Baggot Street Bridge, Dublin 2; ☎01-602 4000; fax 01-855 6821; www.failteireland.ie) can provide a list of hotels to enquirers looking for work in hospitality.

WORKING AS AN AU PAIR

There are a number of au pair and nanny recruitment agencies in Ireland seeking to put au pairs and nannies in touch with families in need of their services. Local and national agencies can be found in the telephone directory service Golden Pages classified under 'Au Pair Agencies' or through a search on the Internet using a search engine such as google.com or a web directory such as yahoo.com. More information on the work permit requirements for au pairs can be found in the *Residence and Regulations* section of this book. *The Au Pair and Nanny's Guide to Working Abroad* by Susan Griffith (Vacation Work; www.vacationwork.co.uk), contains invaluable information for anyone looking to find work in childcare.

AGRICULTURE & FISHING

These days, due to the tightening of the labour laws, potential employers can't even consider hiring seasonal workers without knowing that they qualify to work legally in the country and have the correct documentation and a work permit. For those looking to find casual work fruit picking, the bad news is that it is not possible to arrange a work permit for such work, although those from EU member states do not need a permit to work in Ireland.

For those who can work legally in Ireland there are opportunities for fruit picking on farms. Basic free accommodation may be provided and wages will depend on the ability and experience of the picker. Expect to work hard for your money, and expect to work a six-day week. Most fruit pickers are paid piecework, which means that they are paid by how much fruit they pick. Faster workers can earn a lot more money.

Because of the relatively small size of farms in Ireland and the need by many a farming household to come by part of its annual income by engaging in work outside of agriculture, work on farms is hard to come by. However, opportunities do come about, and are often best found by asking around locally. The type of work available will depend on the time of year and the type of crop grown.

There are two agencies that help to place people keen to work on organic farms with farmers and growers in Ireland. WWOOF (Willing Workers On Organic Farms) organises work stays on over 70 organic farms and smallholdings in Ireland. A current list of WWOOF smallholdings in Ireland can be obtained by writing to WWOOF, Harpoonstown, Drinagh, Co. Wexford. Another organisation offering a similar experience is the Irish Organic Farmers and Growers Association (Harbour Building, Harbour Road, Kilbeggan, Co. Westmeath; ☎ 0506-32563; fax 0506-32063; www.irishorganic.ie), which holds a placement list of farms willing to offer work experience to those interested in learning about organic farming. In both cases, food and accommodation, and occasionally pocket money, is provided by the host family in return for help on the smallholding.

The western seaboard of Ireland, from Donegal to west Cork, is the location for 75% of all seafood industry but this region is also one the poorest in the country. Seasonal jobs do exist in the fishing industry, but the vast majority will be taken by locals.

SECRETARIAL & CLERICAL

Temporary clerical and secretarial work can be found throughout the year through employment agencies (listings in the Golden Pages).

Agencies will generally require staff to be available to work at short notice in order to provide cover for employees on sick leave, holidays, etc. It is a good idea to register your services with as many agencies as you can. Once you have been on a few assignments for an agency and they have taken stock of you, you will be given more regular work. Earnings can be good and the more skills you can offer, the better the hourly rate you can command. Agencies tend to prefer to take on women rather than men. Good word processing and typing skills are required for many clerical and, above all, secretarial jobs. Fluency in a second language is also very useful.

TRAINING, WORK EXPERIENCE & EXCHANGE SCHEMES

There are several organisations that offer training and work experience schemes within Ireland to foreign nationals and a selection of the larger concerns are listed below. Although some of these organisations have age restrictions, many do not, and some can arrange work permits and sort out the necessary red tape if the need arises. Another national organisation that can provide information and place volunteers is Volunteering Ireland, an independent, not-for-profit establishment that matches individuals who wish to volunteer with organisations in Ireland that offer suitable opportunities. Volunteering Ireland has its headquarter in Coleraine House, Coleraine Street, Dublin 7 (☎01-872 2622; fax 01-872 2623; www.volunteeringireland.com) where there is also a volunteer resources centre and a reference library that can be viewed by appointment. Also in Dublin, the Community and Youth Information Centre of Dublin City Council on Sackville Place, Dublin 2 (☎01-878 6844; www.dublincity.ie) has a voluntary work notice board and produces a concise guide to voluntary work opportunities in Ireland.

BUNAC

The British Universities North America Club (BUNAC) runs a programme authorized by the Irish government to allow US students to travel and work in Ireland for a period of up to four months. The sponsor in Ireland is USIT; the programme is administered in the USA by BUNAC.

BUNAC USA, PO Box 430, Southbury, CT 06488; ☎(203) 264-0901; fax (203) 264-0251; www.bunac.org.

USIT NY, New York Student Centre, 895 Amsterdam Avenue, New York NY10025; ☎(212) 663 5435; www.usit.ie.

CIEE

The Council on International Educational Exchange (CIEE) run a similar scheme to BUNAC, offering a four-month programme for US citizens or permanent US residents who are full-time college/university students, or graduates (who must apply for the scheme within six months of graduating). Contact CIEE at 7 Custom House Street, Floor 3 Portland ME 04101; ☎1-800-407-8839; www.ciee.org.

SWAP

Canadians who are full-time post-secondary students and/or graduates of the year in which they apply for the scheme have an option to take part in a one-year Irish work visa for students (you can choose the date the visa begins) or one-year Irish work visa for non-students (in which case the visa begins on the date of issue in Canada). There is a minimum age limit of eighteen, though no upper age limit. Contact Travel-cuts SWAP Ireland, at Suite 100, 45 Charles Street East, Toronto, ON M4Y 1S2; ☎(416) 966 2887; www.swap.ca.

i-i

Another possibility for those looking to stay in Ireland on a programme of study or on an internship, is to book a place on an i-to-i Venture Placement. i-to-i runs placements in 25 countries across the globe, including Ireland and volunteers can become involved in teaching, building, health, media, conservation work and community development projects. Placements run from four to twenty four weeks and are open to everyone aged 18 to 70. Volunteers are charged a fee to participate.

i-to-i Ireland, Exploration House, 26 Main Street, Dungarvan, Co. Waterford; ☎058-40050; fax 058-40059; www.i-to-i.com.

i-to-i North America, 190 E. 9th Ave, Suite 320, Denver, CO 80203; ☎(303) 765-5325; fax (303) 765-5327; www.i-to-i.com.

i-to-i UK, Woodside House, 261 Low Lane, Leeds LS18 5NY; ☎0113-205 4620; fax 0113-205 4619; www.i-to-i.com.

Sources of Advice

A number of books are available which detail opportunities for temporary and casual work, internships and volunteer placements in many countries worldwide, including Ireland. Vacation Work publish a large selection of such books including *The Directory of Jobs and Careers Abroad, Green Volunteers, Taking a Gap Year, Teaching English Abroad, The Au Pair and Nanny's Guide to Working Abroad, Summer Jobs Abroad, The International Directory of Voluntary Work, Working in Tourism* and *Working with the Environment*. The Vacation Work website (www.vacationwork.co.uk) also has a good links page to a variety of organisations dealing in work and travel abroad.

BUSINESS & INDUSTRY REPORT

Despite the deceleration in the growth of Ireland's economy over the first few years of the 21st century, it is still growing at a rate faster than that of most other EU member states. On a per capita basis Ireland, at €33,000 per person, has the highest rate in the EU after Luxembourg. Gross National Product (GNP) has almost doubled since 1992 and unemployment has fallen from 15.7% to 4.9%. This is economic growth on a massive scale in so short a period, especially when you consider that in 1973, when Ireland joined the EEC, it was the poorest member of that Community.

Reversing years of population decline, Irelands population today of around 4 million is at the highest level it has been for 130 years and with an annual increase of 1.3% over the years 1996-2002 Ireland had the fastest rate of growth in the whole of the EU. In addition, Ireland has the second highest proportion of its population under the age of 15 in Europe (after Iceland) and the lowest proportion of under 65s.

During the period 1991-2000 productivity growth in manufacturing averaged 8% annually (the EU average was 1.6%; the USA average was 4.3%); while 85% of products manufactured in Ireland are exported. Export growth has played a key role in Ireland economic boom, accounting for almost half of the country's annual economic growth. According to World Trade Organisation statistics for the year 2001 Ireland was the world's third largest merchandise exporter on a per capita basis after Singapore and Hong Kong. Much of this manufacturing industry is foreign-owned, and is based around high technology products – computer giants Microsoft, Dell and Intel all have operations in Ireland – which has led to the creation of a more export orientated and highly skilled industry sector specialising in electronics, healthcare and pharmaceuticals. The services sector has tended to concentrate on telemarketing, software development, and financial and corporate services.

The Irish government has liberalised the telecommunications market and invested in Broadband Internet Technology and as a result Ireland has the most e-commerce-friendly regulatory environment in Europe. It is hoped that the country will become a, if not the, major eBusiness hub in Europe.

Ireland has become a truly global economy and a recent report by the Global Entrepreneurial Monitor (GEM), a research program that annually assesses levels of entrepreneurial activity around the world, rated Ireland as one of the best countries in the world in which to establish a business, along with the USA, and ahead of the UK, France and Germany.

Useful Addresses

Enterprise Ireland, Glasnevin, Dublin 9, Ireland; ☎01-808 2000; ☎01-808 2020; www.enterprise-ireland.com.

Arthur M. Blank Center for Entrepreneurship, Babson College, Babson Park, MA, 02457-0310, USA; ☎+1 781 239 4420; www.gemconsortium.org.

World Trade Organization, Centre William Rappard, Rue de Lausanne 154, CH-1211, Geneva 21, Switzerland; ☎(41-22) 739 51 11; fax (41-22) 731 42 06; www.wto.org.

REGIONAL EMPLOYMENT GUIDE

Traditionally, Ireland is a country of 32 counties within the four provinces of Connaught, Munster, Leinster and Ulster. The Republic is made up of 26 counties; the other six are located in Northern Ireland. Under the provisions of the Local Government Act, eight Regional Authorities were established in Ireland, which has changed the traditional boundaries somewhat and, in addition, regionalisation arrangements for government structural funding purposes has resulted in a further demarcation of the country into two regions. What follows is a breakdown of employment information by county.

PROVINCE: CONNAUGHT

County Galway

Local Authority: *Galway County Council*, County Buildings, Prospect Hill, Galway; ☎091-509 000; www.galway.ie.

Chamber of Commerce: *Galway Chamber of Commerce and Industry*, Commerce House, Merchant's Road, Galway; ☎091-563536; fax 091-561963; www.galwaychamber.com.

FÁS Office: FAS Island House, Cathedral Square, Galway; ☎091-534400; fax 091-562718.

Regional Newspapers: *The Galway Advertiser*, 41/42 Eyre Square, Galway; ☎091-530900; 091-567079; www.galwayadvertiser.ie. *Galway Independent*, Prospect House, Prospect Hill, Galway; ☎091-569000; fax 091-569333; www.galwayindependent.com. *The Galway Advertiser*, 41/42 Eyre Square, Galway; ☎091-530900; fax 091-567079; www.galwayadvertiser.ie. *The Tuam Herald*, Dublin Road, Tuam; ☎093 24183; fax 093 24478; www.tuamherald.ie.

Industry: Agriculture, tourism, IT, manufacturing and services are the main economic activities of the county. Manufacturing – of computer software and healthcare products – together with food production and telecommunications play an increasingly important role in the county's employment sector. Galway City is the business centre of the county.

County Leitrim

Local Authority: *Leitrim County Council*, Carrick-on-Shannon, Co. Leitrim; ☎071-962 0005; fax 071-962 1982; www.leitrimcoco.ie.

Chamber of Commerce: *Carrick-on-Shannon Chamber of Commerce and Industry*, Main Street, Carrick-on-Shannon; ☎078-59500; fax 078-59503; www.carrickonshannon.ie.

FÁS Office: Government Buildings, Shannon Lodge, Carrick-on-Shannon; ☎078-20503; fax 078-20505.

Regional Newspaper: *Leitrim Observer*, St.Georges Terrace, Carrick-on-Shannon; ☎071-96 20025; fax 071-96 20112; www.leitrimobserver.ie.

Industry: Marginal agricultural land is being given over to forestry to support the sawmilling industry and manufacturers of furniture and other timber products in the county. Organic farming, of vegetables and meat, is increasingly being practised. Light engineering, food production and IT are all areas of employment in the county. Masonite, the US moulded door facings company, has built their 75-acre, 138 million dollar European plant near Carrick-on-Shannon.

County Mayo

Local Authority: *Mayo County Council*, Áras an Chontae, The Mall, Castlebar, Co.Mayo; ☎094-902 4444; www.mayococo.ie.

Chambers of Commerce: *Ballina Chamber of Commerce*, Moy Valley Business Centre, Cathedral Road, Ballina; ☎096-72800; fax 096-72801; www.ballinachamber.com. *Castlebar Chamber of Commerce*, Spencer Street, Castlebar; ☎094-24845; fax 094-24971; www.castlebar.ie. *Erris Chamber of Commerce*, Main Street, Belmullet; ☎097-20977. *Westport Chamber of Commerce and Industry*, Bridge Street, Westport; ☎098-27375; fax 098-27916; www.westportireland.com.

FÁS Offices: Unit 7 & 8, Humbert Mall, Main Street, Castlebar; ☎094-34300; fax 094-22832.

Riverside, Church Road, Ballina; ☎096-24017; fax 096-70608.

Regional Newspaper: *The Mayo News*, The Fairgreen, Westport; ☎098-25311; fax 098-26108; www.mayonews.ie.

Industry: Agriculture – dairy, beef and sheep farming – is still the main source of employment in the county. The tourism industry also provides employment and there may be employment opportunities in manufacturing and engineering.

County Roscommon

Local Authority: *Roscommon County Council*, The Courthouse, Co. Roscommon; ☎090-663 7100; Fax: 090-663 7108; www.roscommoncoco.ie.

Chamber of Commerce: *Roscommon Chamber of Commerce*, The Square, Roscommon; ☎0903-26171; fax 0903-26954.

FÁS Office: Lanesboro Street, Roscommon, ☎0903-26802; fax 0903-25399.

Regional Newspapers: *Roscommon Herald*, St. Patrick's Street, Boyle; ☎071-9662004; fax 071-9662926; roscommonherald.ie. *Roscommon Champion*, Abbey Street, Roscommon; ☎090-66 25051; fax 090-66 25053.

Industry: Farming accounts for 30% of employment in the county. Farming related industries such as bacon production, dairy production, poultry and meat products provide further employment opportunities together with agricultural, commercial and industrial engineering. Tourism is not yet a major industry for the county.

County Sligo

Local Authority: *Sligo County Council,* County Hall, Riverside, Sligo, Co. Sligo; ☎071-915 6666; fax 071-914 1119; www.sligococo.ie.

Chamber of Commerce: *Sligo Chamber of Commerce and Industry,* 16 Quay Street, Sligo; ☎071-9161274; fax 071 9160912; www.sligochamber.ie.

FÁS Office: Government Buildings, Cranmore, Sligo; ☎071-43 390; fax 071- 44120.

Regional Newspapers: *Sligo Champion*, Wine Street, Sligo; ☎071-9169222; fax 071-9169140; www.sligochampion.ie. *Sligo Weekender*, Waterfront House, Bridge Street, Sligo; ☎071-9174912; fax 071-9142255; www.sligoweekender.ie.

Industry: The county is noted for its precision engineering, tool making and design. Multinational companies such as the Korean videotape manufacturer Saehan Media, German precision rubber formparts producer Bruss GMBH and the US pharmaceutical company, Abbot Laboratories all have plants in the Sligo. The county produces beef and dairy products.

PROVINCE: MUNSTER

County Clare

Local Authority: *Clare County Council*, New Road, Ennis, Co. Clare; ☎065-682 1616; fax 065-682 8233; www.clare.ie.
Chambers of Commerce: *Ennis Chamber of Commerce,* 54 O' Connell Street, Ennis; ☎065-6842988; fax 065-6821544; www.ennischamber.ie. *Shannon Chamber of Commerce,* Town Centre, Shannon; ☎061-360611; www.shannonchamber.com.
FÁS Offices: 42 Parnell Street, Ennis; ☎065-6829213; fax 065 6828502. *FÁS Training Centre*, Shannon Industrial Estate, Shannon; ☎061-471133; fax 053-23177.
Regional Newspaper: *The Clare Champion*, Barrack Street, Ennis; ☎065 682 8105; fax 065 682 0374; www.clarechampion.ie.
Industry: Agriculture, especially dairy and beef farming, with a smaller emphasis on organic and market gardening, is a big feature of County Clare. Tourism is also a major employer. The Shannon Free Zone, Ireland's premier industrial park located at Shannon Airport, is home to over 100 international companies employing over 7,500 people. Manufacturers of healthcare products, electronics firms, food producers and engineering companies are all important employers in the county.

County Cork

Local Authority: *Cork County Council*, County Hall, Cork City, Co. Cork; ☎021-427 6891; fax 021-4276321; www.corkcoco.ie.
Chambers of Commerce: *Bantry and District Chamber of Commerce Ltd.,* Reenrour, Bantry; ☎027-50346; fax 027-51065. *Cork*

Chamber of Commerce, Fitzgerald House, Summerhill North, Cork; ☎021-4509044; fax 021-4508568; www.corkchamber.ie.

FÁS Offices: Government Buildings, Sullivan's Quay, Cork; ☎021-4856200; fax 021-4968389. Warner Centre, Barrack Street, Bantry; ☎027-50 464; fax 027-50203.

Regional Newspapers: *The Corkman,* 5 Chapel Lane, Mallow; ☎022 42394; fax 022 43183; www.corkman.ie. *The Southern Star*, Ilen Street, Skibbereen; ☎028 21200; fax 028 21071; www.southernstar.ie.

Industry: The principal industries of the county are agriculture, forestry and tourism. The larger towns also support tourism, food production and brewing, engineering, chemical production and shipping. The economic boom of the 1990s brought great prosperity to the county and outside Dublin, Cork offers the best opportunities for employment and businesses.

County Kerry

Local Authority: *Kerry County Council,* Rathass, Tralee, Co. Kerry; ☎066-712 1111; fax 066-712 9764; www.kerrycoco.ie.

Chambers of Commerce: *Killarney Chamber of Commerce and Tourism,* 2nd Floor, Tourist Information Office, Beech Road, Killarney; ☎064-37928; fax 064-36623; www.killarney-chamber.com. *Tralee Chamber of Commerce,* 20 Denny Street, Tralee; ☎066-7121472; fax 066-7128608.

FÁS Offices: Unit 1, Kenmare Place, Killarney; ☎064-32466; fax 064-32759. 17 Lower Castle Street, Tralee; ☎066-7123065; fax 066-7122954.

Regional Newspapers: *The Kerryman,* Clash, Tralee; ☎066 714 5500; fax 066 714 5570; www.kerryman.ie. *Kerry's Eye,* 22 Ashe Street, Tralee; ☎066 714 9200; fax 066 712 3163; www.kerryseye.com.

Industry: Agriculture (dairy and sheep) and the food production industry employs around 25% of the county's labour force and is the county's largest income generator. Fishing, aquaculture and forestry are also important employment sectors, as is the building and construction industry, electricity and gas providers and mining. Tourism is a major source of revenue, business opportunities and employment for the county. The service industry – restaurants, shops, accommodation provision, leisure centres and specialist tourist attractions – is a growing sector for the county.

County Limerick

Local Authority: *Limerick County Council,* County Hall, Dooradoyle, Limerick City, Co. Limerick; ☎061-496 000; fax 061-496 001; www.limerickcoco.ie.
Chamber of Commerce: *Limerick Chamber of Commerce,* 96 O' Connell Street, Limerick; ☎061-415180; fax 061-415785; www.limchamber.ie.
FÁS Office: 18 Davis Street, Limerick; ☎061-487915; fax 061-412326.
Regional Newspapers: *Limerick Chronicle,* 54 O'Connell Street, Limerick; ☎061 214500; fax 061 401422. *Limerick Leader,* 54 O'Connell Street, Limerick; ☎061 214500; fax 061 401422.
Industry: The IDA National Technological Park in Limerick is the location for over 90 businesses, including Dell Computers, Johnson & Johnson, Cabletron Systems and Vistakon, employing over 3,000 people. In addition, dairy, beef and poultry farming, mushroom growing and forestry are all important employers in the county. Other important industries include engineering, aluminium production, electronics and tourism.

County Tipperary

Local Authority: *North Tipperary County Council,* Courthouse, Nenagh, Co.Tipperary; ☎067-44500; www.tipperarynorth.ie. *South Tipperary County Council,* County Hall, Emmet Street, Clonmel; ☎052-34455; fax 052-25173; southtippcoco.ie.
Chambers of Commerce: *Clonmel Chamber of Commerce,* 8 Sarsfield Street, Clonmel; ☎052-26500; fax 052-26378; www.clonmel.ie. *Nenagh Chamber of Commerce,* 94 Silver Street, Nenagh; ☎067-34900; fax 067-34088; www.nenagh.net.
Thurles Chamber of Commerce*,* 1st Floor, Lar Na Pairce, Slievenamon Road, Turles; ☎0504-23407; fax 0504-20179;

www.thurleschamber.com.

FÁS Offices: 6 Mary Street, Clonmel; ☎052-24422; fax 052-24565. 79 Connolly Street, Nenagh; ☎067-31879; fax 067-31167.

Regional Newspaper: *Tipperary Star*, Friar Street, Thurles; ☎0504 21122; fax 0504 21110; www. tipperarystar.ie.

Industry: Arable and dairy farming have traditionally been the principle industries of South Tipperary, which have been augmented with the manufacturing of food and beverages, healthcare products, electronics and pharmaceuticals. The tourism industry also employs a significant number of people throughout the county.

County Waterford

Local Authority: *Waterford County Council*, Civic Offices, Dungarvan, Co. Waterford; ☎058-22000; fax 058-42911; www.waterfordcoco.ie.

Chambers of Commerce: *Dungarvan and West Waterford Chamber of Commerce*, The Courthouse, Dungarvan; ☎058-45054; fax 058-45622; www.dungarvanchamber.com. *Waterford Chamber of Commerce*, George's Street, Waterford; ☎051-872639; fax 051-876002; www.waterfordchamber.ie.

FÁS Office: 56 Parnell Street, Waterford; ☎051-862900; fax 051-862916.

Regional Newspaper: *Waterford News & Star*, 25 Michael Street, Waterford; ☎051-874 951; fax 051-855281; www.waterfordnews.ie.

Industry: Bausch & Lomb, Allied Signal, Smithkline Beecham, and Hasbro all have operations in Waterford. The world famous Waterford Crystal employs over 1600 people. Engineering, the manufacturing of construction materials and components and dairy, arable and poultry farming are all prominent employers in the county. The more urban areas of Waterford have highly developed retail and business services sectors. Waterford has very good port and shipping facilities.

PROVINCE: LEINSTER

County Carlow

Local Authority: *Carlow County Council*, County Offices, Athy Road, Carlow City, Co. Carlow; ☎0503-70300; fax 0503-41503; www.carlow.ie.

Chamber of Commerce: *County Carlow Chamber of Commerce*, Upper Floor, Haddens Centre, Tullow Street, Carlow; ☎0503-32337; fax 0503-30625; www.carlowchamber.com.

FÁS Office: Carlow Shopping Centre, Kennedy Avenue, Carlow; ☎0503-42605; fax 0503-41759.

Regional Newspaper: *Carlow People*, Rowe Street, Wexford; ☎053 40100; fax 053 40191/2; www.peoplenews.ie.

Industry: Major employers in the county include Braun Ireland Ltd and the precision engineering firm, Lapple Ireland Ltd. A number of companies – both international and local – all have operations producing food, electronics, computers, IT solutions and crafts in the county. Agriculture remains the most important sector in the county and farms produce cereal crops and sugar beet as well as dairy products, beef, lamb and wool.

County Dublin

Local Authorities: *South Dublin County Council*, Town Centre, Tallaght, Dublin 24; ☎01-414 9217; fax 01-414 9110; www.sdcc.ie. *Fingal County Council*, County Hall, Main Street, Swords, Fingal, Co. Dublin; ☎01-890 5650; fax 01-890 5669; www.fingalcoco.ie. *Dun Laoghaire Rathdown*, County Hall, Marine Road, Dun Laoghaire, Co. Dublin; ☎01-205 4700; fax 01-230 0299; www.dlrcoco.ie. *Dublin Regional Authority*, 11 Parnell Square, Dublin 1; ☎01-874 5018; fax 01-8788080; www.dra.ie.

Chambers of Commerce: *Dublin Chamber of Commerce*, 7 Clare Street, Dublin 2; ☎01-6447200; fax 01-6766043; www.dublinchamber.ie. *Dun Laoghaire Rathdown Chamber of Commerce*, Kilcullen House, 1 Haigh Terrace, Dun Laoghaire, Co. Dublin; ☎01-2845066; fax 01-2845034; www.dlrchamber.ie. *South Dublin Chamber of Commerce*,

Tallaght Business Centre, Whitestown Business Park, Tallaght, Dublin 24; ☎01-4622107; fax 01-4599512; www.sdchamber.ie. *Swords Fingal Chamber of Commerce,* Albany House, Main Street, Swords, Co. Dublin; ☎01-8900977; fax 01-8900990; www.swordschamber.ie.

FÁS Offices: 27/33 Upper Baggot Street, Dublin 4; ☎01-6070500; fax 01-6070611. 18/21 Cumberland Street, Dun Laoghaire, Co. Dublin; ☎01-2808488; fax 01-2808476. 34 Main Street, Swords, Co. Dublin; ☎01-8405252; fax 01-8403751. Social Services Centre, Square Complex, Tallaght, Dublin 24; ☎01-4525111; fax 01-452 5591.

Regional Newspapers: *Evening Herald*, 90 Middle Abbey Street, Dublin 1; ☎01-705 5416. *Northside People/Southside People/Dublin Advertiser*, The Dublin People Group, 85-86 Omni Park, Santry, Dublin 9; www.dublinpeople.com. *The Fingal Independent*, Main Street, Swords; ☎01-840 7107; fax 01-840 0682; www.fingal-independent.ie. *The Echo,* Village Green, Tallaght, Dublin 24; ☎0459-8513; fax 0459-8514; www.tallaght.com/theecho.

Industry: Dublin has been the most effected by the boom of the1990s and is home to the headquarters of Ireland's largest financial and business institutions. Dublin offers the most possibilities for employment and businesses. The city is home to international financial, eBusiness and IT companies such as Citibank, Hertz, Hewlett-Packard, IBM, Intel, Microsoft, Xerox, etc., and is rated as a world-class technology location. Irish software companies such as Iona Technologies, Baltimore Technologies and Smart Force also have operations in Dublin. Dublin port, with regular scheduled services to Britain and mainland Europe, is Ireland's major port and caters for container and roll-on/roll-off cargo.

County Kildare

Local Authority: *Kildare County Council*, St. Mary's, Naas, Co. Kildare; ☎045-873 800; fax 045-876 875; www.kildare.ie.

Chambers of Commerce: *Athy Chamber of Commerce,* c/o Duke Street, Athy; ☎059-8631663. *Naas Chamber of Commerce,* 32 North Main Street, Naas; ☎045-894074; fax 045-897060.

FÁS Office: Georges Street, Newbridge; ☎045-431372; fax 045-434446.

Regional Newspaper: *Leinster Leader*, 19 South Main Street, Naas; ☎045 897302; fax 045 897647; www.leinster-leader.ie.

Industry: Home to more than 100 stud farms County Kildare is central to Ireland's blood stock industry, which employs around 5,000 people. Computer software companies and those involved in the IT industry are major employers of the county. Intel Ireland employs over 4,000 at its Collinstown Industrial Park site in Leixlip and Hewlett-Packard employ arounds 1,500 people. Telemecanique Ltd., AHP Manufacturing and Oral-B Laboratories all have important European operations based in Kildare.

County Kilkenny

Local Authority: *Kilkenny County Council*, County Hall, John Street, Kilkenny City, Co. Kilkenny; ☎056-779 4000; fax 056-779 4004; www.kilkennycoco.ie.

Chamber of Commerce: *Kilkenny Chamber of Commerce and Industry*, Lower Walkin Street, Kilkenny City; ☎056-52767; fax 056-56379; www.kilkennychamber.ie.

FÁS Office: Irishtown, Co. Kilkenny; ☎056-65514; fax 056-64451.

Regional Newspaper: *Kilkenny People*, 34 High Street, Kilkenny; ☎056 77 21015; fax 056 77 21414; www.kilkenny-people.ie.

Industry: Agri-business is a major industry and employer in Kilkenny with one of the world's largest cheese manufacturers, Glanbia plc, basing its headquarters in the county. It is good farming country – arable, sugarbeet and beef and dairy are important to the county and food processing is the main industry. Budweiser and Kilkenny beer are brewed by Guinness in the county. Kilkenny is also the home to a large number of engineering firms including Duggan Steel and NN Ball and Roller. County Kilkenny is also well-known for its thriving craft industry and there are approximately 60 craft-related businesses operating in the county. Financial services companies are also important employers in the county.

County Laois

Local Authority: *Laois County Council*, Áras an Chontae, Portlaoise, Co. Laois; ☎0502-640 00; fax 502 22 313; www.laois.ie.
Chamber of Commerce: *Laois Chamber of Commerce Ltd.*, Coliseum Lane, Portlaoise; ☎0502-21598; fax 0502-63452; www.laoischamber.ie.
FÁS Office: 4 Meehan House, James Fintan Lawlor Avenue, Portlaoise; ☎0502-21462; fax 0502-20945.
Regional Newspaper: *The Laois Nationalist*, Coliseum Lane, Portlaoise; ☎0502–60265; fax 0502-61399; www.laois-nationalist.ie.
Industry: The county has an agricultural-based economy from which has grown a fair-sized food industry producing beverages, bread and confectionery. The manufacturing industry in Laois is small. Employment opportunities exist in the public sector and in the telecommunications industry. Existing national/international companies in the county include Tretorn Sports Ltd, DIS Enbi Seals, ICM UniComp, and ebm Industries.

County Longford

Local Authority: *Longford County Council*, Great Water Street, Longford; ☎043-46231; fax 043-41233; www.longfordcoco.ie.
Chamber of Commerce: *Longford Chamber of Commerce and Industry*, Harbour House, Longford; ☎043-45829; fax 043-47455; www.longford-chamber.com.
FÁS Office: 7 Market Square, Longford; ☎043-46820; fax 043-45702.
Regional Newspapers: *Longford Leader*, Leader House, Dublin Road, Longford; ☎043 45241/41488; fax 043 41489; www.longford-leader.ie.
Longford News, Earl Street, Longford; ☎043 41147; fax 043 41549.
Industry: The services sector and food and textiles manufacturing industries are very important to the county's economy and employ much of the available workforce. In addition, Longford is home to a number of engineering firms and is the location for a number of inter-

national companies such as Cameron Ireland Ltd., Cardinal Health, Donnelly Electronics, Triad Systems and Wessel Cable. One of the world's largest healthcare companies, Abbott Laboratories, is opening a site in Longford in 2004 which is expected to create 950 new jobs, mainly at graduate level, over the next five years.

County Louth

Local Authority: *Louth County Council*, County Hall, Millennium Centre, Dundalk, Co. Louth; ☎042-933 5457; fax 042-933 4549; www.louthcoco.ie.

Chambers of Commerce: *Drogheda Chamber of Commerce,* Chamber Buildings, 10 Dublin Road, Drogheda; ☎041-9833544; fax 041-9841609; www.droghedachamber.com. *Dundalk Chamber of Commerce*, Hagan House, Ramparts Road, Dundalk; ☎042-9336343; fax 042-9332085; www.dundalk.ie.

FÁS Office: 79 Park Street, Dundalk; ☎042-9331608; fax 042-9336311.

Regional Newspaper: *Dundalk Argus*, Park Street, Dundalk; ☎042 933 4632; fax 042 933 1643; www.argus.ie.

Industry: County Louth is fast becoming one of Ireland's principal industrial centres, situated as it is on the busiest economic corridor in Ireland. Additionally, the proximity of deep-sea ports continues to attract new growth in the engineering and IT sectors. Dundalk is one of the largest urban centres in Ireland and, according to the IDA, primed to become Ireland's first new city of the 21st century. The county is the home of international companies such as Quantum, Littelfuse (General Electric), Heinz 57, Guinness Group (DIAGEO), ABB, and more recently Xerox. Drogheda is Ireland's largest provincial town and some of the best-known international brand leaders including Coca-Cola, Brother, and Becton Dickinson have operations there.

County Meath

Local Authority: *Meath County Council*, County Hall, Navan. Co. Meath; ☎046-902 1581; www.meath.ie.

Chambers of Commerce: *Kells Chamber of Commerce,* Maudlin

Street, Kells; ☎046-40055; www.kellschamber.ie. *Navan Chamber of Commerce,* Church Hill, Navan; ☎046-23330; fax 046-72873; www.navanchamber.com.

FÁS Office: Tara Mall, Trimgate Street, Navan; ☎046-23630; fax 046-21903.

Regional Newspaper: *Meath Chronicle,* Market Square, Navan; ☎046 90 21442; fax 046 90 23565; www.meath-chronicle.ie.

Industry: County Meath, with its proximity to the employment opportunities in Dublin, is Ireland's fastest growing county and Navan is Ireland's fastest growing town. Farming and agri-business are large employers in the county as is manufacturing and engineering. New companies to base operations in the county include General Insurance, Europ Assist and the US company Pemstar Electronics.

County Offaly

Local Authority: *Áras an Chontae,* Charleville Road, Tullamore, Co. Offaly; ☎0506-46800; fax 0506-46868; www.offaly.ie.

Chamber of Commerce: *Tullamore and District Chamber of Commerce,* Esker House, Patrick Street, Tullamore; ☎0506-23698; fax 0506-23258; www.tullamorechamber.com.

FÁS Office: Church Street, Tullamore; ☎0506-51176; fax 0506-21964.

Regional Newspapers: *The Offaly Independent,* Hayden House, 19 Dominick Street, Mullingar, Co. Westmeath; ☎044 48426; fax 044 40640. *The Midland Tribune,* Syngfield, Birr; ☎0509-20003; fax 0509-20588. *The Tullamore Tribune,* Church Street, Tullamore; ☎0506 21152; fax 0506-23100; www.tullamoretribune.ie.

Industry: Agriculture – dairy and milk production, beef and sheep – is an important sector of the economy in Offaly. Tullamore town is an important industrial manufacturing and services centre and home to national and international companies such as Tyco Healthcare (the largest employer), Isotron Ireland, Boston Scientific Namic and Sennheiser Ireland. The clothing and textiles industry is also important to the county. The Irish Peat Board (Bord Na Mona) employs over 300 people at its commercial peat plant. Public services, the building and construction and electricity generation are all important sectors in Offaly.

County Westmeath

Local Authority: *Westmeath County Council*, County Buildings, Mullingar, Co. Westmeath; ☎044-40861; fax 044-42330; www.westmeathcoco.ie.

Chambers of Commerce: *Athlone Chamber of Commerce*, Lloyd's Lane, Athlone; ☎090-6473173; fax 090-6473330; www.athlonechamber.ie. *Mullingar Chamber of Commerce*, ACC House, Dominick Street, Mullingar; ☎044-44044; fax 044-44045; www.mullingar-chamber.ie.

FÁS Offices: Townhouse Centre, St. Mary's Square, Athlone; ☎0902-75291; fax 0902-78288.

Church Avenue, Mullingar; ☎044-48805; fax 044-43978.

Regional Newspaper: *The Westmeath Independent*, Irishtown, Athlone; ☎0902 72003; fax 0902 74474; www.westmeathindependent.ie.

Industry: Agriculture is still one of the principle employers in the county with a variety of mixed drystock, tillage and related agri-businesses and meat production. Multinational companies in Westmeath include the Swedish software giant, Ericsson, two medical manufacturers from the US – Utah Medical Products and Mallinckrodt Medical, and Iralco Ltd from Germany. Westmeath has strong industrial bases both in Athlone and Mullingar. A diverse range of industries throughout the county include the manufacture of plastics, engineering, milling, IT and the servicing of urban areas.

County Wexford

Local Authority: *Wexford County Council*, County Hall, Spawell Road, Wexford Town, Co. Wexford; ☎053-76500; fax 053-43406; www.wexford.ie.

Chamber of Commerce: *Wexford Chamber of Industry and Commerce*, The Ballast Office, Crescent Quay, Wexford; ☎053-22226; fax 053-24170; www.wexfordchamber.ie.

FÁS Office: Crescent Mall, Henrietta Street, Wexford; ☎053-23126; fax 053-22785.

Regional Newspaper: *Wexford People*, Channing House, Rowe Street, Wexford; ☎053 40100; fax 053 40191; www.peoplenews.ie.

Industry: County Wexford is well known for its engineering, stainless steel manufacturing and tooling and has a thriving tourism industry. The funds administration company PFPC International, Equifax Database Co, Lake Region Manufacturing Co., Sola ADC Lenses, ABS Pumps, Irish Driver Harris Co. Ltd and Waters Technology Ltd all have operations in Wexford town. Major road infrastructural improvements – ongoing until 2006 – will facilitate access to Rosslare Port (the main seaport of southern Ireland) and encourage increased business activities in the County. The 65-acre Wexford Business Park is being developed in order to draw overseas manufacturing industry and internationally traded services. Dairy farming and fruit growing has produced a successful food processing industry.

County Wicklow

Local Authority: *Wicklow County Council*, County Buildings, Whitegates, Wicklow Town, Co. Wexford; ☎404-20100; fax 404-67790; www.wicklow.ie.

Chamber of Commerce: *Wicklow and District Chamber of Commerce*, Wicklow Enterprise Centre, The Murrough, Wicklow; ☎0404-66610; fax 0404-66607; www.wicklowchamber.ie.

FÁS Office: The Boulevarde, Quinnsborough Road, Bray; ☎01-286 7912; fax 01-2864170.

Regional Newspapers: *Wicklow People*, Channing House, Upper Row Street, Wexford; ☎053 40100; fax 053 40192; www.peoplenews.ie. *The Bray People*, Channing House, Upper Row Street, Wexford; ☎053 40100; fax 053 40192; www.peoplenews.ie.

Industry: Because of the county's proximity to Dublin many of its inhabitants commute into the city to work. Agriculture in County Wicklow comprises cereals, dairy and sheep rearing. Agri-businesses include two grain drying companies and meat processors. Tourism in County Wicklow is one of the principle industries. General manufacturing is the second largest industry in the county Dell Direct and Schering-Plough having plants in Bray. Proximity to Dublin seaports and airport makes the county an ideal location for enterprise.

PROVINCE: ULSTER

County Cavan

Local Authority: *Cavan County Council*, Courthouse, Cavan, Co. Cavan; ☎049-4331799; fax 049-4361565; www.cavancoco.ie.
Chamber of Commerce: *Cootehill Chamber of Commerce,* White Star Centre, Market Street, Cootehill; ☎049- 555 2417; fax 049-555 9033.
FÁS Office: 49 Church Street, Cavan; ☎049-4331767; fax 049 4332527.
Regional Newspaper: *The Anglo Celt*, Station House, Cavan; ☎049-4331100; fax 049-32280; www.anglocelt.ie.
Industry: Primarily a rural county, much of Cavan's workforce are employed in food processing and other agri-businesses. International companies based in County Cavan include Abbott Laboratories (USA), ATA Tools and Abrasives Ltd., Boxmore Plastics, Pauwels Trafo (Belgium) and the synthetic fibre manufacturer Wellman International (USA). One of Ireland's oldest crystal producers, Cavan Crystal, is based in the county.

County Donegal

Local Authority: *Donegal County Council*, County House, Lifford, Co. Donegal; ☎074-917 2222; fax 074-914 1640; www.donegal.ie.
Chamber of Commerce: *Letterkenny Chamber of Commerce and Industry,* Chamber of Commerce House, 40 Port Road, Letterkenny; ☎074-25505; fax 074-26678; www.letterkennychamber.com.
FÁS Office: *FÁS Training Centre,* Ballyraine Industrial Estate, Ramelton Road, Letterkenny; ☎074-20500; fax 074-24840.
Regional Newspapers: *Donegal News*, St. Anne's Court, High Road, Letterkenny; ☎074-91 21014; fax 07491 22881; www.donegalnews.com. *Tirconaill Tribune,* Milford; ☎074-915 3600; fax 074-915 3607; www.tirconaill-tribune.com.
Industry: Fishing is an important sector of the Donegal economy (25% of the national catch comes through the port of Killybegs) and the county has a successful aquaculture industry. Agriculture – sheep,

cattle and arable farming along with the growing of potatoes – is still the largest employer in the county. Donegal is also known for its textile industry – tweed, linen and wool. Since the early 1980's Donegal has attracted a number of foreign direct investment projects. International firms in the county include Abbott Ireland (blood glucose monitoring products), Unifi Ltd (textured yarns), Medisize Donegal Healthcare (medical devices), PacifiCare International (health claim processing) and Prumerica Systems of Ireland Ltd (software development). The Belleek Pottery Group, comprising Belleek Pottery, Galway Irish Crystal, Aynsley China and Donegal Parian China, employs 800 people.

County Monaghan

Local Authority: *Monaghan County Council*, County Offices, The Glen, Monaghan, Co. Monaghan; ☎047-30500; fax 047-82739; www.monaghan.ie.

Chamber of Commerce: *Monaghan Chamber of Commerce and Industry*, 5 North Road, Monaghan; ☎047-71218; fax 047-71241.

FÁS Office: Market Street, Monaghan; ☎047-81511; fax 047-83441.

Regional Newspaper: *The Anglo Celt*, Station House, Cavan; ☎049-4331100; fax 049-32280; www.anglocelt.ie.

Industry: Agriculture and food production is still the main component of the county's economy and accounts for over 60% of employment. Poultry production in the county represents some 40% of the national quota and agri-businesses involving dairy products, beef and mushrooms are important sectors of the county's economy. Manufacturers of furniture are also major employers in Monaghan. Examples of existing national and international companies based in the county include Bose (electrical manufacturing), Norbrook Laboratories, Virgin Cola, Kerry Group (Rye Valley Foods) and Monaghan Mushrooms. The Armagh-Monaghan Digital Corridor is an initiative to provide two centres (one in Monaghan and one in Armagh in Northern Ireland) offering facilities, services and supports to projects in the International Services sector and providing accelerated start up facilities for high technology and knowledge based industries.

REGIONAL AUTHORITIES

In 1994, the Irish Government established eight Regional Authorities to promote the co-ordination of the provision of public services and regional development.

Border Regional Authority, Athbara House, Cavan; ☎049-436 2600; fax 049-437 2044 www.border.ie. The Authority comprises the administrative areas of Donegal, Leitrim, Cavan, Monaghan, Louth and Sligo.

Dublin Regional Authority, 11 Parnell Square, Dublin 1; ☎01-874 5018; www.dra.ie. The Authority comprises the administrative areas of Dublin, Dun Laoghaire-Rathdown, Fingal and South and represents approximately 30% of the population of Ireland.

Mid-East Regional Authority, St. Manntan's House, Kilmantin Hill, Wicklow; ☎0404-66058. The Authority comprises the administrative areas of Kildare, Meath and Wicklow.

Midland Regional Authority, Bridge Centre, Bridge Street, Tullamore, Co. Offaly; ☎0506-52996; www.midlands.ie. The Authority comprises the administrative areas of Laois, Offaly, Longford and Westmeath.

Mid-West Regional Authority, Friar Court, Abbey Street, Nenagh, Co. Tipperary; ☎067-33763; fax 067-34401; www.mwra.ie. The Authority comprises the administrative areas of Clare, North Tipperary & Limerick.

South-West Regional Authority, Innishmore, Ballincollig, Co. Cork; ☎021-4876877; fax 021-4876872; www.swra.ie. The Authority comprises Cork City, County Cork and County Kerry.

South-East Regional Authority, 1 Gladstone Street, Clonmel, County Tipperary; ☎052-26200; www.sera.ie. The South-East Regional Authority covers the five counties of Carlow, Kilkenny, South Tipperary, Waterford and Wexford.

West Regional Authority, Woodquay Court, Woodquay, Galway; ☎091-563 842; www.galwaycoco.ie. The Authority comprises the administrative areas of Galway, Mayo and Roscommon.

City Councils. In addition to these Authorities five cities have City Councils:
Cork City Council, City Hall, Cork; ☎021-496 6222; fax 021-431 4238; www.corkcorp.ie.
Dublin City Council, Civic Offices, Wood Quay, Dublin 8; ☎01-672 2222; fax 01-679 2226; www.dublincity.ie.
Galway City Council, City Hall, College Rd, Galway; ☎091-536 400; fax 091-567 493; www.galwaycity.ie.
Limerick City Council, City Hall, Merchants Quay, Limerick City; ☎061-415 799; fax 061-415266; www.limerickcorp.ie.
Waterford City Council, City Hall, The Mall, Waterford City; ☎051-309 900; fax 051-879 124; ww.waterfordcorp.ie.

REGIONAL ASSEMBLIES

There are two regional assemblies – the Border, Midland and Western Regional Assembly and the Southern & Eastern Regional Assembly. The role of these two bodies is to monitor the general impact of all EU Programmes and to co-ordinate of the provision of public services in their Region.

The Border, Midland and Western Region (BMW Region) comprises the three constituent Regional Authority areas of Border Regional Authority, Midland Regional Authority and West Regional Authority, and covers thirteen counties in total (Cavan, Donegal, Galway, Laois, Leitrim, Longford, Louth, Mayo, Monaghan, Offaly, Roscommon, Sligo and Westmeath).

The Southern and Eastern Region comprises the five constituent Regional Authority areas of Dublin Regional Authority, South-East Regional Authority, South-West Regional Authority, Mid-West Regional Authority and Mid-East Regional Authority, and covers 13 counties in total (Dublin, Carlow, Tipperary, Waterford, Wexford, Kilkenny, Cork, Kerry, Clare, Limerick, Kildare, Meath and Wicklow).

The BMW Region is largely rural with a widely dispersed population and heavy reliance on small-scale and dispersed employment such as agriculture, fisheries, aquaculture and tourism. It is a sparsely populated area and essentially rural in character, containing just

27% of the population. Only 32% of the population reside in concentrations of more than 1,500 people. Galway is the region's only major urban centre.

The region has suffered from high levels of outward migration; the population has had to search for employment opportunities elsewhere as the number of people engaged in agriculture has declined with increased mechanisation. Other factors for economic migration include greater urbanisation and the centralisation of industrial activity. Agriculture, forestry and fishing are still very important industries in the region, though industry (including building and construction) accounts for 40% of output. The proportion of the labour force employed in unskilled occupations is high and the percentage employed in professional occupations is lower than the national average. Only 13% of local graduates are employed within the region's boundaries. The services industry is by far the largest single economic sector and is growing in importance, due to the relatively unspoilt environment, very little congestion and many areas of outstanding natural beauty bringing in increasing numbers of tourists.

The Southern and Eastern Region accounts for 53% of the area of Ireland and is characterised by a rising, predominantly urban, population concentrated in a relatively small number of centres. Almost 76% of Ireland's labour force resides in the Southern and Eastern Region with 21% of the labour force employed in commerce, insurance, finance and business services; around 17% of the population are employed in professional services.

As in much of Ireland, a high proportion of manufacturing industry in the south and east of the region is foreign owned. Overseas industry, which directly employs over 10,000 people in 79 enterprises in the region, is concentrated mainly in electronics and precision engineering, pharmaceuticals and healthcare and in international traded services. The principal large companies in the south-east include: Braun Ireland Ltd., Lapple Ireland Ltd., Merck Sharpe & Dohme, Guidant Ltd., Clonmel Healthcare, AOL Bertlesman, Bausch & Lomb, Honeywell International Ltd., Hasbro Ltd., Garrett Engine Boosting Systems, IVAX, Glaxo Smithkline, ABS Pumps, Equifax Database Company and Sola ADC Lenses. Tourism contributes over

€450 million annually to the regional economy of the south-east and is a high growth sector.

In the mid-west of the region, industry is centred on the urban core of Limerick, Ennis and Shannon Town where the industrial base is dominated by light industry such as electronics, instruments, metals and engineering. Features attractive to industry include the Shannon Industrial Estate, the Shannon Free Trade Zone, Limerick University and the National Technological Park located at Plassey. Shannon Airport is a major gateway for the western seaboard with terminal traffic of over 1.2 million passengers annually, and the deep water port of the Shannon Estuary rivals Dublin and Cork with over 8 million tonnes of cargo handled annually. Employment resulting from foreign direct investment now accounts for more than half the region's total manufacturing base.

The Border, Midland and Western Regional Assembly, The Square, Ballaghaderreen, Co. Roscommon; ☎094-986 2970; fax 094-986 2973; www.bmwassembly.ie.

Southern and Eastern Regional Assembly, Assembly House, O'Connell Street, Waterford; ☎051-860 700; fax 051-879 887; www.seregassembly.ie.

DIRECTORY OF MAJOR EMPLOYERS

Communications

Baltimore Technologies, IFSC House, Custom House Quay, Dublin 1; ☎01-605 4399; fax 01-054 388; www.baltimore.ie

Eircom Ltd, 112/114 St Stephens Green, Dublin 2; ☎1901; www.eircom.ie. Ireland's leading communications company, providing a comprehensive range of advanced voice, data and Internet services.

Ericsson Business Communications, Beech Hill, Clonskeagh, Dublin 4; ☎01-207 3000; fax 01-269 3030; www.ericsson.com.

Logica Aldiscon, 5 Custom House Plaza, Harbourmaster Place, Dublin 1; ☎01-819 3400; fax 01-819 3401; www.aldiscon.ie.

Marconi Sales, BBRS Products, West Pier Business Campus, Old Dunleary Road, Dun Laoghaire, Co. Dublin; ☎01-663 8300; fax 01-663 8333; www.marconi.com.

Motorola Ireland Ltd, Lakeshore Drive, Airside Business Park, Swords, Co. Dublin; ☎01-797 1000; fax 01-797 1060; www.motorola.com.

Vodafone Ireland, MountainView, Leopardstown, Dublin 18; ☎042-933 1999; fax 01-203 7778; www.vodafone.ie.

Computers, IT & Electronics

Amdahl Ireland, Airside Business Park, Swords, County Dublin, ☎01-840 3001; fax 01-840 3776; www.amdahl.com.

Credo Group, Longphort House, Earlsfort Terrace, Lower Leeson Street, Dublin 2; ☎01-676 4600; fax 01-676 0579; info@credogrp.com.

CSK Software (Ireland) Ltd., Lisle House, 33 Molesworth Street, Dublin 2; ☎01-604 6300; fax 01-662 2195; www.csksoftware.com.

Hewlett-Packard (Manufacturing) Ltd., Liffey Park, Barnhall, Leixlip, Co. Kildare; ☎01-615 0000; fax 01-615 0975; www.hp.com. Inkjet Cartridge Manufacturer.

IBM Ireland Ltd, Oldbrook House, 24-32 Pembroke Road, Ballsbridge, Dublin 4; ☎01-815 4000; www.ibm.com.

IONA Technologies, The IONA Building, Shelbourne Road, Ballsbridge, Dublin 4; ☎01-637 2000; fax 01-6372888; www.iona.com.

Kindle Banking Systems, Eastpoint Business Park, Fairview, Co. Dublin; ☎01-636 1000; fax 01-855 4550; www.kindle.com.

Microsoft Distribution Ltd, European Operations Centre, Blackthorn Road, Sandyford Industrial Estate, Dublin 18; ☎01-295 5333; fax 01-295 8354; www.microsoft.com.

Oracle Ireland Ltd, East Point Business Park, Clontarf, Dublin 3; ☎01-803 9000; fax 01-803 1156; www.oracle.com/ie.

Symantec Ltd., Ballycoolin Business Park, Blanchardstown, Dublin 15; ☎01-803 5400; fax 01-820 6138; www. World leader in Internet security technology.

Construction

Architectural Aluminium Ltd, Oak Road, Western Business Park, Dublin 12; ☎01-456 8400; fax 01-456 8480; www.arcal.ie.

Arup Consulting Engineers, 10 Wellington Road, Ballsbridge, Dublin 4; ☎01-614 4200; fax 01-668 3169; www.arup.ie. With offices in Dublin, Cork and Limerick Arup is one of the leading consulting engineering firms in Ireland.

Cleary and Doyle Contracting Ltd, Larkins Cross, Wexford; ☎053-65900; fax 053-65999; www.clearydoyle.com.

Coffey Construction, Moanbaun, Athenry, Co. Galway; ☎091-844 356; fax 091-844 519; www.coffeyconstruction.com.

John Sisk & Son Holdings, Naas Road, Clondalkin, Dublin 22; ☎01-409 1500; fax 01-409 1550; www.sisk.ie.

Rogerson Reddan and Associates, 78 Haddington Road, Dublin 4; ☎01-660 9155; fax 01-660 9694. Project, Construction and Cost Managers.

Finance & Banking

AIB Group, Headquarters, Bankcentre, Ballsbridge, Dublin 4; ☎01-660 0311; fax 01-668 2508; www.aib.ie.

Anglo-Irish Bank, Head Office, Stephen Court, 18/21 St. Stephen's Green, Dublin 2; ☎01-616 2000; fax 01-616 2488; www.angloirishbank.ie.

Bank of Ireland, Lower Baggot Street, Dublin 2; ☎01-661 5933; fax 01-661 5671; www.bankofireland.ie.

Cap Gemini Ernst & Young Ireland, International House, 20/22 Lower Hatch Street, Dublin 2; ☎01-639 0100; fax 01-475 0593; www.cgey.com.

CMG Group, 14 Upper Fitzwilliam Street, Dublin 2; ☎01-661 1245; fax 01-661 1058; www.cmg-group.ie. Chartered Certified Accountants.

Deloitte and Touche, Deloitte and Touche House, Earlsfort Terrace, Dublin 2; ☎01-417 2200; fax 01-417 2300; www.deloitte.com.

Hamill Spence O'Connell, Adelaide House, 90 Upper Georges Street, Dun Laoghaire, Co. Dublin; ☎01-280 8433; fax 01-280 4472;

www.hsoc.ie.
Hibernian Group, Haddington Road, Dublin 4; ☎01-607 8000; fax 01-607 0803; www.hibernian.ie.
Irish Life Assurance plc., Lower Abbey Street, PO Box 129, Dublin 1; ☎01-704 2000; fax 01-704 1900; www.irishlife.ie.
KPMG, 1 Stokes Place, St. Stephen's Green, Dublin 2; ☎01-410 1167; fax 01-412 0067; www.kpmg.ie.
PriceWaterhouseCoopers, Gardner House, Wilton Place, Dublin 2; ☎01-662 6000; fax 01-662 6200; www.pcwglobal.com.

Food & Drink

C&C Group plc, Kylemore Park, Dublin 10; ☎01-616 1100; fax 01-616 1125; www.cantrellandcochrane.com. Non-alcoholic and alcoholic beverages and snack foods.
Cadbury Schweppes Ireland, Malahide Road, Coolock, Dublin 5; ☎01-848 0000; fax 01-847 2905; www.cadbury.ie. Confectionery and soft drinks.
Coca-Cola Bottlers Ireland, Western Industrial Estate, Naas Road, Dublin 12; ☎01-456 5377; fax 01-4602 169; www.coca-colahbc.com. Irelands largest producer and distributor of soft drinks.
Diageo Ireland, St James's Gate, Dublin 8; ☎01-453 6700; fax 01-408 4804; www.diageo.ie. Alcoholic beverages production, sales and distribution.
Ferrero Ireland Ltd, Kinsale Road, Cork; ☎021-311 122; fax 021-317 538; www.kindersurprise.com.
Glanbia plc., Glanbia House, Kilkenny; ☎056-777 2200; fax 056-777 2222; www.glanbia.com.
H.J. Heinz Company Ireland, Stradbrook House, Stradbrook Road, Blackrock, Co. Dublin; ☎01-280 5757; fax 01-280 1957; www.heinz.com. Manufacture, sales & distribution of Heinz product.
International Flavours and Fragrances Limited, Industrial Estate, Donore Road, Drogheda, Co. Louth; ☎041-983 1031; fax 041-983 5119; www.iff.com. The world's leading creator and manufacturer of flavours and fragrances.
Irish Biscuits, Belgard Road, Tallaght, Dublin 24; ☎01-414 1111; fax

01-451 1898. Biscuit Manufacturer & Distributor.

Irish Distillers Group, Bow Street Distillery, Smithfield, Dublin 7; ☎01-872 5566; fax 01-872 3109; www.jameson.ie.

Nestlé, 3030 Lake Drive, Citywest Business Campus, Dublin 24; ☎01-449 7777; fax 01-449 7778; www.nestle.com.

Nutricia Ireland Ltd., Deansgrange Business Park, Deansgrange, Co. Dublin; ☎01-289 0289; fax 01-289 0250; www.nutriciababy.be.

Unilever Ireland, Whitehall Road, Rathfarnham, Dublin 14; ☎01-216 9400; fax 01-296 1598; www.unilever.com. A major international company operating in foods, home and personal care products.

Wyeth Nutritionals, Askeaton, Limerick, Co. Limerick; ☎061-392168; fax 061-392440; www.wyeth.ie.

Fuel & Energy

Bord Gáis, Headquarters, PO Box 51, Gasworks Road, Cork; ☎021-453 4000; fax 021-453 4001; www.bge.ie. Bord Gáis is responsible for the supply, transmission and distribution of natural gas in Ireland.

Electricity Supply Board (ESB), Lower Fitzwilliam Street, Dublin 2; ☎01-858 1486; fax www.esb.ie. National Electricity Company which owns and manages the electricity network in Ireland.

Esso Ireland Ltd, Esso Ireland Limited, Stillorgan, Blackrock, Co. Dublin; ☎01-288 1661; fax 01-288 7303; www.esso.com/eaff/essoireland. One of Ireland's leading energy suppliers.

Shell Ireland, Shell House, Beach Hill, Dublin 4; ☎01-202 8888; fax 01-283-8320; www.shellireland.com. Businesses in oil products, exploration and production, and chemicals.

Statoil, Statoil House, 6 George's Dock, Dublin 1; ☎01-636 8300; fax 01-818 0100; www.statoil.ie. Undertakes the marketing, distribution, exploration, development and production of oil and gas in Ireland.

Hotel, Bar & Restaurant Chains

Campbell Bewley Group, Northern Cross, Malahide Road, Dublin 17; ☎01-816 0606; fax 01-816 0601; www.bewleys.com.

Capital Bars, 39/40 Dawson Street, Dublin 2; tel 01-677 9021; fax 01-677 4056; www.capitalbars.com.

Eddie Rockets Restaurants, 7 South Anne Street, Dublin 2; ☎01-679 7340; fax 01-679 0040; www.eddierockets.ie.

Jurys Doyle Hotel Group, 146 Pembroke Road, Ballsbridge, Dublin 4; ☎01-607 0070; fax 01-667 2370; www.jurysdoyle.com.

Lynch Hotels, Vision House, Clare Road, Ennis, Co. Clare; ☎065-686 9999; fax 065-682 3759; www.lynchotels.com.

Sodexho (Ireland) Ltd, 23 Rock Hill, Main Street, Blackrock, Co. Dublin; ☎01-283 3654; fax 01-283 3991; www.sodexho.ie. Catering services group.

Media

Irish Independent, Middle Abbey Street, Dublin 1; ☎01-705 5333; fax 01-872 0304; www.independent.ie. National daily newspaper.

Radio Telefís Éireann (RTÉ), Donnybrook, Dublin 4; ☎01-208 3111; fax 01-208 3080; www.rte.ie. Irish Public Service Broadcasting Organisation.

The Irish Times, 10-16 D'Olier Street, Dublin 2; ☎01-679 2022; fax 01-679 3910; www.ireland.com. National daily newspaper.

Today FM, 124 Upper Abbey Street, Dublin 1; ☎01-804 9000; fax 01-804 9099; www.todayfm.com. Ireland's licensed independent national radio station.

TV3 Television Network, Westgate Business Park, Ballymount, Dublin 24; ☎01-419 3333; fax 01-419 3330; www.tv3.ie. Ireland's first National, commercial, independent television network.

Public Transport

Aer Lingus, Aer Lingus Head Office, Dublin Airport, Co. Dublin; ☎01-886 2222; fax 01-8863832; www.aetlingus.com. State-owned company providing scheduled air passenger and cargo services.

Aer Rianta, Dublin Airport, Co. Dublin; ☎01-814 1111; fax 01-844 5389; www.aerrianta.ie. Management company for Dublin, Shannon and Cork airports.

Bus Éireann, Broadstone, Dublin 7; ☎01-830 2222; fax 01-830 9377;

www.buseireann.ie. Provides bus services throughout Ireland with the exception of Dublin City.

CIÉ, Córas Iompair Éireann, Heuston Station, Dublin 8; ☎01-6771871; fax 01-7032776; www.cie.ie. The state-owned company responsible for operating rail services in Ireland.

Dublin Bus, Bus Átha Cliath, 59 Upper O'Connell Street, Dublin 1; ☎01-872 0000; www.dublinbus.ie. Bus services for the city and county of Dublin and adjoining areas.

Irish Ferries, Head Office, PO BOX 19, Alexandra Road, Dublin 1; ☎01-855 2222; fax 01-855 2272; www.irishferries.com. Ireland's leading ferry company.

Irish Rail, Iarnród Éireann, Connolly Station, Amiens Street, Dublin 1; ☎01-703 2634; fax 01-703 2515; www.irishrail.ie. National train service.

Ryanair, Ryanair Head Office, Dublin Airport, Co. Dublin; ☎01-609 7800; www.ryanair.ie. Low cost airline.

Stena Line Limited, Dun Laoghaire Ferry Terminal, Dun Laoghaire Harbour, Co. Dublin; ☎01-204 7700; fax 01-204 7620; www.stenaline.ie. Ferry Service operator.

Research & Technology

Abbott Diagnostics Division, PO Box 9244, Dublin 4; ☎01-218 6866; fax 01-218 6886; www.abbott.com.

Siemens Ltd, Ballymoss Road, Sandyford Industrial Estate, Dublin 18; ☎021-494 0688; fax 021-494 0709; www.siemens.ie.

Wyeth Medica Ireland, The Wyeth BioPharma Campus at Grange Castle, BioPharma Jobs, PO Box 1157; Dublin 12; ☎01-409 8330; fax 01-409 2701; www.wyeth.ie. Health care product manufacture.

Retail

Brown Thomas Group Ltd, 92 Grafton Street, Dublin 2; ☎01-605 6666; fax 01-605 6752; www.brownthomas.ie. The holding company for three of Ireland's fashion retailers with twenty six stores and approximately 1600 employees.

Dunnes Stores, Beaux House, Beaux Lane, Mercer Street Lower, Dublin

2; ☎01-475 1111; fax 01-611 2935; www.dunnesstores.com. Ireland's largest and most successful retailer.

Grafton Group plc, Heron House, Corrig Road, Sandyford Industrial Estate, Dublin 18; ☎01-216 0600; fax 01-295 4470; www.graftonplc.ie. Builders and plumbers merchanting, DIY retailing and manufacturing.

Lidl Ireland GmbH, Sales Operations Department, Great Connell Road, Newbridge, Co. Kildare; ☎045-440 400; fax 045-440 556; www.lidl.ie. Discount retail store.

Lifestyle Sports, Unit D1, Airport Business Park, Swords Road, Co. Dublin; ☎01-812 5500; fax 01-844 701; www.lifestylesports.com. Ireland's largest sports retailer.

Musgrave Group, Ballycurreen, Airport Road, Cork; ☎021-452 2222; fax 021-452 2244; www.musgrave.ie. Ireland's largest food and grocery distributor. Manages Ireland's leading cash & carry operation as well as the SuperValu and Centra retail franchises.

Tesco Ireland Ltd, PO Box 3, Gresham House, Marine Rd, Dun Laoghaire, Co. Dublin; ☎01-280 8441; fax 01-280 0136; www.tesco.ie. Over 10,000 employees in Ireland.

THE 50 BEST COMPANIES TO WORK FOR

Every year an international research company, Discovery Research Ltd (Lilmar House, Royal Oak, Santry, Dublin 9; ☎01-862 0155; fax 01-842 4500; www.discovery.ie) runs a survey to find the best company or organisation in Ireland. Workplaces with at least 50 employees are evaluated on the relationship between employees and management; employees and their jobs, and between the employees. Approximately 13,000 employees from 115 companies took part in the 2004 survey. The companies also completed a questionnaire outlining their policies, practices and philosophies regarding employees. The 50 best companies in Ireland for 2004, evaluated on the results of the employee surveys and the company questionnaires, are listed below:

Abbott Ireland Laboratories, Ballytivnan, Sligo; ☎071-915 5600; fax 071-915 5605; www.abbott.ie. Irish subsidiary of the US manufacturer of quality healthcare products.

ACC Bank, Charlement Place, Dublin 2; ☎01-418 4000; fax 01-418 4444; www.accbank.ie. Banking services for customers in business (SME), personal and agri-based sectors.

Allianz Ireland, Burlington House, Burlington Road, Dublin 4; ☎01-613 3000; fax 01-613 4444; www.allianz.ie. One of Ireland's largest indigenous multi-line general insurance companies.

Appleby Jewellers, 5-6 Johnson's Court, Grafton Street, Dublin 2; ☎01-679 9572; fax 01-679 4367; www.appleby.ie. Retailer, now part of Buy4Now.ie, Ireland's first online shopping centre.

Arup Consulting Engineers, 10 Wellington Road, Ballsbridge, Dublin 4; ☎01-614 4200; fax 01-668 3169; www.arup.ie. One of the leading consulting engineering firms in Ireland, with offices in Dublin, Cork and Limerick.

Ballina Beverages, www.coke.com. Currently the largest soft drink manufacturing plant in the world and represents the largest single investment ever made by The Coca-Cola Company.

Bank of Scotland (Ireland), Canada House, 65-68 St. Stephen's Green, Dublin 2; ☎01-408 3500; fax 01-671 7797; www.bankofscotland.ie. The third largest business bank in Ireland.

Boston Scientific Tullamore, www.bsci.com. Medical device manufacturer.

Boston Scientific Ireland, Ballybritt Industrial Estate, Galway; ☎091-756 300; fax 091-701 283; www.bostonscientific.ie. A worldwide developer, manufacturer and marketer of medical devices.

BrightWater Selection, 36 Merrion Square, Dublin 2; ☎01-662 1000; fax 01-662 3900; www.brightwater.ie. Recruitment agency for jobs in HR, banking, IT, Sales and marketing, Insurance, accountancy, etc.

Bupa Ireland, 12 Fitzwilliam Square, Dublin 2; ☎01-662 7662; fax 01-662 7672; www.bupaireland.ie. International healthcare organisation with over 170 staff in its Ireland offices.

Campbell Catering Ltd, Northern Cross, Malahide Road, Dublin 17; ☎01-816 0700; fax 01-816 0681; www.campbellcatering.ie. Ireland's largest contract catering company and part of the Campbell Bewley Group. Offices in Limerick, Dublin and Cork.

Chubb Ireland, Unit 2 Stillorgan Industrial Park, Blackrock, Co. Dublin; ☎01-295 3333; fax 01-295 5779; www.chubb.ie. Leading provider of security and fire protection services to businesses and industry in Ireland, with offices throughout Ireland.

Clontarf Castle Hotel, Castle Avenue, Clontard, Dublin 3; ☎01-833 2321; fax 01-833 0418; www.clontarfcastle.ie.

Corporate Travel Partners, Lincoln House, Lincoln Place, Dublin 2; ☎01-605 3900; fax 01-676 7480; www.ctp.ie. The largest travel management companies in Ireland.

Deloitte, Deloitte & Touche House, Earslfort Terrace, Dublin 2; ☎01-417 2200; fax 01-417 2300; www.deloitte.com/ie. A member firm of Deloitte Touche Tohmatsu and Ireland's largest multi-disciplinary professional services (audit, tax and legal, consulting, and financial advisory) firm employing 700 people in Dublin, Cork and Limerick.

Department of Enterprise, Trade and Employment, Kildare Street, Dublin 2; ☎01-631 2121; fax 01-631 2827; www.entemp.ie.

DePuy Ireland, Loughbeg, Ringaskiddy, Co. Cork; ☎021-491 4000; fax 021-491 4199; www.depuy.com.

Diageo Ireland, St James's Gate, Dublin 8; ☎01-453 6700; fax 01-408 4804; www.diageo.ie.

DMG Services, 53 Park West Industrial Park, Dublin 12; ☎01-438 0200; fax 01-438 0288; www.filestores.com. Document, data management services and document storage for clients from large bluechip companies to small and medium sized enterprises and government bodies.

Dublin Bus, Bus Átha Cliath, 59 Upper O'Connell Street, Dublin 1; ☎01-872 0000; www.dublinbus.ie.

Eagle Star Insurance Company, Eagle Star House, Ballsbridge Park, Dublin 4; ☎01-667 0666; fax 01-667 0660; www.eaglestar.ie. The fifth largest general insurer in Ireland employing 430 people and operating a nationwide branch network with offices in Cork, Drogheda, Galway, Limerick, Waterford, Sligo and Tralee.

EBS Building Society, The EBS Building, 2 Burlington Road, Dublin 4; ☎01-665 9000; fax 01-665 8118; www.ebs.ie. One of Ireland's most successful credit institutions. EBS offers a range of savings, investments, mortgage and insurance products and services and employs over 580 staff.

Fehily Timoney & Company, Core House, Pouladuff Road, Cork;

☎021-496 4133; fax 021-496 4464; www.fehilytimoney.com. The leading engineering and environmental consultancy in Ireland.

Four Seasons Hotel Dublin, Simmonscourt Road, Ballsbridge, Dublin 4; ☎01-665 4000; fax 01-665 4099; www.fourseasons.com.

GE Capital Aviation Services, Aviation House, Shannon, Co. Clare; ☎061-706 500; fax 061-706 884; www.gecas.com. Global aviation solutions, providing a range of fleet, financing and productivity solutions to the airline industry.

GlaxoSmithKline (Ireland), Stonemasons Way, Rathfarnham, Dublin 16; ☎01-495 5000; fax 01-495 5105; http://ie.gsk.com. One of the world's leading research-based pharmaceutical and healthcare companies.

Guidant Corporation, Cashel Road, Clonmel, Co. Tipperary; ☎052-81000; fax 052-81001; www.guidant.com. A world leader in the design and development of cardiovascular medical products.

Halifax Insurance Ireland, Dromore House, East Park Industrial Estate, Shannon, Co. Clare; ☎061-477 000; fax 061-477 019; www.halifax.co.uk.

Heineken Ireland, Lady's Well Brewery, 58 Leitrim Street, Cork; ☎021-450 3371; fax 021-455 1098; www.heineken.ie.

Hibernian Group, Haddington Court, Haddington Road, Dublin 4; ☎01-607 8000; fax 01-607 8112; www.hibernian.ie. One of Ireland's largest and most successful financial organisations offering general insurance, risk management, pensions, life assurance, investment management and personal financial services.

Hilton Dublin, Charlemont Place, Dublin 2; ☎01-402 9988; fax 01-402 9966; www.hilton.com.

Janssen Pharmaceutical, IDA Estate, Little Island, Co. Cork; ☎021-4353321; www.jnj.com.

MBNA Ireland, 46 St. Stephen's Green, Dublin 2; ☎01-619 6000; fax 01-619 6048; www.mbna.com. One of the largest gold card issuers in Ireland.

Mentor Graphics (Ireland) Ltd, Bay 127, Shannon Free Zone, Co. Clare; ☎061-716 200; fax 061-716 202; www.mentorg.ie. Electronic design automation solutions.

Microsoft Ireland, Atrium Building Block B, Carmenhall Road, Sandyford Industrial Estate, Dublin 18; ☎01-295 3826;

www.microsoft.com/Ireland.

O2 Communications, McLaughlin Road, National Technological Park, Limerick; ☎061-203 501; fax 1800-322086; www.o2.ie. Headquartered in Dublin, O2 Ireland employs over 1,450 people in offices in Dublin, Cork and Galway a customer care centre in Limerick.

PEI, M50 Business Park, Ballymount Road Upper, Ballymount, Dublin 12; ☎01-419 6900; fax 01-419 6999; www.pei.ie. A leading medical and surgical sales, marketing and distribution company.

Radisson SAS Group. www.radissonsas.com.

Royal and SunAlliance, 13-17 Dawson Street, Dublin 2; ☎01-677 1851; fax 01-671 7625; www.royalsunalliance.ie. Commercial, household, travel and motor insurance services.

Royal Bank of Scotland Group Technology, www.rsb.co.uk. Software development and financial services.

Sodexho Catering and Support Services, 23 Rock Hill, Blackrock, Dublin; ☎01-283 3654; fax 01-283 3991; www.sodexho.ie. Food and management services.

Statoil Ireland, Statoil House, 6 George's Dock, Dublin 1; ☎01-636 8300; fax 01-818 0100; www.statoil.ie. Marketing, distribution, exploration, development and production of oil and gas. Also involved in power generation in partnership with the ESB.

Superquinn, Newcastle Road, Lucan, Co. Dublin; ☎01-630 2000; fax 01-628 1443; www.superquinn.ie. Market leader in grocery retailing in the greater Dublin area with stores in Kilkenny, Carlow, Clonmel, Dundalk, Waterford and Limerick.

Symantec Ireland, Ballycoolin Business Park, Blanchardstown, Dublin 15; ☎01-803 5400; fax 01-820 6138; World leader in Internet security technology.

The Civil Service Commission, Chapter House, 26/30 Abbey Street Upper, Dublin 1; ☎01-858 7859; www. publicjobs.ie.

Transitions Optical, IDA Industrial Estate, Dunmore Road, Tuam, Co. Galway; ☎093-70713; fax +800 9889 9889; www.transitions.com.

Trócaire, Maynooth, Co. Kildare; ☎01-629 3333; fax 01-629 0661; www.trocaire.ie. Overseas development agency of the Catholic Church in Ireland.

Watson Wyatt LLP, 65/66 Lower Mount Street, Dublin 2; ☎01-661 6448; fax 01-676 0818; www.watsonwyatt.com/europe. Manage-

ment consultancy.
Whirlpool SSC, www.whirlpool.com. Financial services.

Useful Websites

Association of Graduate Careers Services in Ireland (AGCSI), in association with the publisher GTI Ireland, publishes the www.gradireland.com website, which offers career advice for students and graduates in Ireland.

Business World, www.businessworld.ie, is a one-stop business resource with information on the markets, media and business research facilities.

BusinessPro, www.businesspro.ie, is the largest publisher of industry reports in Ireland.

Companies Registration Office, www.cro.ie. Almost all of the information filed with the Companies Registration Office in Ireland is available for public inspection and there is a search facility on the website where information on registered companies may be obtained.

Dunn & Bradstreet, http://dbireland.dnb.com, is the world's leading provider of business information. D&B have a searchable database containing information on 75 million companies worldwide.

EURES, http://europa.eu.int/eures/. The European Employment Services Internet Portal contains information on jobs and learning opportunities in Europe, and includes fact sheets on employment possibilities in Ireland.

The Irish Times' Business Pages, www.ireland.com/business/. *The Irish Times,* in association with Business World, also produces an annual Top 1000 of companies operating in Ireland.

STARTING A BUSINESS

CHAPTER SUMMARY

- Non-EEA nationals wishing to start a business in Ireland must obtain Business Permission from the Minister for Justice, Equality & Law Reform.
- Unless a business premises was previously used for the purpose intended, you will have to apply for planning permission for a 'material change of use'.
- The viability of a Business for Sale is likely to be reflected in the asking price.
- Any contracts relating to a business or a purchase of property should be drawn up or vetted by a qualified solicitor.
- **Self-employment.** People who work for themselves or in partnership with one or more people must inform the local Revenue office.
  - The self-employed are responsible for paying their own tax through the Self-Assessment system.
  - Tax is calculated on profits (after expenses and tax reliefs) for the tax year.
- **Employing staff.** If you employ staff you will need to register with the Revenue for PAYE and PRSI as an employer.
  - Under employment legislation, employers have a number of responsibilities to their employees.

Residence Regulations

Nationals of the European Economic Area (EEA) are allowed to work in any EU member state without the requirement of a work permit. Non-EEA nationals wishing to start a business in Ireland will, with some limited exceptions, need to obtain Business Permission from the Minister for Justice, Equality & Law Reform at the Immigration Division, 72-76 St Stephen's Green, Dublin 2 (☎01-602 8202; fax 01-661 5461; www.justice.ie). To obtain Business Permission the following criteria must be met:

- The proposed business must result in the transfer to the State of Ireland of a minimum capital investment of €300,000
- The proposed business (if a new project) must create employment for at least two Irish (or other EEA) nationals, or at least maintain levels of employment if an existing business
- The proposed business should add to the commercial activity and competitiveness of Ireland
- The proposed business must be a viable trading concern capable of providing the applicant and any dependents with sufficient income
- The applicant must be in possession of valid identity documents and be of good character

Exceptions to the €300,000 minimum capital investment may be considered in instances where the applicant has been legally resident in Ireland in an employed capacity for a period of five or more years or the applicant is the spouse or dependent of an Irish (or EEA) national. An applicant meeting all these eligibility requirements will also need to present a business plan.

CREATING A NEW BUSINESS

It is not difficult, legally, to start your own business. In most cases, there is little to stop you setting up in business overnight, though this would be foolhardy without having done plenty of groundwork beforehand. There are two broad approaches to identifying an idea for a business, depending on personal circumstances and requirements. If you are committed to living in a certain part of Ireland, you should survey the locality to identify services the locals may be lacking and those that are already well catered for. From a survey of this kind you can then come up with an idea for a business which will cater to a demand and which you may be able to provide. Alternatively, if you already have your business idea, the best approach is to decide in which area in Ireland your idea will work best. This may depend on such things as where you are likely to find your customers and suppliers, and whether you will need a good transport infrastructure for your business to work effectively, or whether this is irrelevant for you particular product or service.

Ask yourself whether you have the right background or qualifications to set up the sort of enterprise you are considering. Whether you are prepared to risk almost everything to achieve your goals. You should be completely familiar with your product or service, and have detailed technical knowledge of it. Research is very often the key to success and you would be well advised to find out as much as possible about both your target population and your competition. It is a good idea to look into whether there is a trade association that deals with the product or service you are intending to offer, as this is likely to be a good source of information, advice and assistance.

There is a third approach to setting up in business that does not depend at all on the area in which you live and work. Knowledge-based occupations using computers and the Internet as their supply route can run from the remotest areas of Ireland as long as you have a telephone line, a computer and a modem. Areas of work ideally suited to this area of business include writing, editing, indexing, website design and other computer-based services.

If you are considering a more traditional area of business, changing trends are an important factor to bear in mind. Many people who move to tourist areas of Ireland assume that they will be able to make a reasonable income from offering bed and breakfast in their house. Although this is one of the simplest businesses to establish – the legal and planning requirements to make this sort of use of your family home are minimal – it will not necessarily be a sure-fire income generator and is of course seasonal.

When looking for a location in which to start up a business, it is wise to keep in mind the community relations implications of your proposed venture. For instance, if you plan to move to a small community with the idea of setting up a business in direct competition to an existing business, that has perhaps been in existence for years and is family-run, then you are unlikely to make many friends with a proportion of your new neighbours, and most definitely not with the competition. All businesses in Ireland, depending on the nature of the business and the location, are required to be legally registered and to operate in conformity with the relevant financial, environmental, tax and health and safety regulations.

Planning Permission

If you are planning to run a business from a property (land or buildings) which is going to need a substantial conversion or alteration for the purpose and is likely to impact on the neighbours and/or the local community, then you will be wise to investigate the planning implications before proceeding. It is a good idea to do such research before buying any property intended to be used for business purposes because unless the property was previously used for the purpose intended, you will have to apply for permission for a 'material change of use'. A local authority's Planning Department will be able to advise you about making a planning application and answer questions such as whether your planned development fits in with its own development policies and what documents you will need to submit. Before applying for planning permission, the intention to do so must be published in a newspaper that has a circulation in the same district as the property. In addition, a notice stating the nature of the proposed development must also be placed on the property. There is a fee payable, which depends on the type of development proposed and the type of permission being sought. Generally, the local Planning Department must make a decision on a planning application within eight weeks of receipt, however, things may take a little longer if the local authority needs more information before making a decision; or the decision is appealed against.

BUYING AN EXISTING BUSINESS

One way of avoiding planning problems, and of avoiding the pitfalls of starting a business completely from scratch, is to buy an existing business. This affords the obvious benefits of being able to walk into a going concern (hopefully a profitable and successful one with an established client base) and take up where the previous owner left off. Obviously it will be advisable to do some research locally to discover why the business is being sold, and to find out how long it has been on the market. If the business hasn't been doing too well, you need to work out whether you can turn it around and make it work for you.

The viability of a business is likely to be reflected in the asking price, and a thriving business with 'a genuine reason for sale' is likely to cost you far more than one that has been struggling to make a profit. However, even if a business for sale hasn't been doing too well of late there will often be the necessary plant, equipment and stock in trade already on site, and suppliers will know what is needed and hopefully be willing to continue a business relationship with a new owner.

Not all businesses for sale are on the market for negative reasons. In some cases the owners want to retire, or move on from one venture to set up another, or have become tired of the running of a certain type of business, or need to realise their assets, or wish to move away from the area. However, when investigating a prospective business purchase it is advisable to make an assessment of both the business and the current owner.

When making your assessment take into account the following: location; profitability; local and regional competitors; the market for the type of business; the value of the premises and whether it is to be sold freehold or leasehold, and the age and condition of machinery or equipment included in the sale price. You will need to make sure that all accounts and tax matters relating to the business are up to date before a sale goes through and that all property title documents are in place. Further, if stock is to be transferred, ensure that you have done your own stock take and compare this with the seller's valuation; and agree with the seller on how the legal and professional costs of the sale are to be split.

You should check if the current clientele has a special relationship with the present owner and how long current accounts have been with the business. Will clients take their custom elsewhere when the business passes into new hands? Look at how the business is perceived locally, and in general. Talk to suppliers, competitors, customers, banks and the owners of other businesses in the area.

Buying a franchise is another way into business, which takes some of the risk out of setting up on your own. Franchises have the advantage of offering, in most cases, a tried and tested name and product, training and backup support. The pros and cons of franchises are discussed below.

Finding Premises or an Existing Business for Sale

Commercial properties for sale or rent, as well as existing businesses for sale, can be found through estate agents and commercial agents. Local and regional newspapers will display adverts of properties for sale. There are also a number of companies in Ireland that deal specifically in business retail and acquisition such as Irish Businesses for Sale (17 Casement Square, Cobh, Co. Cork; ☎021-481 2397; www.irish businessesforsale.com), Irish Business Sales and Corporate Investment Company (IBSCI, Harcourt Centre, Block 3, Harcourt Road, Dublin 2; ☎01-418 2287; fax 01-418 2223; www.irishbusinesssales.com) and Boylan & Dodd Corporate Services Ltd (41 Percy Place, Dublin 4; ☎01-660 7166; fax 01-6607193; www.businessireland.net).

PROCEDURES INVOLVED IN STARTING A BUSINESS

When starting up in business it is advisable to open a separate business bank account. People who work for themselves or in partnership with one or more people are classified as self-employed and must inform the local Revenue office. If you are self-employed, and if your taxable turnover (total sales) exceeds a certain threshold (i.e. €25,500 in the case of persons supplying services, €51,000 for persons supplying goods) in any 12-month period, you must also register for value added tax (VAT). You may also be obliged to register for VAT if you receive taxable services from abroad, or if you are a foreign trader doing business in Ireland.

Businesses registered as Limited Companies will need to register for Corporation Tax, Employer's PAYE/PRSI and VAT with the Revenue by filling in Form TR2, available from any tax office and available to download from the Revenue website (www.revenue.ie). Self-employed individuals and partnerships can register for Income Tax, VAT and Employer's PAYE/PRSI by completing Form TR1. A sole trader who is likely to earn less than €126,794 per annum should complete Form STR. Whatever the nature of the business, it is important to keep accurate records, as these are essential for tax purposes and will make it much easier to prepare annual accounts.

Business Structures

There are several different trading structures you can adopt when going into business and your own individual circumstances will dictate whether you should operate as a limited company or as a sole trader or partnership. A sole trader and a partnership are basically taxed the same way, however, because a limited company is a separate legal entity, tax regulations are rather more complex and so limited company taxation is best handled by a properly qualified and certified accountant. In addition to taxation issues you also need to consider the various other practical and legal matters to be taken into account when setting up a company. As always in matters concerning a certain degree of financial risk, you should seek professional advice before jumping into negotiations.

Sole Trader. This is the simplest form of business structure. As its name suggests, this is a 'one-man' or 'one-woman' business. There is no need to register the business with anybody, other than notifying the Revenue Commissioners that you are self-employed. You will be liable to pay your PRSI contributions unless your earnings are very low, in which case you may be able to elect not to pay contributions until your earnings reach the statutory level. Sole traders are liable for income tax on a similar basis to an employee in a company, though the calculation of taxable income is slightly more complicated due to the deduction of business costs and allowances. There is a risk involved if you go into business as a sole trader in that, if the business should fail, you will personally be liable for all debts, which means the possibility of losing all your assets.

Partnership. Where two or more people run a business together, they may set up a partnership. Partners can establish a business as informally as a sole trader, with nothing more than a verbal agreement and a handshake between them. However, this may not be advisable, as even the best of friends or colleagues who work well together might have disagreements once they enter into a business relationship, and this could lead to disputes in the future. For this reason, a formal deed of partnership, outlining the financial arrangements regarding the business, should be drawn up by a solicitor and signed by all parties involved. Then, if the business should fail or one of the partners decides to leave, there will be no misunderstanding about how the profits and losses are to be dealt with.

Limited Company. Setting up a company is a far more complicated procedure than starting in business as a sole trader or partnership, and if the business is small and still finding its feet it may not always be necessary or worthwhile to turn it into such a formal and highly regulated structure.

One of the biggest advantages of a company is that, in most cases, a director's or member's liability for debts is limited, so personal assets are not at risk if a company is wound up. Also, The only income taxable on the owners of the business is any salaries or dividends taken from the business. There are four main types of company:

- **Private company limited by shares**. Members' liability is limited to the amount unpaid on shares they hold.
- **Company limited by guarantee not having a share capital**. Members' liability is limited to the amount they have agreed to contribute to the company's assets if the company is wound up.
- **Company limited by guarantee having a share capital**. Members' liability is limited to the amount, if any, which is unpaid on the shares they hold and on the amount they have undertaken to contribute to the assets of the company if it is wound up.

○ **Public limited company (PLC)**. The company's shares may be offered for sale to the general public and members' liability is limited to the amount unpaid on shares held by them.

Briefly, all companies must have a minimum of two directors and a company secretary. The business of the company and the way it will be run is laid out in a memorandum and articles of association. These itemise such matters as the minimum and maximum number of directors it should have, how many of these constitute a quorum at meetings, and the procedure should the company be wound up at any time. Companies are legally obliged to hold regular, minuted meetings for members, and to deliver full annual accounts and an annual return to Companies Registration Office (Parnell House, 14 Parnell Square, Dublin 1; ☎01-804 5200; fax 01-804 5222; www.cro.ie). The names, addresses and occupations of all directors must be notified to Companies Registration Office, and any changes must be notified immediately. These details are available for public inspection by anyone who asks. Company officers have wide responsibilities and obligations in law, so it is a good idea to take advice from a solicitor or an accountant as to whether an incorporated company is the best way to run your business.

SOURCES OF FINANCE

There are a number of sources of funding available to assist with the formation or expansion of a business, although unless you have some personal capital to invest, whether from savings or through financial help from friends and relatives, you may find it difficult to lever further funds from external sources. Broadly, the formal sources of finance are banks, venture capitalists and the public sector. As part of the move to encourage the formation of businesses of all sizes in Ireland, a variety of public bodies have funds available to assist the establishment of new businesses and to develop or expand existing businesses.

City & County Enterprise Boards

The 35 City & County Enterprise Boards were established as an initiative of the Department of Enterprise, Trade and Employment and are funded with the assistance of the European Union. Their remit is to support, develop and assist indigenous potential and to stimulate economic activity at a local level, primarily through the provision of financial and technical assistance. Enterprise Boards support individuals, firms and community group projects deemed to be commercially viable, and offer advice and training for the development of small businesses.

Useful Addresses
Carlow County Enterprise Board, 98 Tullow Street, Carlow; ☎0503-913 0880; fax 0503-913 0717; www.carlow-ceb.com.
Cavan County Enterprise Board, Dublin Road, Cavan; ☎049-437 7200; fax 049-437 7250; www.cavanenterprise.ie.
Clare County Enterprise Board, Enterprise House, Mill Road, Ennis, Co. Clare; ☎065-684 1922; fax 065-684 1887; www.clare-ceb.ie.
Cork City Enterprise Board, 1-2 Bruach na Laoi, Union Quay, Cork; ☎021-496 1828; fax 021-496 1869; www.corkceb.ie.
Cork North Enterprise Board, The Enterprise Office, 26 Davies Street, Mallow; ☎022-43235; fax 022-43247; www.theenterpriseoffice.com.
Cork South Enterprise Board, Unit 6a, South Ring Business Park, Kinsale Road, Cork; ☎021-497 5281; fax 021-497 5287; www.sceb.ie.
Cork West Enterprise Board, 8 Kent Street, Clonakilty; ☎023-34700; fax 023-34702; www.wceb.ie.
Donegal County Enterprise Board, The Enterprise Fund Centre, Ballyraine Industrial Estate, Letterkenny; ☎074-916 0735; fax 074-916 0783; www.donegalenterprise.com.
Dublin City Enterprise Board, 17 Eustace Street, Dublin 2; ☎01-677 6068; fax 01-677 6093; www.dceb.ie.
Dublin South Enterprise Board, 3 Village Square, Old Bawn Road, Tallaght; ☎01-405 7073; fax 01-451 7477; www.sdenterprise.com.
Dunlaoghaire/Rathdown Enterprise Board, Nutgrove Enterprise Centre, Nutgrove Way, Rathfarnham, Dublin 14; ☎01-494 8400; fax 01-494 8410; www.venturepoint.ie.
Fingal County Enterprise Board, Upper Floor Office Suite, Mainscourt, 23 Main Street, Swords; ☎01-890 0800; fax 01-813 9991; www.fingalceb.ie.

Galway City & County Enterprise Board, Wood Quay Court, Wood Quay, Galway; ☎091-565 269; fax 091-565 384; www.galwayenterprise.ie.

Kerry County Enterprise Board, County Buildings, Tralee; ☎066-712 1111; fax 066-712 6712; www.kerryceb.ie.

Kildare County Enterprise Board, The Woods, Clane, Kildare; ☎045-861 707; fax 045-861 712; www.kildareceb.ie.

Kilkenny County Enterprise Board, 42 Parliament Street, Kilkenny; ☎056-52662; fax 056-51649; www.kceb.ie.

Laois County Enterprise Board, IBS House, Dublin Road, Portlaoise; ☎0502-61800; fax 0502-61797; www.laoisenterprise.com.

Leitrim County Enterprise Board, Carrik-On-Shannon Business Park, Dublin Road, Carrick-On-Shannon; ☎078-20450; fax 078-21491; www.leitrimenterprise.ie.

Limerick City Enterprise Board, The Granary, Micheal Street, Limerick; ☎061-312611; fax 061-311889; www.limceb.ie.

Limerick County Enterprise Board, County Buildings, 79/84 O'Connell Street, Limerick; ☎061-319319; fax 061-319318; www.lcoeb.ie.

Longford County Enterprise Board, 38 Ballymahon Street, Longford; ☎043-42757; fax 043-40968; www.longfordceb.ie.

Louth County Enterprise Board, Partnership Court, Enterprise House, The Ramparts, Dundalk; ☎042-932 7099; fax 042-932 7101; www.lceb.ie.

Mayo County Enterprise Board, McHale Retail Park, McHale Road, Castlebar; ☎094-24444; fax 094-24416; www.mayoceb.com.

Meath Enterprise Board, Navan Enterprise Centre, Trim Road, Navan; ☎046-907 8400; fax 046-902 7356; www.meath.com.

Monaghan County Enterprise Board, M:TEK Building, Knockaconny, Monaghan; ☎047-71818; fax 047-84786; www.mceb.ie.

Offaly County Enterprise Board, Cormac Street, Tullamore; ☎0506-52971; fax 0506-52973; www.offaly.ie.

Roscommon County Enterprise Board, Abbey Street, Roscommon; ☎0903-26263; fax 0903-25474; www.roscommon.ie.

Sligo County Enterprise Board, Sligo Development Centre, Cleveragh Road, Sligo; ☎071-914 4779; fax 071-914 6793; www.sligoenterprise.ie.

Tipperary North Enterprise Board, Connolly Street, Nenagh; ☎067-

33086; fax 067-33605; www.tnceb.ie.

Tipperary South Enterprise Board, 1 Gladstone Street, Clonmel; ☎052-29466; fax 052-26512; www.southtippcoco.ie.

Waterford City County Enterprise Board, Enterprise House, New Street Court, Waterford; ☎051-852883; fax 051-877494; www.waterfordceb.com.

Waterford County Enterprise Board, The Courthouse, Dungarvan; ☎058-44811; fax 058-44817; www.enterpriseboard.ie.

Westmeath County Enterprise Board, Business Information Centre, Church Avenue, Mullingar; ☎044-49222; fax 044-49009; www.westmeath-enterprise.ie.

Wexford County Enterprise Board, 16/17 Mallin Street, Cornmarket, Wexford; ☎053-22965; fax 053-24944; www.wexfordceb.ie.

Wicklow County Enterprise Board, 1 Main Street, Wicklow; ☎0404-67100; fax 0404-67601; www.wicklowceb.ie.

Loan Finance

Loans account for 40% of total external funding for new businesses. Most new businesses receiving external finance get it mainly in the form of loans, usually from the banks. Loans are also available at competitive rates from some other sources. City and County Enterprise Boards may offer low interest loans for certain items or buildings. The Bank of Ireland Enterprise Support Unit (ESU) (Haddington Centre, Percy Place, Dublin 4; ☎01-665 3300; fax 01-665 3755; www.bankofireland.ie) can provide small business loans to the start-up and developing SME sector, as can many of the other banks in Ireland such as AIB (Bankcentre, Ballsbridge, Dublin 4; ☎01-641 3090; fax 01-641 3045; www.aib.ie) and ACCBank – now part of Rabobank – (Business Banking Unit, Charlemont Place, Dublin 2; ☎01-418 4000; www.accbank.ie).

Whether you can obtain a loan from any of these institutions will depend on the quality and viability of your business plan, the amount of revenue your business is likely to generate, the security you can provide and your own personal credibility. As the main concern of any lender will be your ability to repay the loan and meet the interest charges, your main concern must be to convince them that you are a 'safe bet'.

  Be aware that those businesses that apply for and receive a loan are in the minority. In reality, fewer than 30% of start-ups depend on loans, either because they do not wish to take on the risks and costs involved, or because they are unable to raise external finance. However, it is often those that do rely on this sort of financial assistance that end up getting into difficulties, so you need to think carefully about whether you actually need a loan or can manage without. It is better to start small and expand as and when you are in a financial position to do so, rather than spend money that you do not have on a business that has yet to prove itself in the marketplace, acquire a client base and pay for itself.

Equity Capital

This is the core capital of any business, which helps to establish it in the first place and subsequently keeps it going. If a business has a good equity base it can help to secure other sources of funding such as loans or grants. If you have enough equity capital from personal and informal sources all well and good. If not, then there are other sources of equity capital available, but these are not easy to access and secure, and may involve you losing some control over the running of the your proposed business.

  Private individuals, venture capitalists and the public sector may inject funds if you can convince them your business is a sure-fire winner. However, the risks involved in helping to bankroll an unknown start-up are high, so financiers will generally expect a high return on their investment. Venture capitalists are professional investors looking for a good return on their money, and will therefore only back businesses capable of earning them significant financial returns. Many VCs avoid start-up businesses, seeing them as too great a risk, and concentrate instead on developing existing businesses with a strong track record. Further information on sources of venture capital is available from the Irish Venture Capital Association (☎ 01-230 1725; fax 01-280 9396; www.ivca.ie), the representative body of the venture capital industry in the Republic of Ireland and Northern Ireland.

  Another promising route to part-funding a new business is to approach public sector venture funders who may be prepared to invest where a private venture capitalist would not, or provide grants. Some City and County Enterprise Boards (see above) can also assist in this area. Not only can they inject funds but they may also play a role in encouraging other private sector investors to take part. Funding may also be available under the National Development Plan, which aims to improve Ireland's economic and social infrastructure, foster balanced regional development and sustain national economic and employment growth through the investment of public, EU and private funds. A guide to schemes under the NDP is available from the NDP Information Office (15 Lower Hatch Street, Dublin 2; ☎ 01-639 6280; fax 01-639 6281; www.ndp.ie) and can assist in the identification of possible sources of funding available to support various projects.

WRITING A BUSINESS PLAN

Before deciding whether to lend or grant you monies for your business, potential financial backers will require a business plan which lays out in detail your proposal, together with projected costs and income generated.

Whether you are applying for finance from a public or private organisation they will need to be assured that they will generate a return on their investment, either in the short or the long term – although the nature of such a return may be calculated in different ways: for example a bank or a venture capitalist will be looking at their investment in purely monetary terms whereas a public organisation such as a local enterprise company or a local council may classify a good return on their investment in other ways, such as the creation of a number of new jobs in the area, or the provision of a much needed service in a particular geographical area. Both groups will be looking to avoid risk, and may have several investment options from which to choose, of which yours will be just one. Therefore, a business plan that sets out your proposal clearly and concisely, and predicts a favourable return on investment is essential to help beat the competition.

A completed business plan is a summary and evaluation of your business idea. It is the written result of the planning process and a blueprint for your business operations. Your ability to make it work depends on checking your progress against the plan and reviewing that plan as your business evolves. In the early stages of development, when you are seeking finance, your business plan may well be the only tangible aspect of your intentions. The business plan should contain a fully considered financial plan, including a budget for at least the first 18 months. You should make sure that you include an allowance for unexpected and intangible expenses, in particular taxes, as one of the most common reasons for the failure of new businesses is the lack of planning for such contingencies. A business plan would normally include the following elements, though the names and the order of subjects may vary from plan to plan:

A BUSINESS PLAN

1. Commercial Section
- Title page
- Table of contents
- Introduction
- Description of the business and market
- Products and services
- History of you and your team
- Objectives of the business

2. Financial Section
- Profit budget
- Cash-flow forecast
- Current financial circumstances
- Past accounts
- Future accounts
- Financial requirements: amount requested; purpose of funding; use of funds; description of security (if seeking a loan)

3. Appendices and Supporting Documentation
- Photographs
- Samples
- Letters
- Forms
- Documents concerning legalities, taxes, etc.

When preparing a business plan, make it as clear and concise as possible. Aim for a plan of about ten to twelve pages, excluding appendices. While putting forward the 'best case scenario' regarding the prospects of the business, don't be tempted to exaggerate. Backers may hold you accountable for any statements that prove to be false or untenable. Try to see the whole enterprise from the backers' point of view, which is likely to be far narrower and more cautious than your own. Focus on those aspects of the business which will be important or relevant to them and, most importantly, get the figures right. Providers of finance will want to know how much the business will make after paying expenses and salaries, how long it will take the business to break even, and they will compare your personal finances with the proposed business finances. It is advisable to have your figures verified by a qualified accountant and this in itself will carry some weight with potential backers.

There are a number of publications available which can help when preparing your business plan, and assistance is also available from your nearest small business development corporation, industry associations, chambers of commerce, and from business advisors and accountants.

IDEAS FOR NEW BUSINESSES

Tourism

The tourism industry supports one job in every twelve in Ireland. International visitor numbers annually exceed six million, bringing with them billions of euros in revenue to the Irish economy. Domestic tourism – the Irish exploring their own back yard – further increases these figures. A number of areas of potential growth have been identified by *Fáilte Ireland* for investment, including tourism attractions and special interest activity holiday centres. For 2004 alone, €4.5million has been allocated to 13 projects in counties Kerry, Wicklow, Clare, Wexford, Donegal and Offaly under *Fáilte's* Tourism Product Development Scheme. This Scheme was set up to address gaps in the tourism industry and focuses in particular on less developed areas of the country.

Fáilte Ireland publishes a range of guides drawing on extensive market research carried out and commissioned by the organisation to look into the Irish tourism industry. These guides are a good place to start when researching the market for business opportunities in tourism and can be obtained from Fáilte Ireland by telephone (01-602 4193) or post (Baggot Street Bridge, Dublin 2). Talking to individual Regional Tourism Authorities will also give you a good idea of what is already available and what gaps there are in the tourism industry regionally.

Tourists will always need somewhere to sleep and somewhere to eat and opening a Bed & Breakfast establishment can be a good way to cater for both of these needs. During the height of the summer season temporary accommodation is always in short supply, especially in the west and south-west of the country. Location is very important for a B&B business and can mean the difference between earning a good and a mediocre living. Placing your establishment on accommodation lists, in guides and on the Internet will all help to market your business, but depending on the listings organisation there may be a fee involved and/or certain criteria and standards to be met. Trade is seasonal and running a successful B&B, depending on the number of guests you can cater for, is hard work – though if you can make enough money over the summer months to see you through the winter it can be well worth the effort.

Retail

Opening a retail outlet, such as a general grocer's, newsagent or gift-shop, which aims to supply local residents as well as holidaymakers can make a viable business proposition. Market research is essential to ensure that you won't be opening a mini-supermarket in an area already well supplied with them. Arts and craft shops also do well in tourist areas, especially if you can supply quality and original goods rather than offering the same cheap and cheerful souvenirs that can be found nationwide.

If you are producing your own art and craft works it is a good idea to set up your own retail outlet (and this can be in addition to having a presence on the Internet), but aim to keep overheads down. If possible arrange to share space in co-operative premises with others who are producing in a similar vein. In areas popular with tourists almost any shop or craft centre will attract business and sales over the season. Coach parties and families on holiday are looking to take home souvenirs of their stay and want places to visit and browse in, especially on a rainy day.

An alternative option to setting up shop in a town or village is to consider running a mobile shop, which will give you the advantage of reaching a wider customer base by travelling to small communities and out into the more rural areas. If you know your trade and can research the market you could become a travelling grocer, fishmonger, butcher, fish & chip seller, bookseller, Aran sweater purveyor, mobile art studio, etc. Another option is to tour the markets and county shows of Ireland with a mobile stall selling sandwiches, burgers, baked potatoes, etc. This can be a very good way to earn a living over the summer months as people at such events are always looking for somewhere to eat and drink.

Garages

Garages that sell fuel and can carry out vehicle repairs are essential even in the remotest areas of Ireland and like any other business, if run well and offering a good standard of service, running a garage can be a viable way of earning a living. Always look at the full cost implications of buying an existing business premises carefully: a filling station which has been inoperative for some time will need to have its tanks checked and passed as suitable before you can trade. Upgrading or other work may be required to satisfy government regulations. If you can operate as a mechanic from out of your own home-based garage, costs can be kept down, and a client base built up quickly if word gets around that your hourly rate is less than a commercial concern down the road.

Franchises

Franchising is a technique used by a variety of businesses in retailing, domestic services, car repairs and fast food. The franchiser offers a complete package of support including advertising, training, assistance to launch the business and instructions about its day-to-day running. The company offering the franchise will also help the franchisee obtain, equip and stock the business premises. The main advantage of franchising is that the business concept and name is already established and has a proven track record in the marketplace. In essence, franchising can be considered as going into business with an experienced partner.

The disadvantages are that franchises still require a large amount of start-up capital (although usually less than would be involved in setting up in business independently) and that inevitably the franchisee never has complete control over the business. Also, if the franchiser gets into difficulties this can affect the franchisee. Generally, franchise agreements involve up-front support during the initial start-up phase, helping with establishing a reputation and building up a client base, which reduces as the business becomes established. However, the royalties that the franchiser receives (proportional to sales) continue for the full length of the franchise agreement. Inevitably this means that the returns that you would get as a franchisee will never be as good as those you could get running your own autonomous business, but then you will not have the risk involved in setting up a totally unproven commodity.

As with all business ventures, make sure that you do your homework before going into this type of venture. Franchise terms vary greatly among companies, and some may not be so favourable. The position of the franchise in the market in which it trades should be carefully assessed. You should not only look at the particular franchised business in relation to its own activities, but also make an assessment of the prospects for the industry as a whole. The franchise will be dealing in goods, products or services and you should consider whether these are offering something new or have distinct advantages over the competition. Check that the franchised business has been thoroughly proven in practice, or whether it is merely exploiting a fad or current fashion, which may be transient or short-lived. If the product is strongly associated with a celebrity name, remember that a person's fame can fade as quickly as it came, and that your business, built as it is on a name, may fade with it. You should consider whether you have the expertise to handle the product or service that you will be offering, and make sure that you are convinced of the franchiser's financial buoyancy and reliability.

Franchises for sale can be found advertised alongside other businesses for sale in newspapers and estate agents' publications. Franchise Direct (Unit 27, Guinness Enterprise Centre, Taylor's Lane, Dublin 8; ☎ 01-410 0667; fax 01-410 0733; www.franchisedirect.ie) is a dedicated resource for both franchisees and franchisers and holds a directory of franchisers seeking partners in Ireland.

Computer Services

With the increasing domination of computers in the world of communication and business activities, there are always opportunities for those offering support services to home and business computer users or who have expertise in areas such as hardware and software design, production and website design. Computer-users continue to regularly upgrade both hardware and software to keep up with technological advances and those with the know-how to supply, fit and service new components, or who can offer assistance and advice at the end of a telephone or modem, are an invaluable asset to a community, particularly in the more remote areas far from the large towns.

Trades

Skilled trades people are always in demand just about everywhere. Builders, plumbers, hairdressers, gardeners, painters and decorators should be able to find employment either with existing businesses or on a self-employed basis in rural and urban areas throughout Ireland.

Working as a Freelance

There is a wide range of work you can do from home by making use of technological advancements to find and keep in contact with clients. Occupations such as writing, editing, proofreading, indexing, translating, technical authoring, distance teaching, graphic and illustration work, web design, computer programming and music composition can all be carried out successfully by individuals working from their own homes. Such occupations come with the advantage that you can adjust your working hours and work-rate to suit your situation, whether working full-time, or using freelance work as a part-time source of income and fitting it around your other commitments.

If you have talents in these areas but are not formally trained in them, there are distance-learning courses you can take from home, completing assignments sent to you by post or via the Internet. If you prefer more personal contact with tutors and fellow students, there are short and longer-term day and residential courses available in all manner of creative fields. Some courses allow you to work towards a formal qualification or diploma assisting you in finding work once you are qualified, while others concentrate on assisting you to find markets for your work to launch you on to the freelance path.

E-COMMERCE

Whichever business you decide to establish, effective marketing is always going to be an integral part of making it a success. The Internet has opened up new marketing possibilities and even the most traditional business can, so long as they have access to a telephone line and a computer equipped with a modem, an internet browser and e-mail software (which almost all computers possess as standard features these days), make good use of technology to reach a wider – and international – customer base.

The simplest of websites will act as an on-line brochure, announcing the business and containing information about the company's activities together with contact information. This can then be improved by adding images of products and services offered (photographs can be taken using digital cameras scanned onto the site) as well as logos and graphics, etc. With the introduction of a secure payment facility customers can carry out their business with the company remotely, buying on-line and paying by credit card over the Internet. Even if the cost of providing on-line shopping facilities proves too high for the start-up business the speed and ease of use of e-mail, together with simple devices such as a downloadable booking/payment form, can work almost as well to make booking and buying easier.

You will want to publicise your website by putting your website address on as much business paraphernalia as possible and registering the site with Internet search engines so that your website comes out on the search results page ahead of businesses offering similar services to yours. In addition, if you have the finance to spend, you can advertise your site on other websites. Remember that the best websites are those that are updated regularly and offer up-to-the-minute information about the company and its activities. Updating also brings return visits from existing customers.

The domain name (website address) that you choose should be as distinctive as possible and should either include the name of your business or describe the product that you are offering. Domain names ending in the suffix '.ie' refer to those registered with the Irish national Internet registry, IE Domain Registry LTD (Windsor House, 14 Windsor Terrace, Sandycove, Co. Dublin; ☎ 01-230 0797; fax 01-230 0365; www.iedr.ie).

Websites are fairly cheap to create. Registering a domain name costs between €50 and €150; site hosting around €50 a month. Site design costs range from zero (if you do it yourself) into the thousands of euros mark depending on how flash you want the site to look. On-line shop software, which will allow you to offer secure pay-online facilities, costs around €600.

Setting up you own website is a cheap and direct way to reach potential clients overseas. For even the smallest B&B or self-catering cottage, setting up a dedicated website or advertising on a community or commercial site is cost-effective. For larger businesses, the returns are potentially even greater. The Internet has opened up whole new fields of enterprise and successful businesses can be established which would not have been possible or profitable any other way. Internet auctions are popular worldwide, and increasing numbers of people are finding they can make a good income by dealing in all kinds of goods and services by using the Internet as a cyber-shop window, selling through the Internet auction sites and those devoted to specific products (such as second hand books, records, DVDs, etc) and shipping products across the world.

RUNNING A BUSINESS

Taxation

When you establish a business you will need to advise the tax office by completing Form STR if you are a sole trader whose turnover is expected to be less than €127,000 per annum; Form TR1 if you are a sole trader or a Partnership or Trust with an annual turnover exceeding €127,000; and Form TR2 if you are registering a company. These forms will register you and your business for Income Tax, employer's PAYE/PRSI and, if applicable, VAT. Form TR2 will also register a company for Corporation Tax. You must register for VAT if you are a taxable person and the turnover of your business is likely to exceed €51,000 in respect of supply of goods or €25,500 in respect of the supply of services. You will need a Personal Public Service (PPS) number to register which, if you are without, you will have to obtain from the Department of Social and Family Affairs.

As a self-employed person you will be responsible for paying your own tax through the Self-Assessment system. Your tax assessment for any year is normally based on actual income earned in the tax year (i.e. from 1 January to 31 December). If your income consists of profits from a trade, profession or vocation, and your annual accounts are normally made up to a date other than 31 December your assessment will be based on the profits of your accounting year which ends in the tax year. It is up to you to decide the date to which you prepare your accounts. You can prepare your accounts from the date your business started to the following 31 December (i.e. the end of the tax year) or a date which is 12 months after the date on which you started, or some other date appropriate to your business. Most businesses work out their profits once a year, usually to the same date each year.

Tax is calculated on your profits for the tax year. If there is any other income that has accrued over the year, such as income from investments, property rental, etc., then this is added to give a total income. Personal tax reliefs, expenses and allowances are deducted from this figure to give the total taxable income and this is taxed at the relevant tax rate.

Certain expenses can be claimed against profit, the general rule being that expenses must be 'wholly and exclusively' incurred for the purpose of the business. Expenses are normally referred to as revenue expenditure (the day-to-day running costs) and covers items such as purchase of goods for resale, salaries, rent, rates, repairs, lighting and heating, etc., running costs and lease payments of vehicles or machinery used in the business, accountancy fees, and interest paid on any monies borrowed to finance business expenses. If you are registered for VAT the expenses you claim should be exclusive of VAT.

Under the self-assessment system, Pay and File was introduced in 2002 in order to streamline the filing and payment obligations of taxpayers. On a single date annually – 31 October – taxpayers can file the current year's tax return, pay the estimated Income Tax (Preliminary Tax) for the current year, pay the balance of income tax and any capital gains tax for the previous tax year plus the Capital Gains Tax for the initial period of the current tax year. By filing your income tax return on that date the Revenue will compute and issue you with a final tax assessment for the relevant tax year. The balance of tax is payable by the 31st of January the year after the annual tax return has been submitted and agreed. Alternatively you can file and pay your tax online using the Revenue On-line Service (ROS). Failure to submit tax returns on time results in a fine being added to the amount of tax that you owe.

Companies pay Corporation Tax. This tax is charged on a company's profits, which include both income and chargeable gains. There are two rates of Corporation Tax: 12.5% for trading income (there are exceptions – certain land dealing, mining and petroleum businesses all pay the higher tax of 25%); and 25% for non-trading income (i.e. from rental or investment income, etc). For small and medium-sized enterprises where the trading income does not exceed €253,948, the rate of Corporation Tax is 12.5%. This rate is fixed to the year 2010 and has been guaranteed by the Irish Government with the agreement of the European Commission. For full details on all matters referring to tax and business access the Revenue website (www.revenue.ie) or contact the local tax office:

Addresses of Main Revenue Offices.

Collector General's Division, Apollo House, Tara Street, Dublin 2;

☎01-671 6998.
Dublin Regional, Apollo House, Tara Street, Dublin 2; ☎01-633 0600.
Border Midlands West Regional, Custom House, Flood Street, Galway; ☎091-536 300.
East & South East Regional, Government Offices, The Glen, Waterford; ☎051-862 100.
South West Regional, Government Offices, Sullivan's Quay, Cork; ☎021-432 5000.

Employing Staff

If you decide to employ staff for your business you will need to register with the Revenue for PAYE and PRSI as an employer. If your business is registered as a company, rather than as a sole trader or partnership, then the company must register as the employer. The relevant forms can be obtained from your local tax office or in writing from Taxes Central Registration Office, Arus Brugha, 9-15 Upper O'Connell Street, Dublin 1, or by telephoning the Revenue Forms and Leaflets Service (Lo-Call 1890-306 706). Once the Revenue has processed the forms you will receive confirmation of your registration as an employer, a registered number for PAYE purposes and information regarding PAYE/PRSI. The tax deducted from an employee's pay, plus the total amount of PRSI contributions paid by employer and employee, must be forwarded with form P30 by the employer on a monthly basis to the Collector General. At the end of every tax year an employer must complete and return forms P35, P35L to the Collector-General by 15 February. A guide (No. IT50) to the PAYE system aimed at employers is available from tax offices and from the Revenue website (www.revenue.ie).

Employers also have a number of responsibilities to their employees under employment legislation, with regard to such things as contracts of employment, working hours, conditions of working, health and safety, and sexual and racial equality of opportunity. For fuller details of these, see the *Aspects of Employment* section above or contact the Department of Enterprise, Trade and Employment (Kildare Street, Dublin 2; ☎01-631 2121; fax 01-631 2827). The Department's website (www.entemp.ie) also contains leaflets and fact sheets on aspects of employers responsibilities.

Business Insurance

Insurance for most types of small to medium sized businesses is available from the main insurance companies. If you need specialist insurance for your particular business, an insurance broker should be able to source a company giving the cover you need at a competitive price.

Insurance companies tend to rate risks in different ways, but the various kinds of insurance available to businesses include: Fire, Theft, Public Liability, Product Liability, Employer's Liability and Motor Insurance. The majority of insurance companies can offer any or all of these options in a single business policy. It is a good idea to discuss your needs with an insurance broker who will be able to find you the right policy by looking at the different options offered by a number of different insurance companies.

Apart from insurance to cover buildings and contents, you can insure your business for a range of other eventualities including business interruption, stock and goods in transit protection, legal fees protection, credit insurance, computer equipment, travel, patents and life insurance. Taking out health insurance for you and your staff will cover your business against possible loss of earnings through illness and incapacity. Ask your broker or insurance agent if it is possible to reduce premiums by paying an excess and whether the premiums can be paid monthly or quarterly rather than annually. In the final analysis, the insurance you decide to take out will depend on the risk you are willing to take and the budget you have available.

Data Protection

If you keep computer records of names and addresses and other personal data regarding people you employ and do business with, you may be required to notify the Data Protection Commissioner. If you are classed as a data controller who is processing personal data you are obliged to notify unless you are exempt.

The Data Protection Acts of 1988 and 2003 apply to data controllers and data processors and govern the collection, processing, storing and disclosure of personal data in Ireland, and regulate dealings in personal data in both electronic and manual form. Under the legislation, data controllers must ensure that personal data is collected and processed fairly, that it is kept only for specified and lawful purposes and is not kept for longer than necessary. Data processors are also under obligations to take appropriate measures to ensure the security of the data and must only process data in accordance with the instructions of the data controller. Data must also be kept up to date and accurate. Further details can be obtained from the Data Protection Commissioner (Office of the Data Protection Commissioner, 3rd Floor, Block 6, Irish Life Centre, Lower Abbey Street; Dublin 1; ☏ 01-874 8544; fax 01-874 5405; www.dataprivacy.ie). The Commission's website also includes a self-assessment section which will help you to identify whether you need to notify.

Intellectual Property

Intellectual property rights (of patents, copyrights, trade marks, industrial designs, etc.) are governed and protected in Ireland by various different pieces of legislation. There are two types of patent protection available in Ireland: a long-term patent lasting for 20 years, and a short-term patent, which lasts for 10 years. Inventions are patentable if they are new, involve an inventive step and are susceptible of industrial application. The right to a patent belongs to the inventor or to his successor in title.

Copyright exists in all original literary, dramatic, musical and artistic works, sound recordings, films, broadcasts and programmes; the typographical arrangements of published editions; and original databases. There are no registration or deposit formalities to obtain copyright protection in a work and copyright of a work generally lasts for a period of 70 years from the year of death of an author.

A trademark of both goods and services is registerable if it is capable, by words, designs, letters, numbers, sounds or the shape of the goods or their packaging, to distinguish the goods or services of one undertaking from those of other undertakings. A trademark is protected for an initial period of ten years, and then renewable for further periods of ten years. An industrial design, if it is new and has individual character, can be protected in Ireland under the Industrial Designs Act of 2001.

Irish Patents Office, Government Buildings, Hebron Road, Kilkenny; ☎056-7720111; fax 056-7720100; www.patentsoffice.ie.
Copyright Association of Ireland, Broom House, 65 Mulgrave Street, Dun Laoghaire, Co. Dublin; www.cai.ie.
Irish Music Rights Organisation (IMRO), Copyright House, Pembroke Row, Lower Baggot Street, Dublin 2; ☎01-661 4844; fax 01-676 3125; www.imro.ie.
National Software Directorate, Merrion Hall, Strand Road, Sandymount, Dublin 4; ☎01-206 6310; fax 01-206 6278; www.nsd.ie.

Accountancy and Legal Advice

A good accountant can help you to order your business affairs most efficiently, and can prepare your tax return on the basis of information you supply. The amount of tax they may be able to save you is usually well worth what they would charge in fees and anyone considering operating a business in Ireland is advised to engage the services of a suitably qualified Irish attorney. Any contracts relating to your business or a purchase of property should be drawn up or vetted by a qualified solicitor.

Qualified accountants can be found through the Institute of Chartered Accountants in Ireland (ICAI) or the Association of Chartered Certified Accountants (ACCA). Solicitors can be found through the Law Society of Ireland. Addresses of practitioners of both professions in your area can be obtained from the local Phone Book and Business Pages. Free advice on many aspects of living and working in Ireland can be obtained from Comhairle, Ireland's Citizen's Advice Bureau, which runs 80 Citizen's Information Centres across the country.

Useful Addresses
Association of Chartered Certified Accountants, ACCA Ireland, 9 Leeson Park, Dublin 6; ☎01-498 8900; fax 01-496 3615; http:

//ireland.accaglobal.com/. ACCA is Ireland's fastest growing professional accountancy body.

Institute of Chartered Accountants in Ireland, CA House, 87/89 Pembroke Road, Dublin 4; ☏01-637 7200; fax 01-668 0842; www.icai.ie. The ICAI website includes a searchable database of registered chartered accountants in Ireland.

The Institute of Certified Public Accountants in Ireland, 9 Ely Place, Dublin 2; ☏01-676 7353; fax 01-661 2367; www.cpaireland.ie.

The Law Society of Ireland, Blackhall Place, Dublin 7; ☏01-672 4800; fax 01-672 4801; www.lawsociety.ie.

Comhairle, Head Office, 7th Floor, Hume House, Ballsbridge, Dublin 4; ☏01-605 9000; fax 01-605 9099; www.comhairle.ie.

SOURCES OF ADVICE & ASSISTANCE

There are a number of sources of support, information and advice available for those who wish to establish a business in Ireland or who are already doing so and are looking to expand their current operations. Below are some of those sources; all are good starting points.

Business Innovation Centres. A B.I.C. (Business Innovation Centre) is a local or regional partnership structure providing SMEs, through public and private resources, with a range of services, usually on favourable terms. BICs tend to focus on identifying budding entrepreneurs with ideas for innovative solutions for industry or services to industry.

Cork BIC, NSC Campus, Mahon, Cork; ☏021-230 7005; fax 021-230 7020; www.corkbic.com. Identifies, selects and develops around twelve start-ups annually.

Dublin BIC, The Tower, TCD Enterprise Centre, Pearse Street, Dublin 2; ☏01-671 3111; fax 01-671 3330; www.dbic.ie.

Limerick BIC, National Technological Park, Limerick; ☏061-338 177; fax 061-338 065; www.shannon-dev.ie/innovation/.

South East Business & Innovation Centre Ltd, Unit 1b, Industrial Park, Cork Road, Waterford; ☏051-356300; fax 051-354415; www.sebic.ie.

West BIC, Galway Technology Centre, Mervue Industrial Estate,

Galway; ☎091-730850; fax 091-730853; www.westbic.ie.
European BIC Network, Avenue de Tervuren 168, B-1150 Brussels, Belgium; ☎+32 2 772 89 00; fax +32 2 772 95 74; www.ebn.be.

BASIS Project, Department of Enterprise, Trade & Employment, 4th Floor, Earlsfort Centre, Lower Hatch Street, Dublin 2; ☎01-631 2787; fax 01-631 2563; www.basis.ie. BASIS (Business Access to State Information and Services) was established in 2000 as part of the Irish Government Action Plan *Implementing the Information Society in Ireland* to deliver Government information and services to businesses.

Chambers of Commerce of Ireland (CCI), 17 Merrion Square, Dublin 2; ☎01-661 2888; fax 01-661 2811; www.chambersireland.ie. The Chambers of Commerce of Ireland represents over 11,000 businesses nationwide. CCI runs several business development projects sub-contracting from state agencies and the EU to provide low-cost training to its businesses and is able to secure discounts in areas such as electricity and telecommunications for its members.

Enterprise Ireland, Glasnevin, Dublin 9, ☎01-808 2000; fax 01-808 2020; www.enterprise-ireland.com. Enterprise Ireland is the government organisation charged with assisting Irish businesses to develop competition, sales, exports and employment and at the same time act as a conduit for international businesses seeking to trade with Irish companies. The organisation provides a range of services to help both Irish and international businesses. An additional 13 offices are located throughout Ireland in Dublin, Athlone, Cork, Dundalk, Killarney, Galway, Letterkenny, Shannon, Sligo and Waterford.

Fáilte Ireland, Baggot Street Bridge, Dublin 2; ☎01-602 4000; fax 01-855 6821; www.failteireland.ie. Fáilte Ireland, the National Tourism Development Authority, was established in 2003 by merging Bord Fáilte (the Tourist Board) and CERT (the Government trainee body for people in tourism). The Authority provides strategic and practical support in order to sustain Ireland as a high-quality tourist destination, and by doing so to increase the contribution of tourism to the economy of the country.

FÁS, PO Box 456, 27-33 Upper Baggot Street, Dublin 4; ☎01-607 0500; fax 01-607 0600; www.fas.ie. FÁS is Ireland's national training and employment authority and runs specific programmes to assist businesses (small, medium and large firms, both national and international, in all sectors of industry) and provides a regional training advisory service. In addition, FÁS runs training programmes of relevance to employers, and a recruitment service.

IBEC, Head Office, Confederation House, 84/86 Lower Baggot Street, Dublin 2; ☎01-605 1500; fax 01-638 1500; www.ibec.ie. The Irish Business and Employers Confederation acts as the national voice of Irish businesses and employers. With a head office in Dublin and regional offices in Cork, the Mid-West, the North-West, the South-East and the West of the country, as well as a Brussels office, IBEC provides a comprehensive human resource and industrial relations service, as well as a forum for networking, to its 7,000 members.

IDA Ireland, Wilton Park House, Wilton Place, Dublin 2; tel 01-603 4000; fax 01-603 4040; www.ida.ie. With offices throughout Ireland and the world, the Irish Industrial Development Agency is a Government initiative with responsibility for marketing Ireland as an attractive base for businesses and securing new investment from overseas, mainly in the sectors of manufacturing and internationally traded services. The IDA focuses on attracting sophisticated businesses in sectors such as e-Business, engineering, information communications technologies, medical technologies, pharmaceuticals, and financial and international services.

Irish Small & Medium Enterprise Association, 17 Kildare Street, Dublin 2; ☎01-662 2755; fax 01-661 2157; www.isme.ie. The Irish Small and Medium Enterprises Association was formed in 1993 to assist small and medium enterprises and owner-managed businesses in Ireland. There are regular regional business briefing sessions, which act as a good networking forum and bring members up to date on issues relating to their business activities. Group Schemes help to reduce members' individual expenses. ISME also publishes a monthly newsletter, bulletins and employment related guides.

Regional Development Agency, Údarás na Gaeltachta, Na Forbacha, Gaillimh; ☎091-503 100; fax 091-503101; www.udaras.ie. The Regional Development Agency holds responsibility for the economic, social and cultural development of the Gaeltacht regions and supports businesses promoting and developing the use of the Irish language in their activities.

Small and Medium Enterprise Unit, Room 522 Department of Enterprise Trade and Employment, Kildare Street, Dublin 2; fax 01-631 2801; www.entemp.ie. The Small and Medium Enterprises (SME) Unit looks after the needs of small business and entrepreneurs at national and international level and produces a number of publications that will be of use to anyone looking to establish a business enterprise in Ireland.

The Bank of Ireland, Customer Care Unit, Bank of Ireland Head Office, Lower Baggot Street, Dublin 2; ☎01-661 5933; www.bankofireland.ie. The Bank of Ireland produces a series of business management guides such as *Starting Your Own Business – A Guide to Building your own Business* for people thinking of starting or expanding a business in Ireland, covering areas such as market testing, product identification, the business plan, employment and finances.

The Small Firms Association, Confederation House, 84-86 Lower Baggot Street, Dublin 2; ☎01-6051500; fax 01-661 2861; www.sfa.ie. The Small Firms Association (SFA) in an invaluable asset to small enterprises in Ireland, representing the needs of it members and providing economic, commercial, employee relations, and social affairs advice and assistance.

Irish Business Magazines

Accountancy Ireland, CA House, 87/89 Pembroke Road, Ballsbridge, Dublin 4; ☎01-637 7240; fax 01-668 5685; www.icai.ie. A magazine focusing on accountancy matters, business and management information, taxation, information technology, general news, leisure and lifestyles, etc.

Adworld, Bellrock Communication Group, Glencormack Business Park, Kilmacanogue, Co. Wicklow; ☎01-276 5717; fax 01-276 5718; www.adworld.ie. The Irish marketing journal.

Business Plus, 30 Morehampton Road, Dublin 4; ☎01-660 8400; www.bizplus.ie. Business Plus is the largest circulation business magazine in Ireland. A monthly magazine focusing on the activities of Irish and Ireland-based companies.

ComputerScope and *PC Live!*, Scope Communications Group, Prospect House, 3 Prospect Road, Dublin 9; ☎01-882 4444; fax 01-830 0888; www.techcentral.ie. Two of Ireland's leading IT magazines.

Enterprise Network, www.enterprisenetwork.ie. The Sunday Times' business information resource.

The Irish Entrepreneur, Morrissey Media Ltd, Clondaw House, Clondaw Lower, Ferns, Co. Wexford; ☎053-36884; fax 053-36881; www.irishentrepreneur.com. With articles on starting, running and growing a business.

The Sunday Business Post, 80 Harcourt Street, Dublin 2; ☎01-602 6000; fax 01-679 6498; www.sbpost.ie. Ireland's financial, political and economic newspaper.

PERSONAL CASE HISTORIES

FREYA FORREST

Freya Forrest trained in 3-Dimensional Design at Manchester Polytechnic and went on to complete a Masters degree in Furniture Design at the Royal College of Art in London. After a career designing furniture for Habitat and other companies in London she decided to move into theatre design and toured India and England with a horse-drawn theatre company for five years. In 1991 Freya went to Ireland for St. Patrick's Day and decided that she didn't want to leave. She initially worked with a theatre company in Galway before training in TV Set Design in Connemara. Freya now works as a freelance Film and TV Designer and Art Director, as a Scenic Artist for theatre and, on occasion, as a painter and director in private houses. Currently Freya lives in Co. Wicklow with her two children aged seven and five.

Where do you live in Ireland and why have you chosen to live in that particular province/county?
I lived and worked for eight years in the West of Ireland near Galway. Four years ago I moved to Greystones, Co. Wicklow – about sixteen miles away from Dublin. I live near Ardmore Film Studios in Bray and it is easier to find work in Film and TV on the East Coast. The East coast is much more densely populated and affluent, so work is easier to find, but it also means that the cost of living is in general higher.

What were your first impressions of Ireland? What have you found to be the main differences between Ireland and the UK?
I first visited Ireland in 1987, straight from four months in India. I

came over here to set up a tour for a theatre company that I was working for at that time. I find the country open and rural – more like a big village – and at that time more reminiscent of India than England. It's great horse country and there is easy access to the sea and beautiful countryside. The music and set dancing were also a great attraction and the reputed Irish craic is always here to be found. Above all, I love the Irish sense of humour and turn of phrase. People still have time for you over here, particularly in the rural areas.

Were there any difficulties with red tape – work and residence permits, etc?

I personally had no problems with immigration. I was allotted an RSI number on my first job and was fed into the tax system. The first few years I was here I signed on the dole during the winter without difficulties. If your income is below a certain level you are entitled to a Medical Card to cover visits to the doctor and hospital. Dental treatment is more expensive over here than it is in England, and car insurance and car tax are expensive. I have always run a commercial vehicle and get commercial insurance and tax. I receive Child Benefit of c. €235 pcm as both my children were born here.

How did you go about finding work?

I have always got work by word of mouth (and still do). I had the advantage of having toured the west coast with the theatre company and had met a number of people during holidays I had taken over here before I came to live here. Ireland is a small country and the arts community is small and quite tight knit. Film and TV jobs also tend to function on personal contacts.

Have you found it easy to make friends? What is your general impression of the Irish?

Although the Irish are extremely friendly on the surface, I find they take a long time to get to know well. They are a more complex and hidden people than the English, with deep roots of religion running through the community. Their sense of humour and values always win me over and I have a strong network of friends in many different walks of life.

What do you like best about living in Ireland?
The ability of the people here to make me laugh. Also, in Ireland I can sustain a fulfilling lifestyle between town and country relatively easily.

What do you like least about living in Ireland?
What I like least about living here is the begrudgery and gossip, and people appearing to prefer it when you're down than when you are being successful: their 'me fein' attitude [self obsession – from the Irish for 'myself']. I make a concerted effort not to join in. I miss the gorgeous vernacular architecture of Britain.

How does the quality of life in Ireland differ to that in the UK?
I think the quality of life is very good here despite the high cost of living and housing. I play flute in a local symphony orchestra and there is an endless choice of films/theatre/classes to go to. There are also a lot of activities and sport for children to become involved in, despite the lack of playgrounds. The equine community is thriving and it is easy to find horses to ride – to borrow even if you don't have your own. The standard of education is very good, if rather lacking in art and non-denominational schools. The country is being forced to open up with the many immigrants and asylum seekers moving here, which I really welcome. I feel less of a 'blow-in' on the homogenised east coast that I did in the west, but that is also due to having lived here long enough to adapt.

Have you any advice to offer those considering making a permanent move to Ireland?
At present the cost of living in Ireland is very high and Dublin is now a more expensive city than Helsinki. The cost of housing and rents in this area are exorbitant with very little cheap housing available. Ireland still has an island mentality and it is more expensive to get out of than Britain. For me though, I love living here and could not contemplate living back in Britain. I have never regretted the move, and it is a conscious choice to bring my children up here.

JAMES PENGELLY

James Pengelly spent his working life commuting between London and his home in the South of England. He first went to Ireland on holiday with his family and fell in love with the country and its people and decided that it was where he wanted to end his days. After a divorce and early retirement, James moved to Ireland to live full-time in 1988.

Where do you live in Ireland and why have you chosen to live in that particular province/county?
I live in a cottage in a village outside Killarney in County Kerry. Kerry is a beautiful part of the country and though there are quite a number of tourists over the summer months they don't bother me. This part of Ireland is still 'a bit of old Ireland', picture-bookish. I moved to Ireland because I found England was getting too overcrowded and the South-East of England was becoming just an extension of London and I was after peace and tranquillity.

What were your first impressions of Ireland? What are the main differences between Ireland and the UK?
Ireland has changed a lot since I first moved here in the late 1980s. But the main differences are the lack of traffic; and it's generally more expensive over here. But the people are friendlier, and I love the Irish accent. It's a lot more laid back that England. Ireland has changed in the past 20 years or so, become wealthier.

Have you found it easy to make friends? What is your general impression of the Irish?
The Irish are friendly people. I have been greeted with civility wherever I go. I find the Irish to be pleasant, easygoing people.

What do you like best about living in Ireland?
I love the freedom, and the lack of traffic. I enjoy the Guinness, though I wish the music in pubs started earlier in the evenings.

What do you like least about living in Ireland?
The rain.

How does the quality of life in Ireland differ to that in the UK?
For me I have a much better quality of life. People are not so materialistic. I don't have to keep up with the Jones's all the time. I enjoy the walking and bird watching.

Have you any advice to offer those considering making a permanent move to Ireland?
Come with an open mind and an open heart.

GARY HETZLER

Gary Hetzler was born in St. Louis, Missouri and moved to Boston, Massachusetts in the early 1980s. He met his wife, Janis James, while an actor, but abandoned acting soon after moving to Boston, where he worked for an insurance company for nearly twenty years. He and Janis spent many vacations in Scotland prior to visiting Ireland. Ultimately, they dreamt of 'retiring' in Ireland but couldn't wait that long. So in July 2001, because of its scenery and relaxed lifestyle, the couple moved to Ireland. They moved while they were still relatively young, so they would not later wonder what would have happened if…

Where do you live in Ireland and why have you chosen to live in that particular province/county?
We live in County Clare. For practical reasons, that puts us close to the larger population and job centres of Limerick and Galway. But our real reason is to be close to the scenic beauty of this area, particularly the Burren.

What were your first impressions of Ireland? What have you found to be the main differences between Ireland and the USA?
Our first impressions of Ireland were of the beauty of the landscape in the west. Unlike in the States, the hills and mountains here are predominantly devoid of trees. That reveals more of the wild terrain and craggy rocks, which we find appealing.

Were there any difficulties with red tape – work and residence permits, etc?
There were a few difficulties we encountered with the residency permit process. One document we didn't realise we needed was the original of a letter from the police department of our former town, attesting to our fine moral character. Then, we moved from one county in Ireland to another after our paperwork was already in process. That meant we had to start all over again at a new Gardai station. And of course, our paperwork became lost in the system from time to time. But now that the registration process is computerized, registration and permit renewals are much quicker and don't get lost.

How did you go about finding work?
I work here as an actor, my first career choice. This is difficult to do in any country, and frankly it is more so in Ireland. This is a small country and most work is in Dublin. I'm on the opposite side of the country, but that's my choice. I have an agent, and that helps, but it takes a long time to become known. I audition for parts; that's the process anywhere.

Have you found it easy to make friends? What is your general impression of the Irish?
I have found it far easier to make friends with other blow-ins, probably because we would already have much in common. I think the Irish are very cordial, well read and very helpful. But they take their time to get to know you and take an even longer time to reveal themselves to you. In some ways, that makes them similar to New Englanders. An easy way to make friends is to become involved in local community theatre productions. Ireland has a surprisingly strong and well-established amateur theatrical tradition.

What do you like best about living in Ireland?
What I like best about living in Ireland is the proximity of the countryside to the towns and cities. In ten minutes you can be in the middle of nowhere. That and the beauty of the land itself are what I find most appealing.

What do you like least about living in Ireland?
What I like least about living in Ireland is the lack of certain products that I'm used to. Those could be favourite foodstuffs or everyday household products or hardware items. I also hate the traffic jams and endless construction I find whenever I visit Dublin.

How does the quality of life in Ireland differ to that in the USA?
Quality of life is very subjective. I have to drive further to obtain the goods and services that I need, but I like living in a rural area. I enjoy the lack of a hectic pace here, even in Dublin. This is still a relaxed country, and a small one. No matter what town you mention in a casual pub conversation, you'll soon find someone with a relative there

or some other connection to it. I happen to like that.

Have you any advice to offer those considering making a permanent move to Ireland?
If you're thinking seriously about moving here, visit and visit often – for longer periods each time. Come during seasons of the worst weather and the least daylight. Get out of the vacation mindset and really imagine how your everyday life would be. Ask yourself if the difference is worth enough for you to make that move. If it works out, great. And if it doesn't work out for you after all, that's okay too. You would have tried and will never be left wondering what would have happened if…

Complete guides to life abroad from Vacation Work

Live & Work Abroad

Live & Work in Australia & New Zealand	£10.99
Live & Work in Belgium, The Netherlands & Luxembourg	£10.99
Live & Work in China	£11.95
Live & Work in France	£10.99
Live & Work in Germany	£10.99
Live & Work in Ireland	£10.99
Live & Work in Italy	£10.99
Live & Work in Japan	£10.99
Live & Work in Russia & Eastern Europe	£10.99
Live & Work in Saudi & the Gulf	£10.99
Live & Work in Scandinavia	£10.99
Live & Work in Scotland	£10.99
Live & Work in Spain & Portugal	£10.99
Live & Work in the USA & Canada	£10.99

Buying a House Abroad

Buying a House in France	£11.95
Buying a House in Italy	£11.95
Buying a House in Portugal	£11.95
Buying a House in Spain	£11.95
Buying a House on the Mediterranean	£12.95

Starting a Business Abroad

Starting a Business in France	£12.95
Starting a Business in Spain	£12.95

Available from good bookshops or direct from the publishers
Vacation Work, 9 Park End Street, Oxford OX1 1HJ
Tel 01865-241978 * Fax 01865-790885 * www.vacationwork.co.uk

In the US: available at bookstores everywhere
or from The Globe Pequot Press (www.GlobePequot.com)